LAGUARDIA ™

A Very
Modern
Story of
Immigration

BERGER
BOOKS
™ AN IMPRINT OF
DARK HORSE COMICS

Editor
Karen Berger

Assistant Editor
Rachel Boyadjis

Logo/Book Designer
Richard Bruning

Digital Art Technician
Adam Pruett

President & Publisher
Mike Richardson

« LAGUARDIA »

This volume collects issues #1–4 of LAGUARDIA
from Berger Books.

First Edition: July 2019
ISBN 978-1-50671-075-4
Digital ISBN 978-1-50671-077-8
13 5 7 9 10 8 6 4 2
Printed in China

Published by
Dark Horse Books
A division of Dark Horse Comics LLC
10956 SE Main Street
Milwaukie, OR 97222

Library of Congress Cataloging-in-Publication Data
Names: Okorafor, Nnedi, writer. | Ford, Tana, artist. | Devlin, James
(Comic book artist), colorist. | Cipriano, Sal, letterer.
Title: LaGuardia / written by Nnedi Okorafor ; art by Tana Ford ;
colored by James Devlin ; lettered by Sal Cipriano.
Description: First edition. | Milwaukie, Oregon : Dark Horse Comics LLC, 2019.
| "This volume collects Issues #1–4 of LaGuardia."
Identifiers: LCCN 2019012819 | ISBN 9781506710754 (paperback)
Subjects: LCSH: Comic books, strips, etc. | BISAC: COMICS & GRAPHIC NOVELS /
Science Fiction. | COMICS & GRAPHIC NOVELS / Literary.
Classification: LCC PN6728.L236 038 2019 | DDC 741.5/973--dc23
LC record available at https://lccn.loc.gov/2019012819

WRITER
Nnedi Okorafor

ARTIST
Tana Ford

COLORIST
James Devlin

LETTERER
Sal Cipriano

« DEDICATIONS »

To all the extraterrestrials who have come,
are currently here, and will arrive.
Including my cat Periwinkle Chukwu.
You are welcome.
And to my daughter Anyaugo,
who read and loved this story first.
— Nnedi Okorafor

For Kirsten-
Who listens and loves,
and reminds me to
water the garden.
— Tana Ford

CHAPTER 1

HOMECOMING

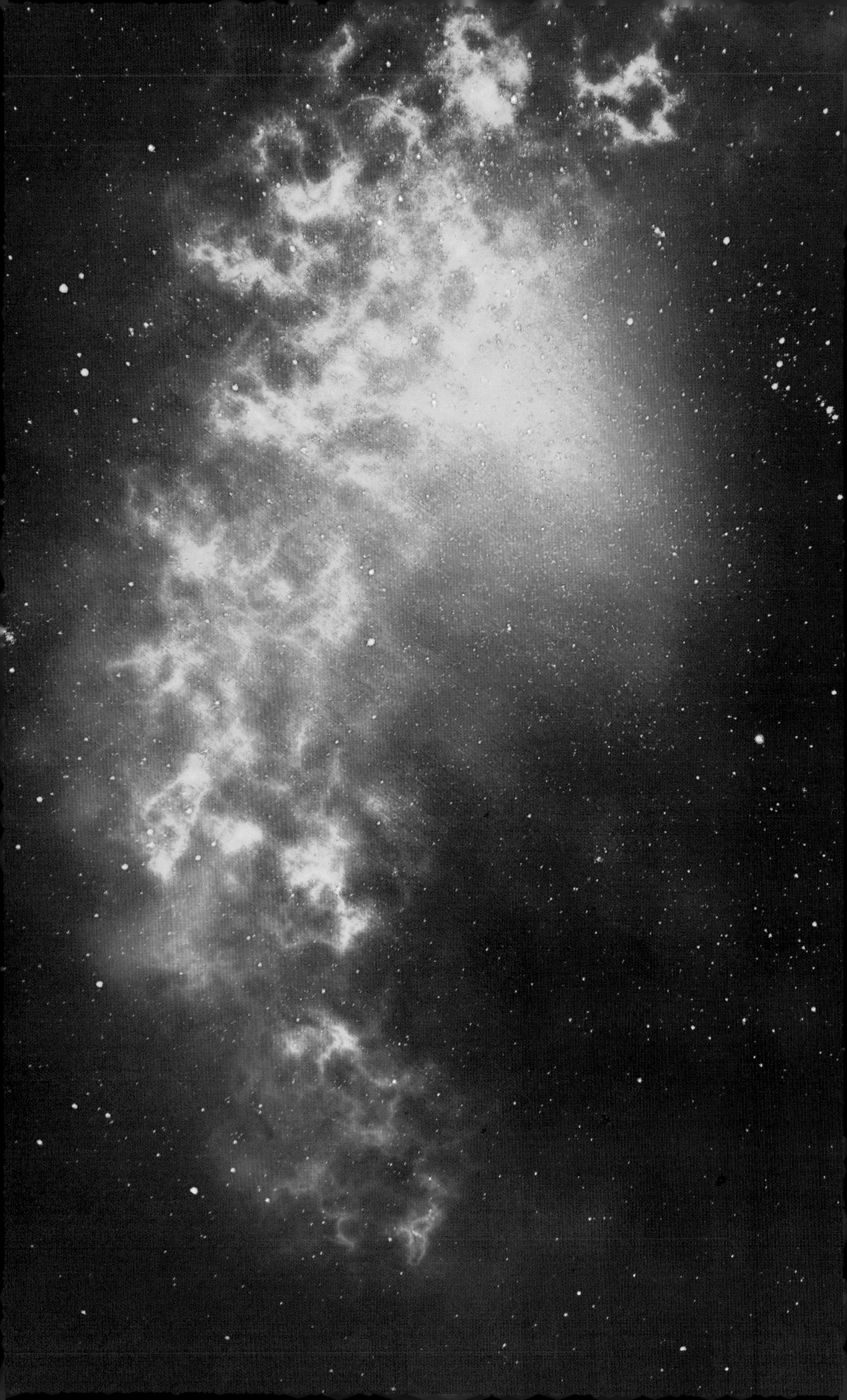

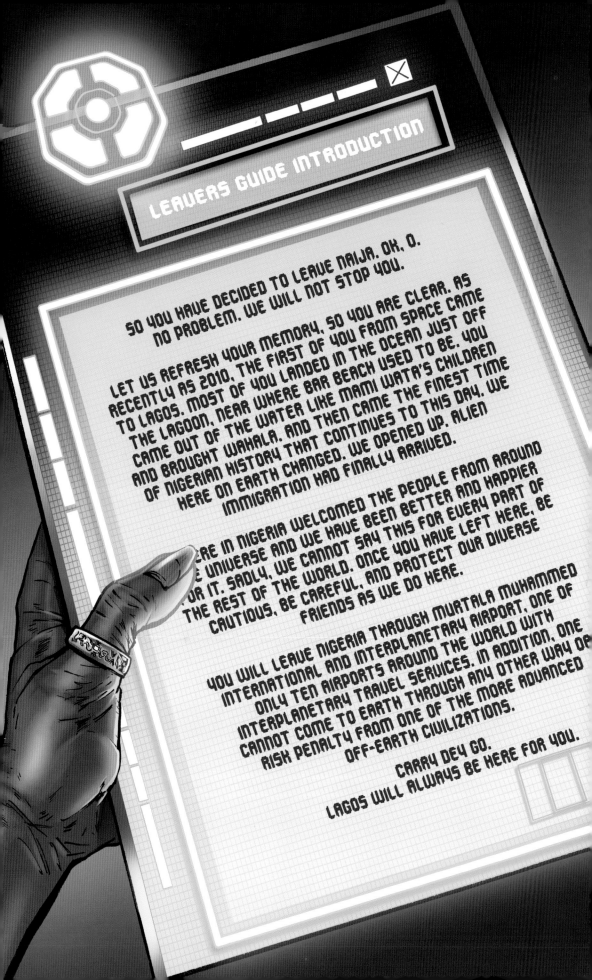

LEAVERS GUIDE INTRODUCTION

SO YOU HAVE DECIDED TO LEAVE NAIJA. OK, O. NO PROBLEM. WE WILL NOT STOP YOU.

LET US REFRESH YOUR MEMORY, SO YOU ARE CLEAR. AS RECENTLY AS 2010, THE FIRST OF YOU FROM SPACE CAME TO LAGOS. MOST OF YOU LANDED IN THE OCEAN JUST OFF THE LAGOON, NEAR WHERE BAR BEACH USED TO BE. YOU CAME OUT OF THE WATER LIKE MAMI WATA'S CHILDREN AND BROUGHT WAHALA. AND THEN CAME THE FINEST TIME OF NIGERIAN HISTORY THAT CONTINUES TO THIS DAY. WE HERE ON EARTH CHANGED. WE OPENED UP. ALIEN IMMIGRATION HAD FINALLY ARRIVED.

[WE] HERE IN NIGERIA WELCOMED THE PEOPLE FROM AROUND [TH]E UNIVERSE AND WE HAVE BEEN BETTER AND HAPPIER [F]OR IT. SADLY, WE CANNOT SAY THIS FOR EVERY PART OF THE REST OF THE WORLD. ONCE YOU HAVE LEFT HERE, BE CAUTIOUS, BE CAREFUL, AND PROTECT OUR DIVERSE FRIENDS AS WE DO HERE.

YOU WILL LEAVE NIGERIA THROUGH MURTALA MUHAMMED INTERNATIONAL AND INTERPLANETARY AIRPORT, ONE OF ONLY TEN AIRPORTS AROUND THE WORLD WITH INTERPLANETARY TRAVEL SERVICES. IN ADDITION, ONE CANNOT COME TO EARTH THROUGH ANY OTHER WAY OR RISK PENALTY FROM ONE OF THE MORE ADVANCED OFF-EARTH CIVILIZATIONS.

CARRY DEY GO.
LAGOS WILL ALWAYS BE HERE FOR YOU.

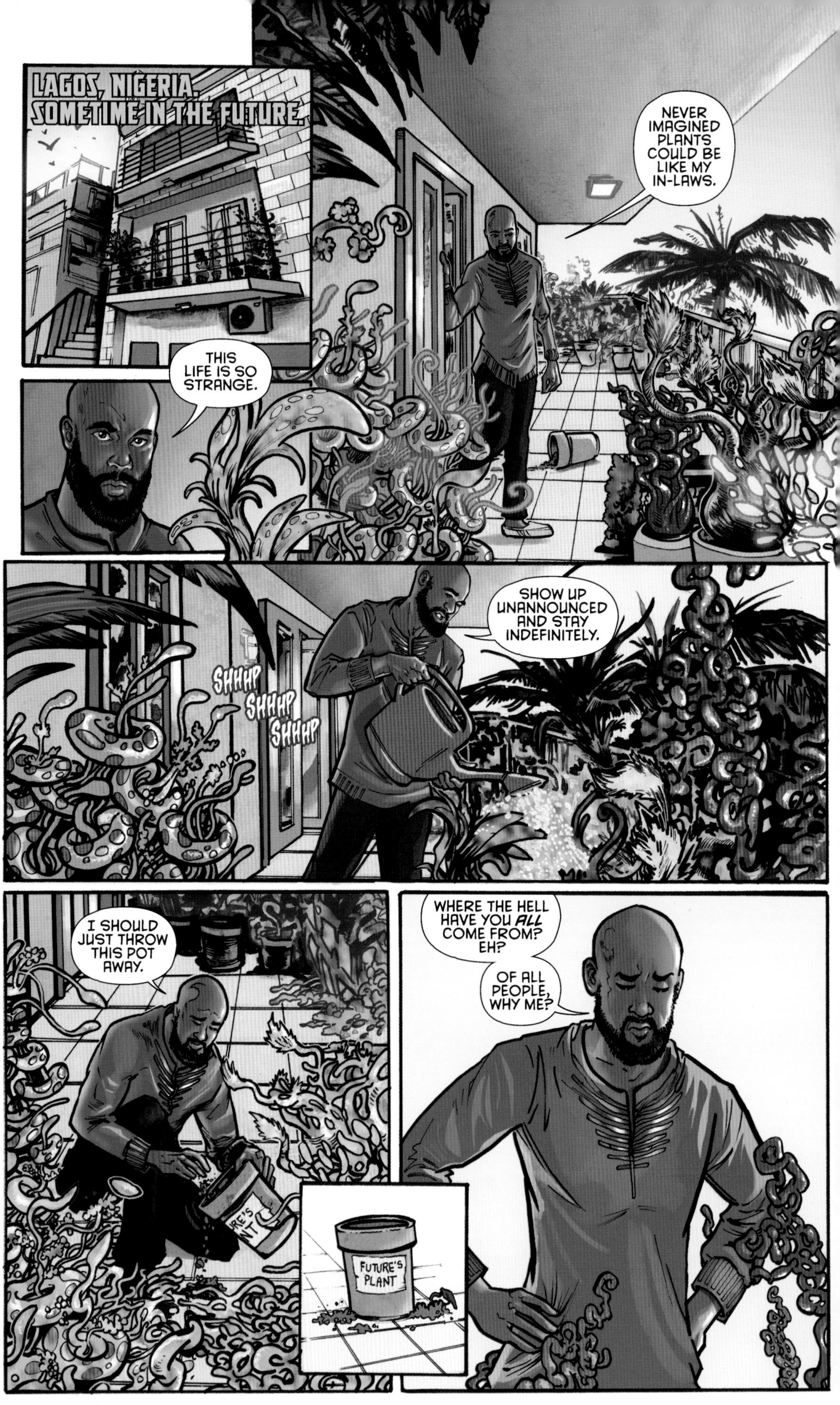
LAGOS, NIGERIA.
SOMETIME IN THE FUTURE.
NEVER IMAGINED PLANTS COULD BE LIKE MY IN-LAWS.
THIS LIFE IS SO STRANGE.
SHOW UP UNANNOUNCED AND STAY INDEFINITELY.
SHHHP
SHHHP
SHHHP
I SHOULD JUST THROW THIS POT AWAY.
FUTURE'S PLANT
WHERE THE HELL HAVE YOU ALL COME FROM? EH?
OF ALL PEOPLE, WHY ME?

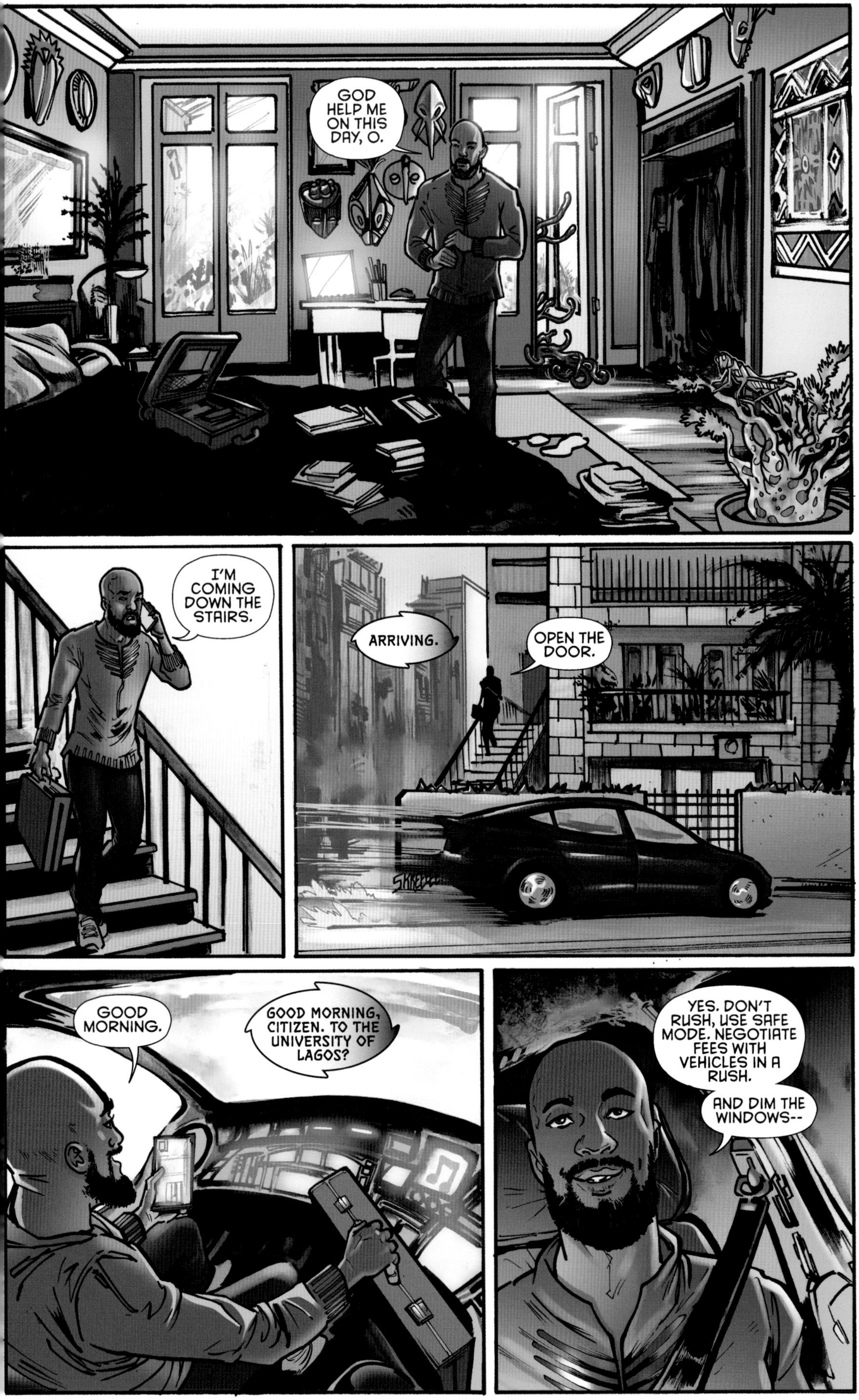
GOD HELP ME ON THIS DAY, O.
I'M COMING DOWN THE STAIRS.
ARRIVING.
OPEN THE DOOR.
GOOD MORNING.
GOOD MORNING, CITIZEN. TO THE UNIVERSITY OF LAGOS?
YES. DON'T RUSH, USE SAFE MODE. NEGOTIATE FEES WITH VEHICLES IN A RUSH.
AND DIM THE WINDOWS--

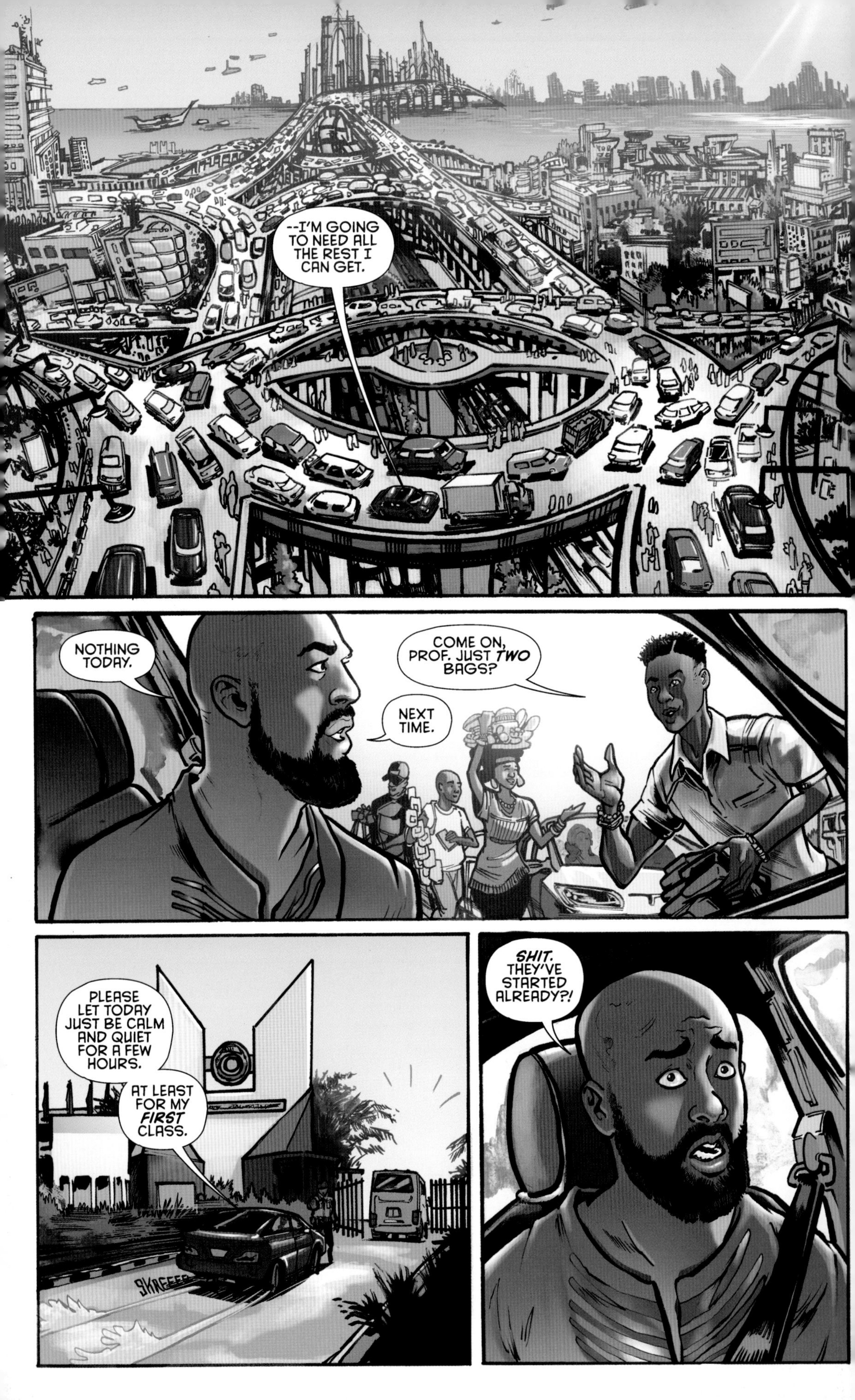
--I'M GOING TO NEED ALL THE REST I CAN GET.
NOTHING TODAY.
COME ON, PROF. JUST *TWO* BAGS?
NEXT TIME.
PLEASE LET TODAY JUST BE CALM AND QUIET FOR A FEW HOURS.
AT LEAST FOR MY *FIRST* CLASS.
SKREEE
SHIT. THEY'VE STARTED ALREADY?!

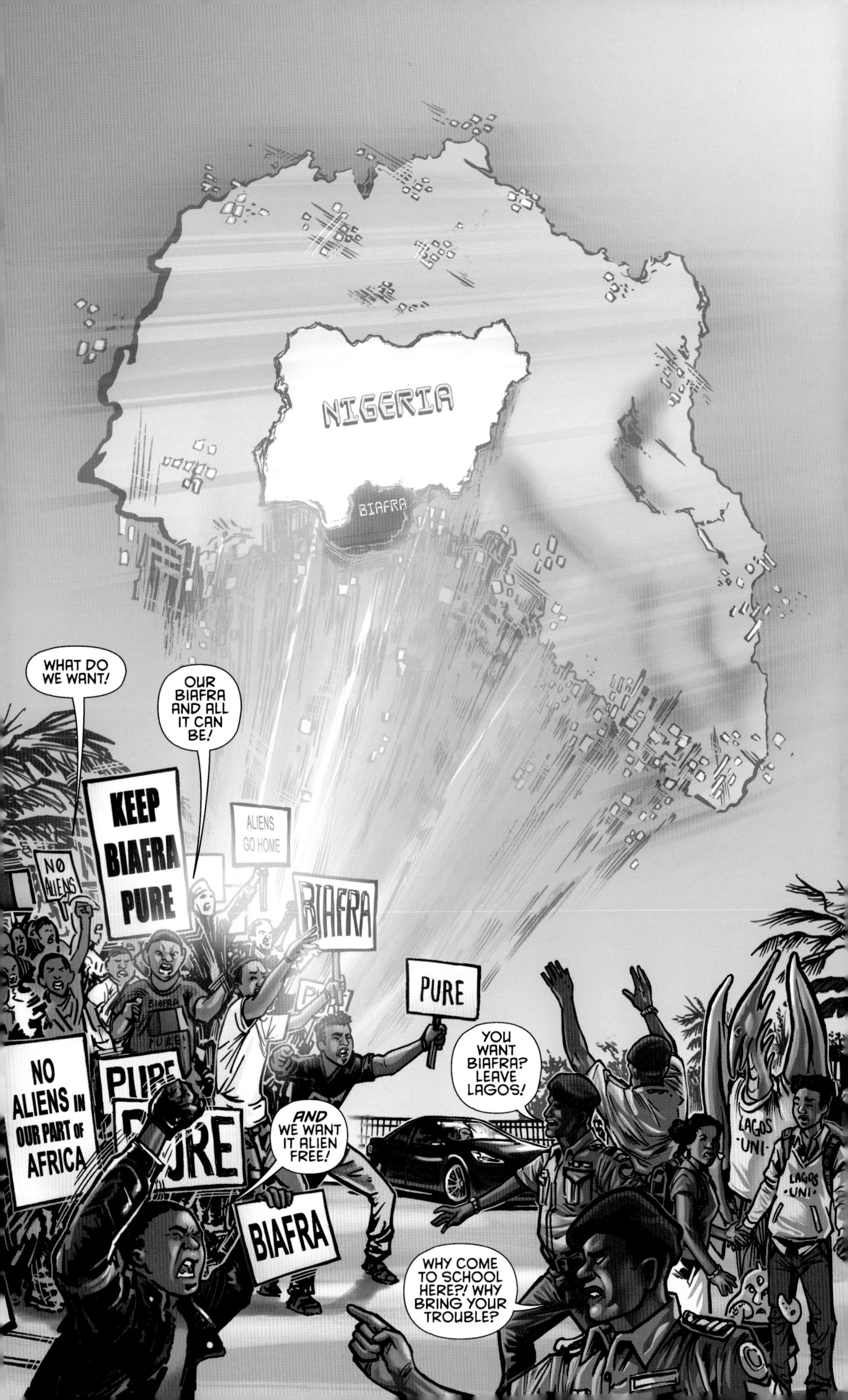
NIGERIA
BIAFRA
WHAT DO WE WANT!
OUR BIAFRA AND ALL IT CAN BE!
KEEP BIAFRA PURE
NO ALIENS
ALIENS GO HOME
BIAFRA
PURE
NO ALIENS IN OUR PART OF AFRICA
PURE
PURE
AND WE WANT IT ALIEN FREE!
BIAFRA
YOU WANT BIAFRA? LEAVE LAGOS!
LAGOS UNI
LAGOS UNI
WHY COME TO SCHOOL HERE?! WHY BRING YOUR TROUBLE?

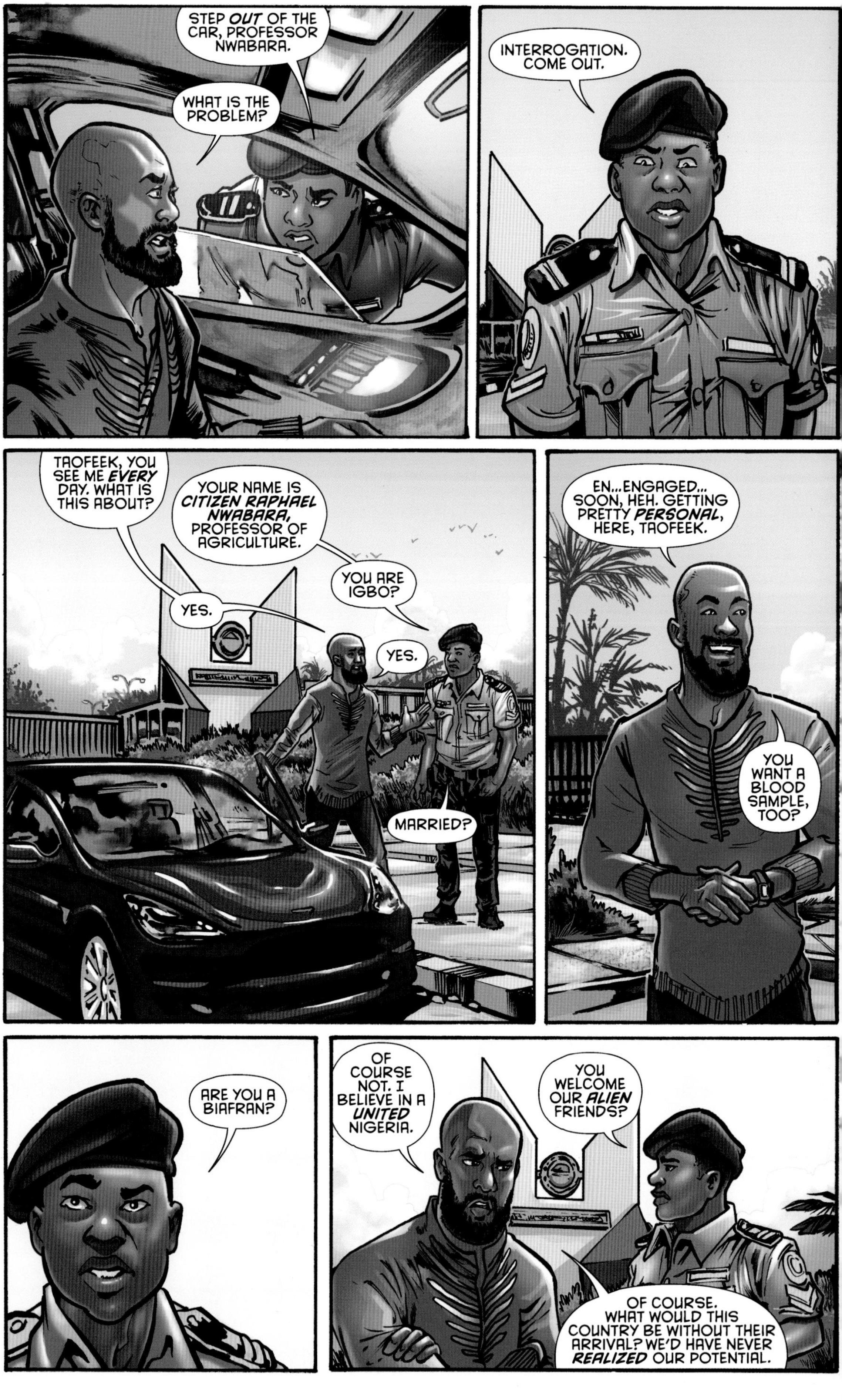
STEP OUT OF THE CAR, PROFESSOR NWABARA.
WHAT IS THE PROBLEM?
INTERROGATION. COME OUT.
TAOFEEK, YOU SEE ME EVERY DAY. WHAT IS THIS ABOUT?
YOUR NAME IS CITIZEN RAPHAEL NWABARA, PROFESSOR OF AGRICULTURE.
YES.
YOU ARE IGBO?
YES.
MARRIED?
EN...ENGAGED... SOON, HEH. GETTING PRETTY PERSONAL, HERE, TAOFEEK.
YOU WANT A BLOOD SAMPLE, TOO?
ARE YOU A BIAFRAN?
OF COURSE NOT. I BELIEVE IN A UNITED NIGERIA.
YOU WELCOME OUR ALIEN FRIENDS?
OF COURSE. WHAT WOULD THIS COUNTRY BE WITHOUT THEIR ARRIVAL? WE'D HAVE NEVER REALIZED OUR POTENTIAL.

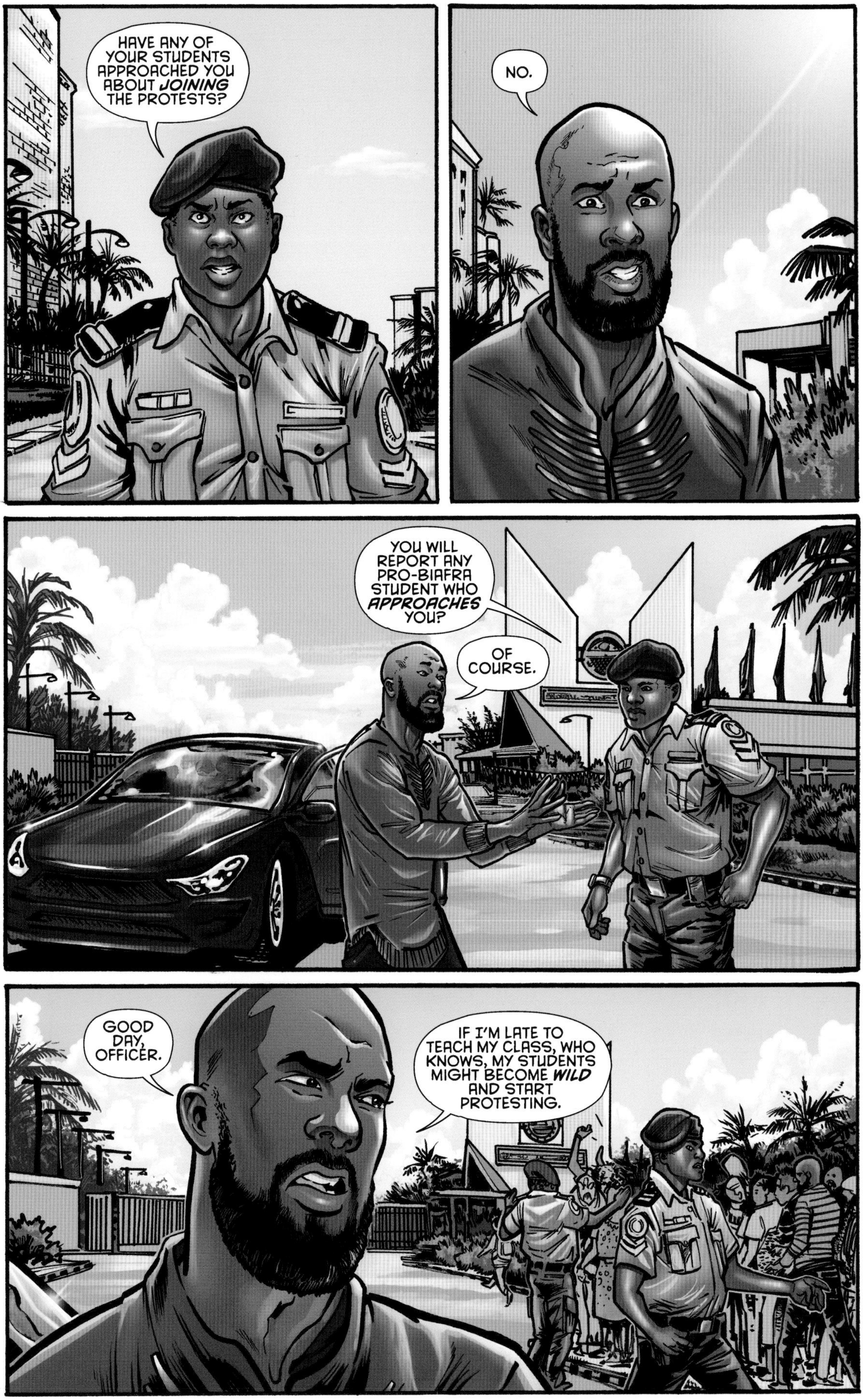
HAVE ANY OF YOUR STUDENTS APPROACHED YOU ABOUT *JOINING* THE PROTESTS?
NO.
YOU WILL REPORT ANY PRO-BIAFRA STUDENT WHO *APPROACHES* YOU?
OF COURSE.
GOOD DAY, OFFICER.
IF I'M LATE TO TEACH MY CLASS, WHO KNOWS, MY STUDENTS MIGHT BECOME *WILD* AND START PROTESTING.

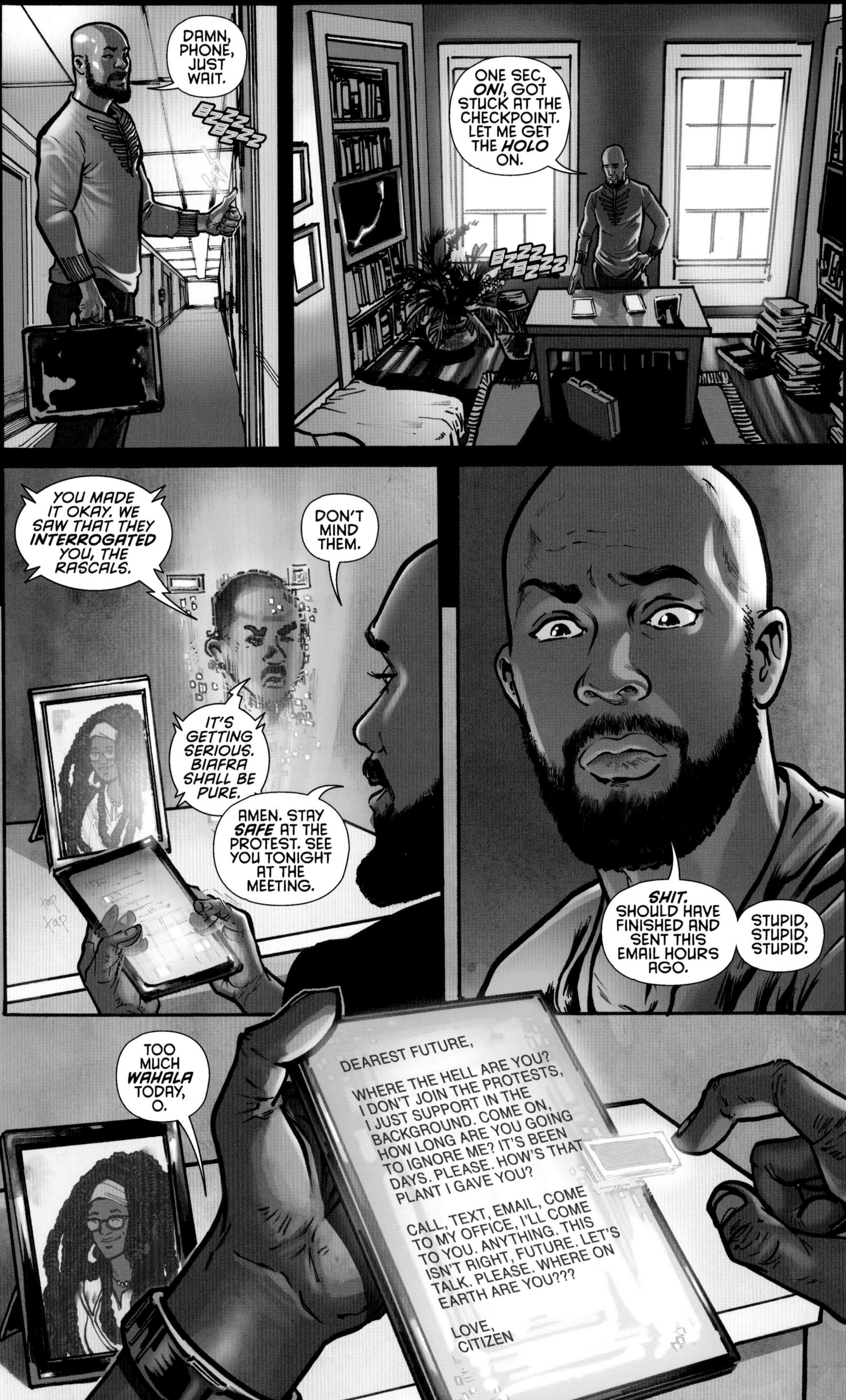
DAMN, PHONE, JUST WAIT.
BZZZZ BZZZZ
ONE SEC, ONI, GOT STUCK AT THE CHECKPOINT. LET ME GET THE HOLO ON.
BZZZZ BZZZZ
YOU MADE IT OKAY. WE SAW THAT THEY INTERROGATED YOU, THE RASCALS.
DON'T MIND THEM.
IT'S GETTING SERIOUS. BIAFRA SHALL BE PURE.
AMEN. STAY SAFE AT THE PROTEST. SEE YOU TONIGHT AT THE MEETING.
tap tap
SHIT. SHOULD HAVE FINISHED AND SENT THIS EMAIL HOURS AGO.
STUPID, STUPID, STUPID.
TOO MUCH WAHALA TODAY, O.
DEAREST FUTURE,
WHERE THE HELL ARE YOU? I DON'T JOIN THE PROTESTS, I JUST SUPPORT IN THE BACKGROUND. COME ON, HOW LONG ARE YOU GOING TO IGNORE ME? IT'S BEEN DAYS. PLEASE. HOW'S THAT PLANT I GAVE YOU?
CALL, TEXT, EMAIL, COME TO MY OFFICE, I'LL COME TO YOU. ANYTHING. THIS ISN'T RIGHT, FUTURE. LET'S TALK. PLEASE. WHERE ON EARTH ARE YOU???
LOVE, CITIZEN

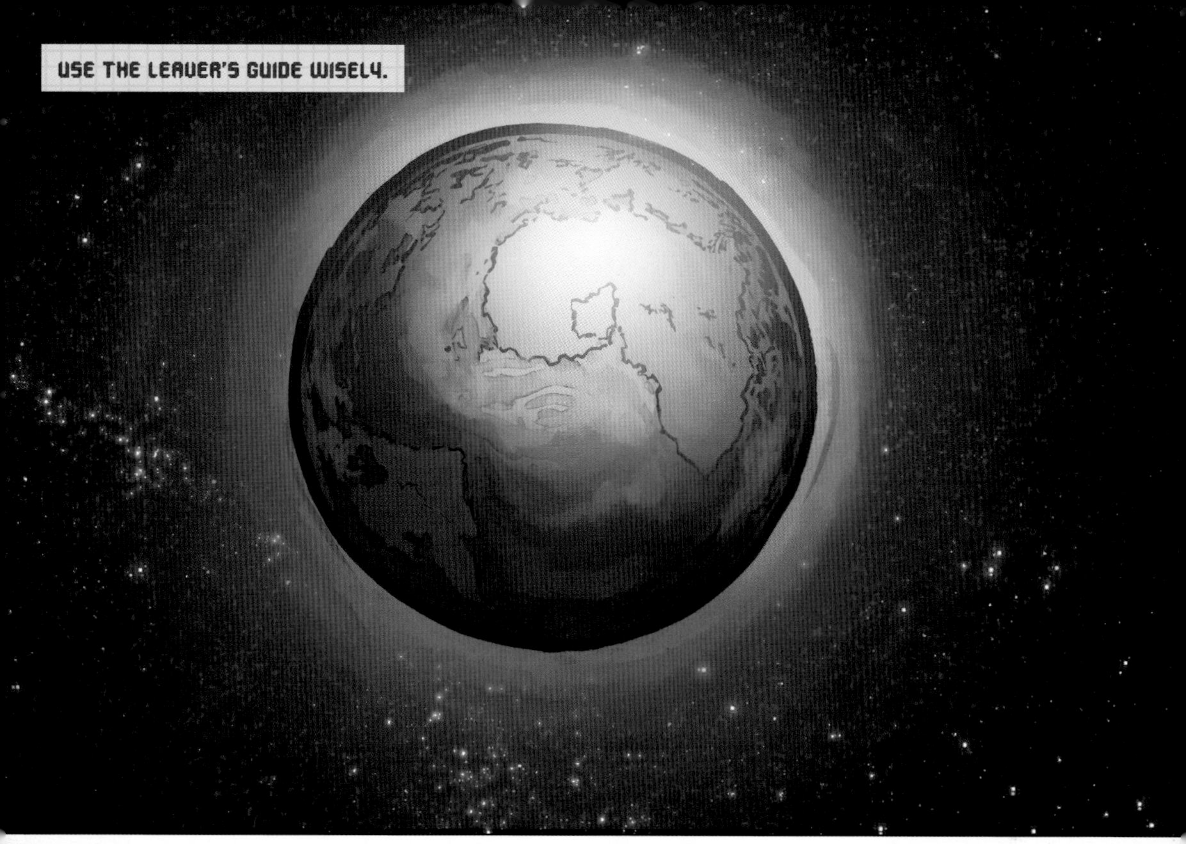
USE THE LEAVER'S GUIDE WISELY.

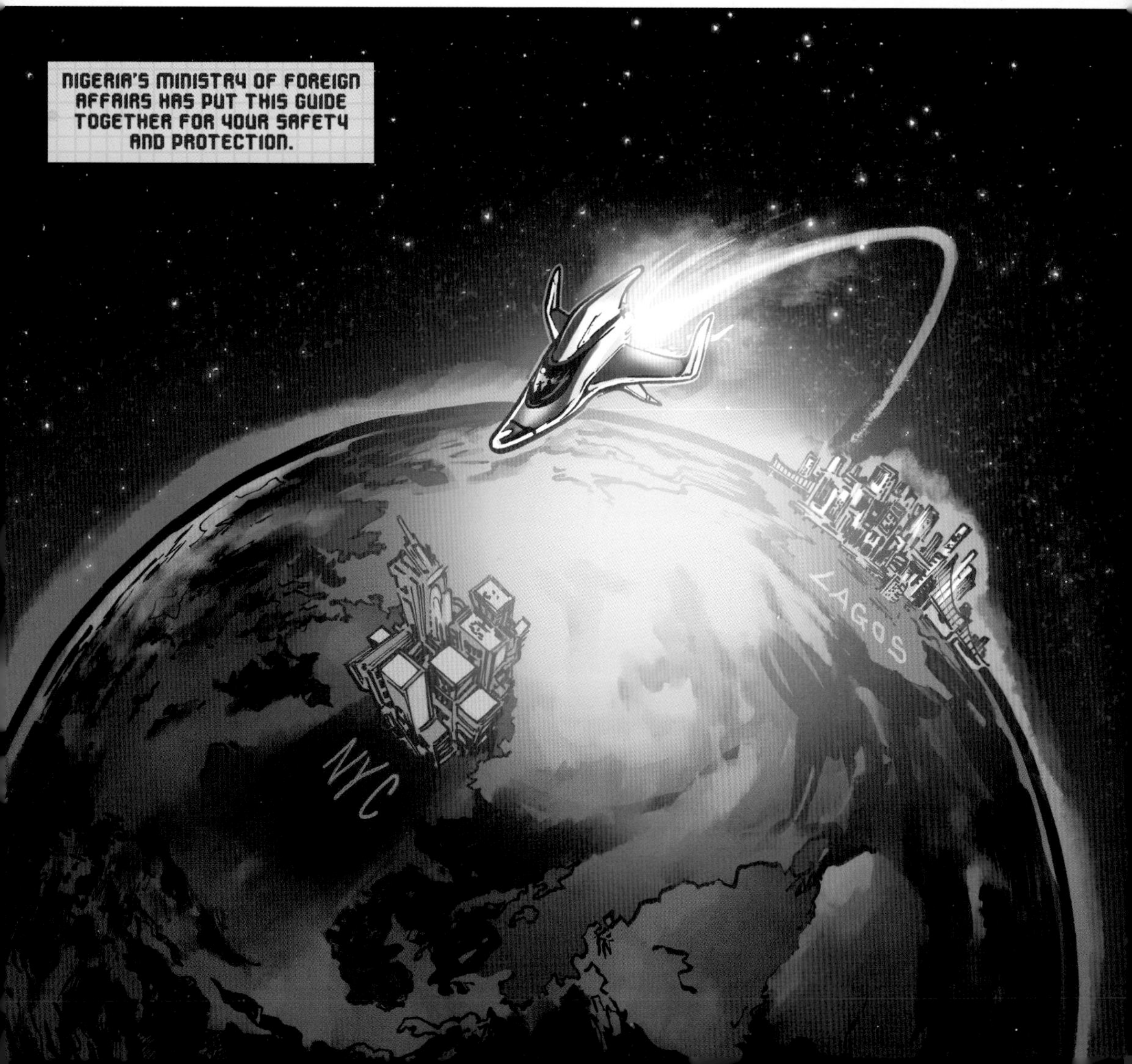
NIGERIA'S MINISTRY OF FOREIGN AFFAIRS HAS PUT THIS GUIDE TOGETHER FOR YOUR SAFETY AND PROTECTION.
LAGOS
NYC

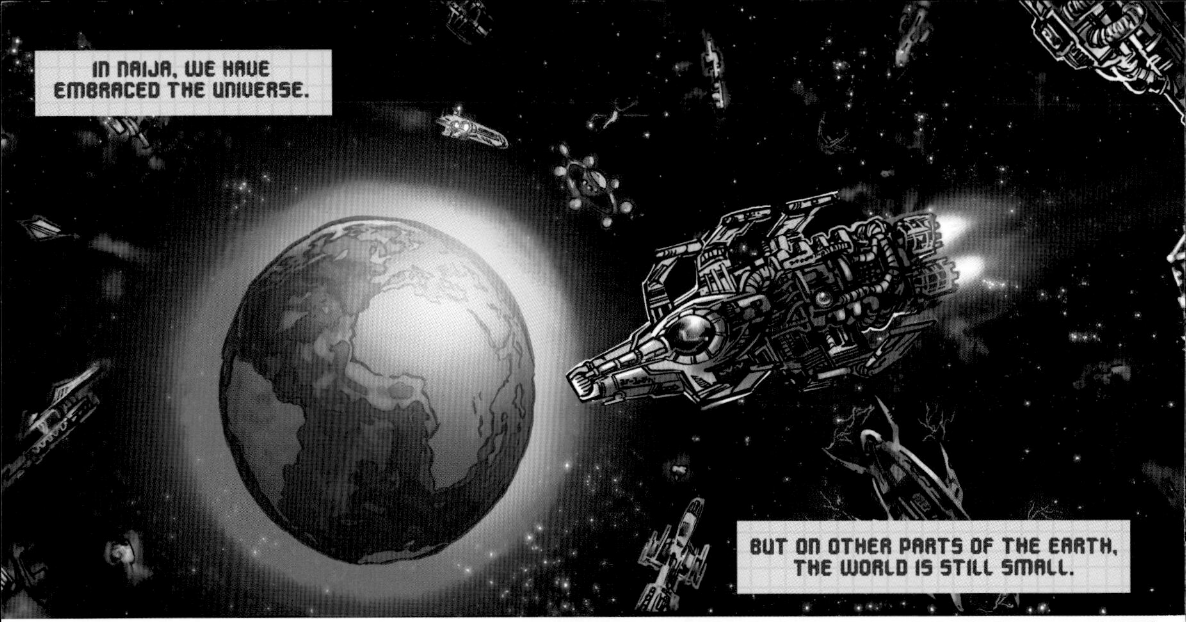
IN NAIJA, WE HAVE EMBRACED THE UNIVERSE.
BUT ON OTHER PARTS OF THE EARTH, THE WORLD IS STILL SMALL.

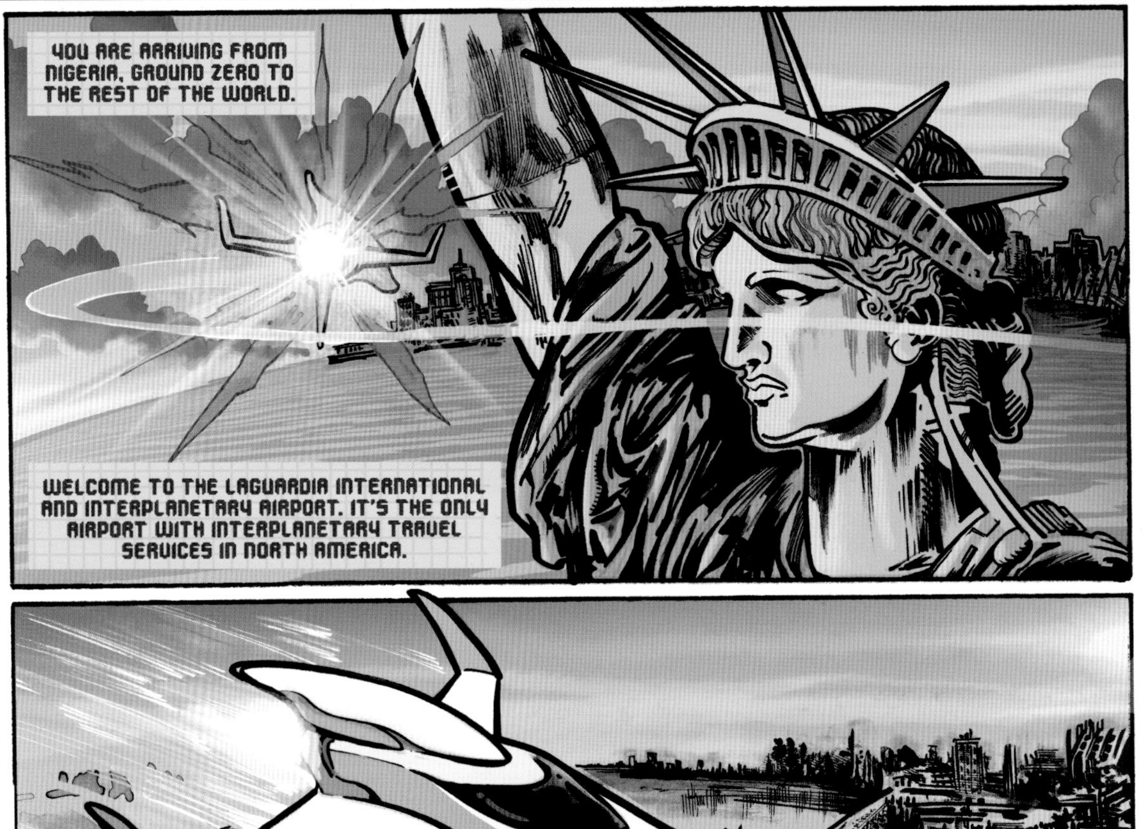
YOU ARE ARRIVING FROM NIGERIA, GROUND ZERO TO THE REST OF THE WORLD.
WELCOME TO THE LAGUARDIA INTERNATIONAL AND INTERPLANETARY AIRPORT. IT'S THE ONLY AIRPORT WITH INTERPLANETARY TRAVEL SERVICES IN NORTH AMERICA.

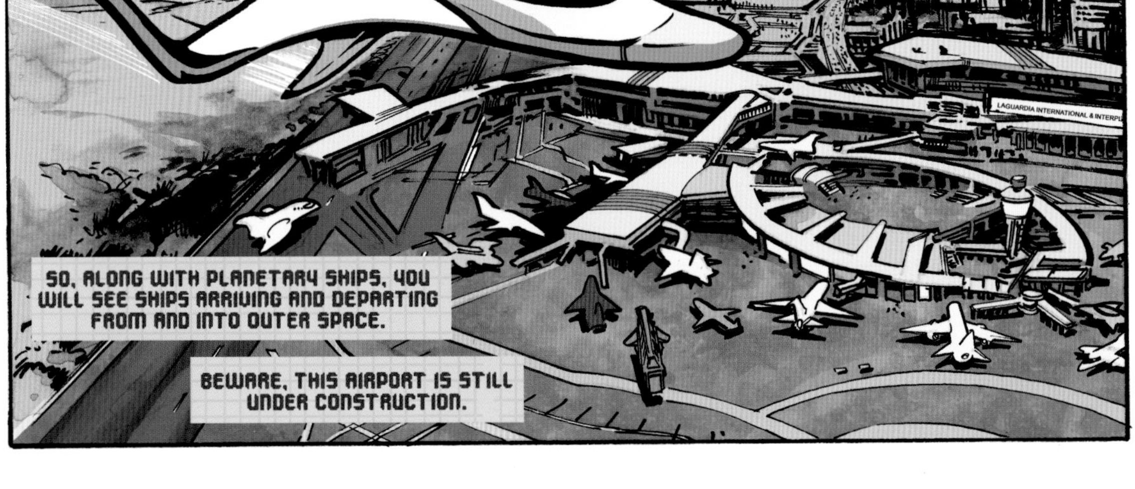
LAGUARDIA INTERNATIONAL & INTERPL
SO, ALONG WITH PLANETARY SHIPS, YOU WILL SEE SHIPS ARRIVING AND DEPARTING FROM AND INTO OUTER SPACE.
BEWARE, THIS AIRPORT IS STILL UNDER CONSTRUCTION.

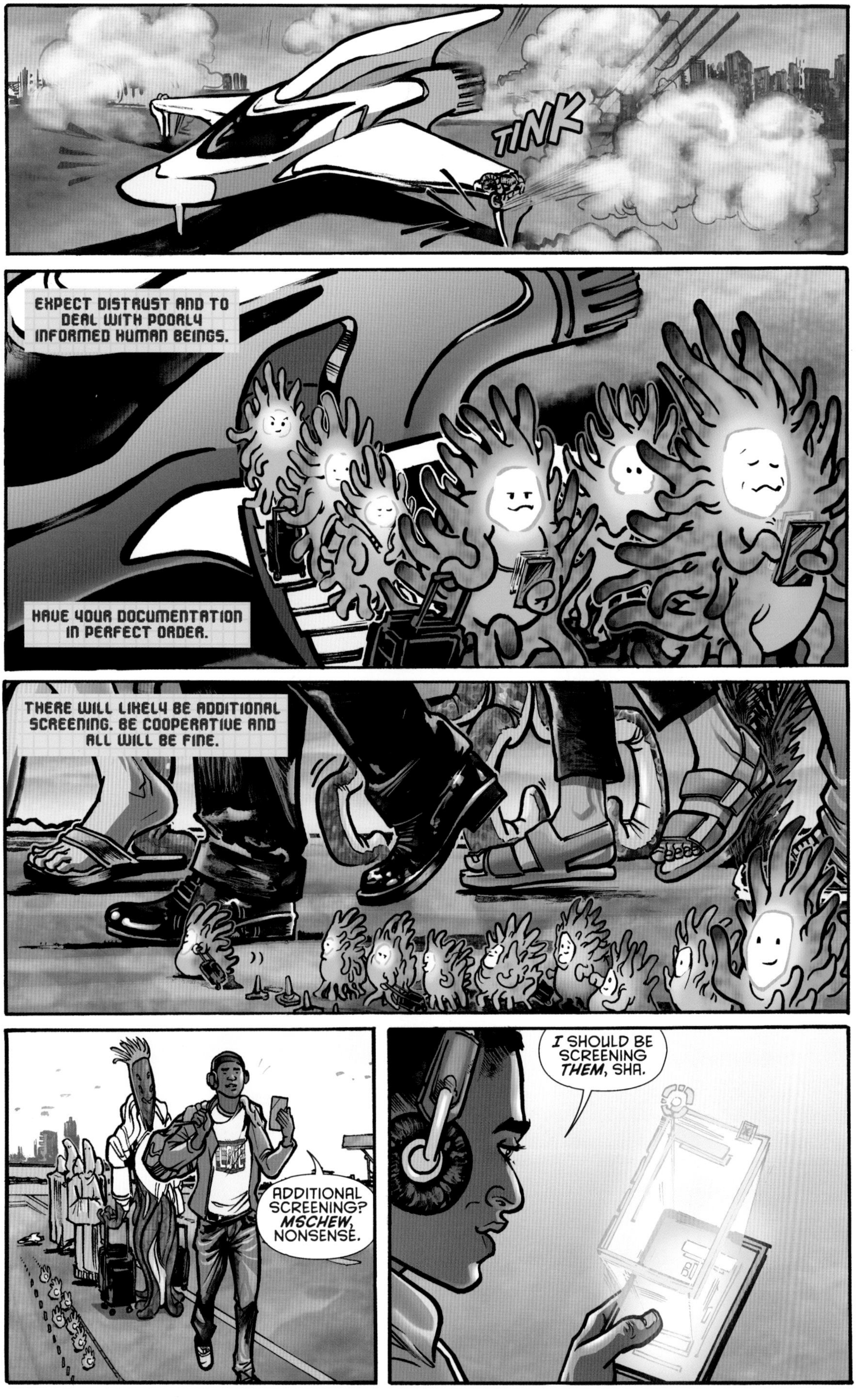
TINK
EXPECT DISTRUST AND TO DEAL WITH POORLY INFORMED HUMAN BEINGS.
HAVE YOUR DOCUMENTATION IN PERFECT ORDER.
THERE WILL LIKELY BE ADDITIONAL SCREENING. BE COOPERATIVE AND ALL WILL BE FINE.
ADDITIONAL SCREENING? *MSCHEW*, NONSENSE.
I SHOULD BE SCREENING *THEM*, SHA.

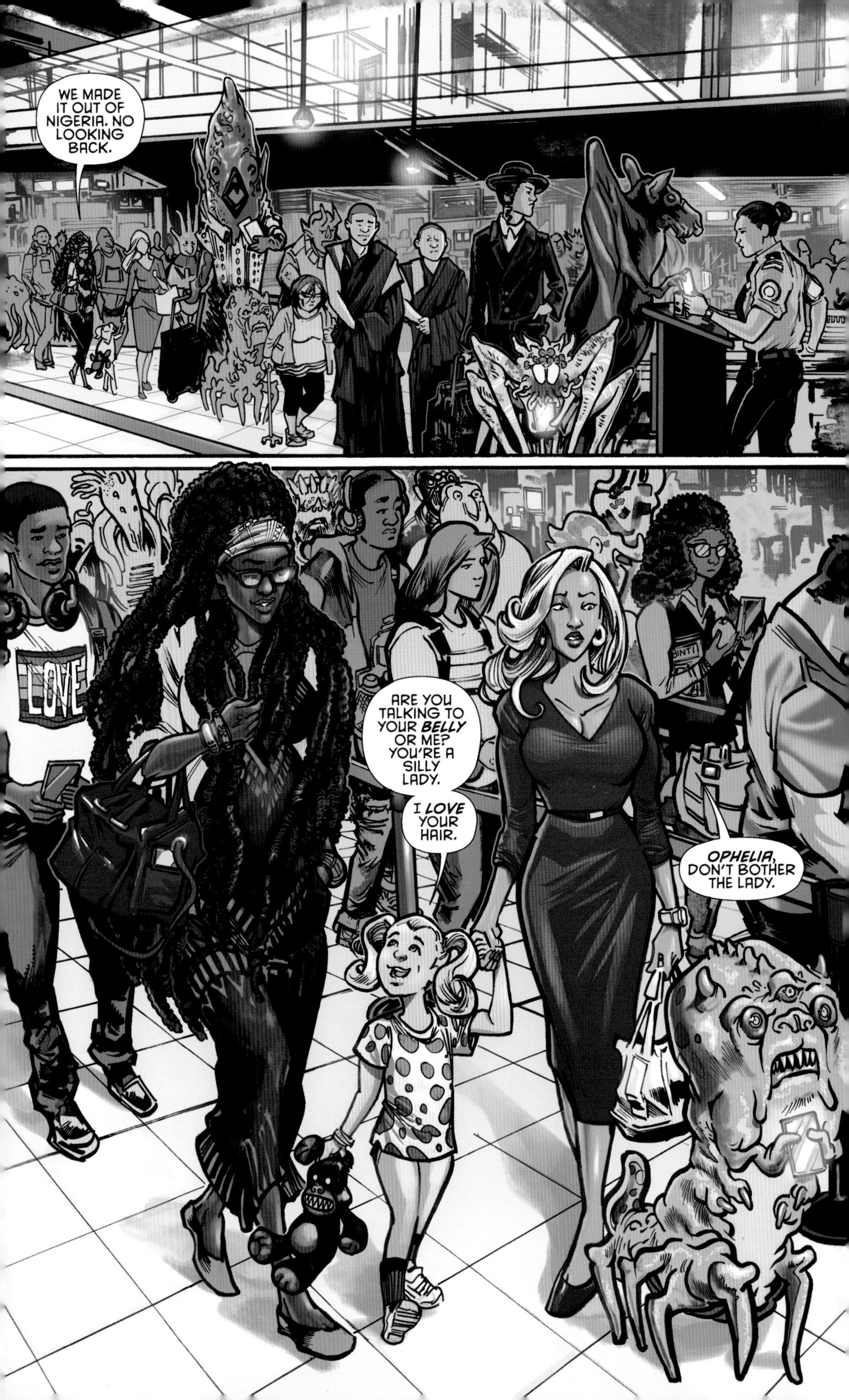
WE MADE IT OUT OF NIGERIA. NO LOOKING BACK.
LOVE
BINTI
ARE YOU TALKING TO YOUR *BELLY* OR ME? YOU'RE A SILLY LADY.
I *LOVE* YOUR HAIR.
OPHELIA, DON'T BOTHER THE LADY.

OH, CAN YOUR BABY SPEAK *ENGLISH* ALREADY?

IS IT AN ALIEN?

THIS DOESN'T LOOK GOOD, BUT DON'T WORRY. I'LL GET US THROUGH.

WAIT UNTIL GRANDMA FINDS OUT ABOUT YOU. THAT'S GOING TO BE FUN.

CAN YOUR *BABY* SEE ME?

I'LL DANCE FOR HIM OR HER. *LOOK!*

ⵣⵣⴰⴷⵃ ⴷⵡⵛⵯⵙⵏⵗ ⵏⵢ

ⴼⵅⴷ ⵣⵏⵙⴷ ⵢⵞⴳⵯ ⵯⵙⴷⵙⵯ

DROP!

AH!

OPHELIA! NO!

YANK

WHAT IS IT WITH *YOU* AND HAIR OR TENTACLES!

REMEMBER WHAT WE TALKED ABOUT, OPHELIA?! IT'S *NOT* POLITE!

I'M *SO* SORRY!

IT'S FINE.

ARE THOSE REAL?

YES.

WOW. THEY'RE BEAUTIFUL!

THANKS.

HERE. SO RIGHT IT SAYS

GO! JUST

NEXT.

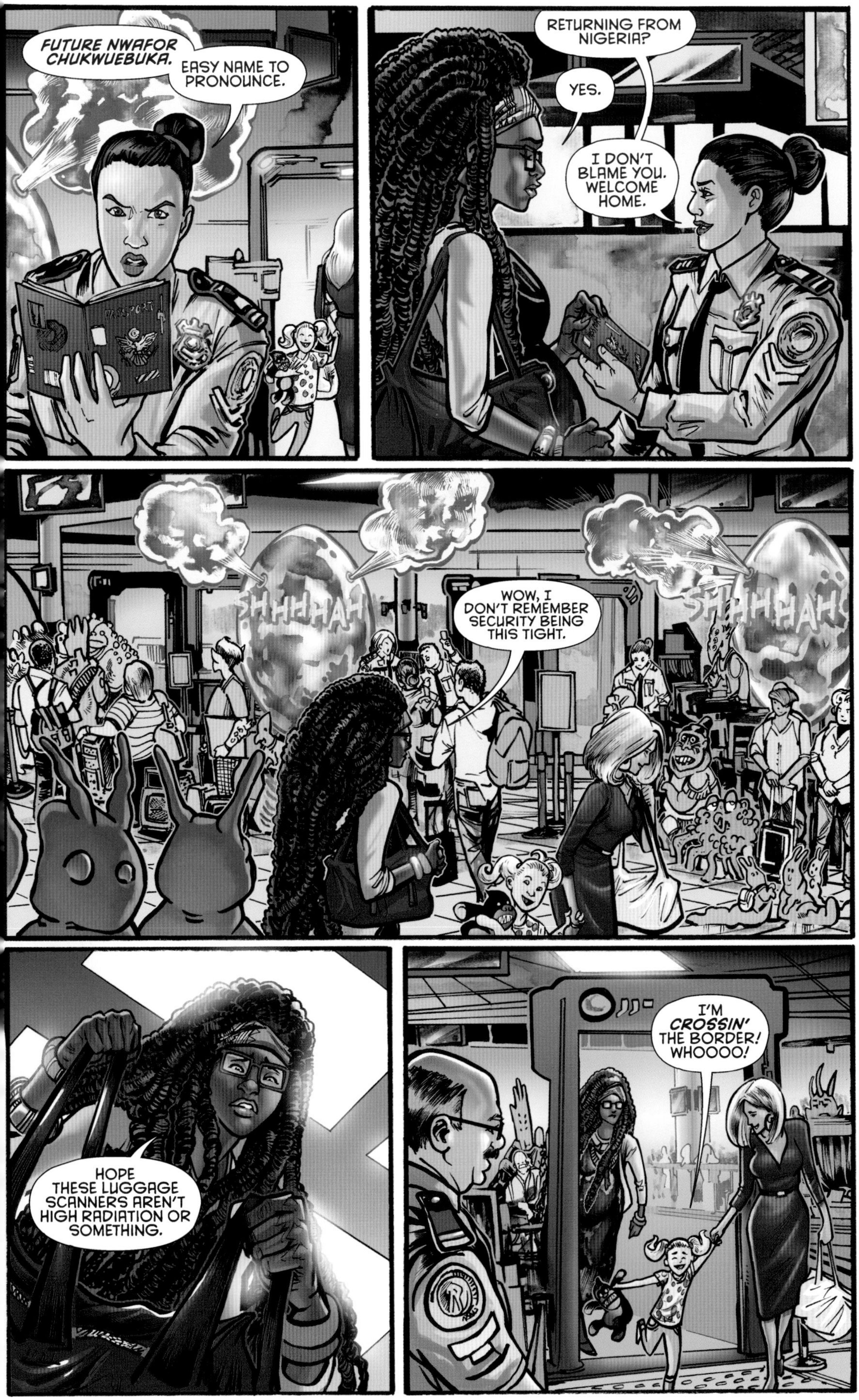
FUTURE NWAFOR CHUKWUEBUKA.
EASY NAME TO PRONOUNCE.
RETURNING FROM NIGERIA?
YES.
I DON'T BLAME YOU. WELCOME HOME.
SHHHHAH
WOW, I DON'T REMEMBER SECURITY BEING THIS TIGHT.
SHHHHAH
HOPE THESE LUGGAGE SCANNERS AREN'T HIGH RADIATION OR SOMETHING.
I'M CROSSIN' THE BORDER! WHOOOO!

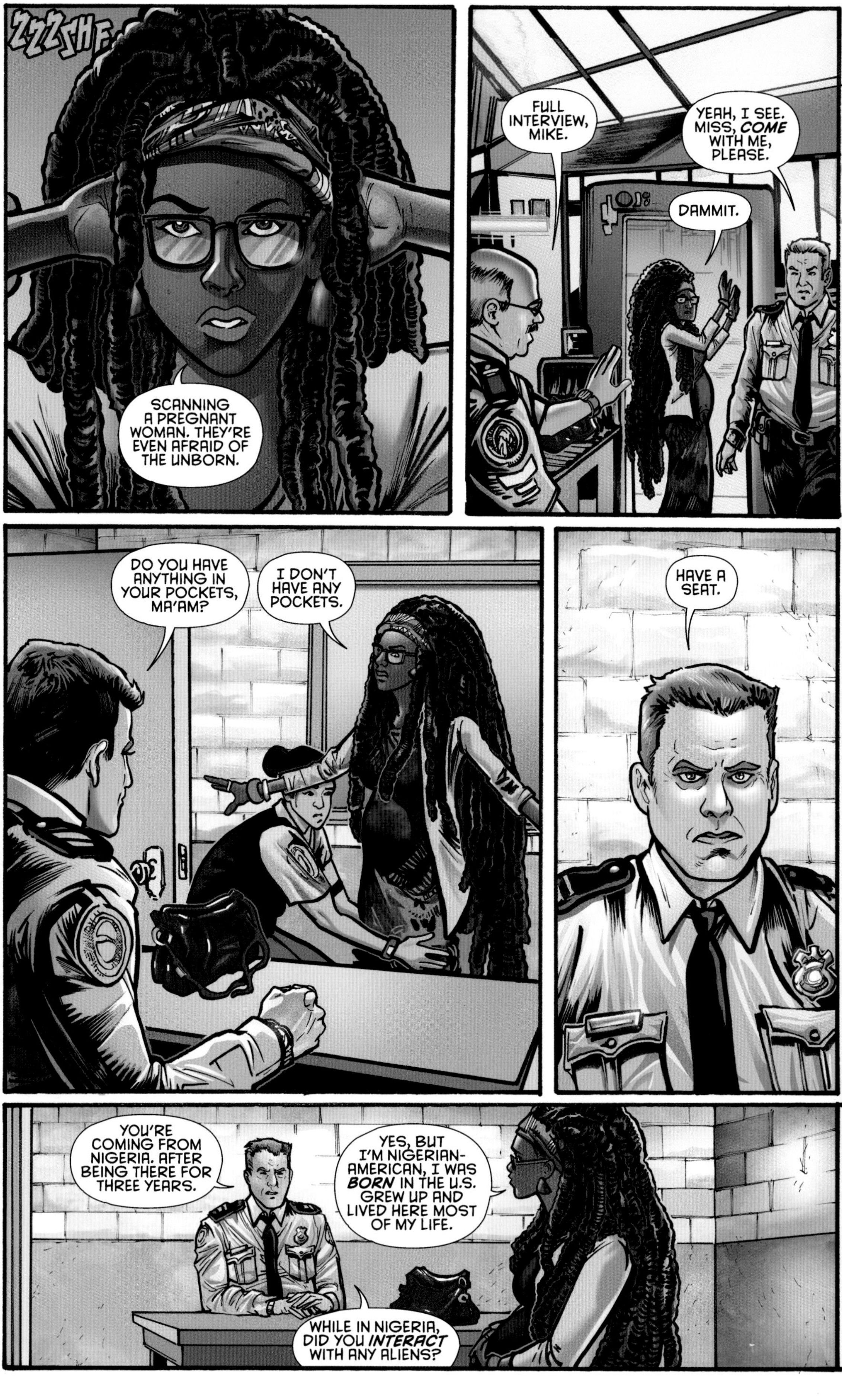
ZZZSHF
SCANNING A PREGNANT WOMAN. THEY'RE EVEN AFRAID OF THE UNBORN.
FULL INTERVIEW, MIKE.
YEAH, I SEE. MISS, COME WITH ME, PLEASE.
DAMMIT.
DO YOU HAVE ANYTHING IN YOUR POCKETS, MA'AM?
I DON'T HAVE ANY POCKETS.
HAVE A SEAT.
YOU'RE COMING FROM NIGERIA. AFTER BEING THERE FOR THREE YEARS.
YES, BUT I'M NIGERIAN-AMERICAN, I WAS BORN IN THE U.S. GREW UP AND LIVED HERE MOST OF MY LIFE.
WHILE IN NIGERIA, DID YOU INTERACT WITH ANY ALIENS?

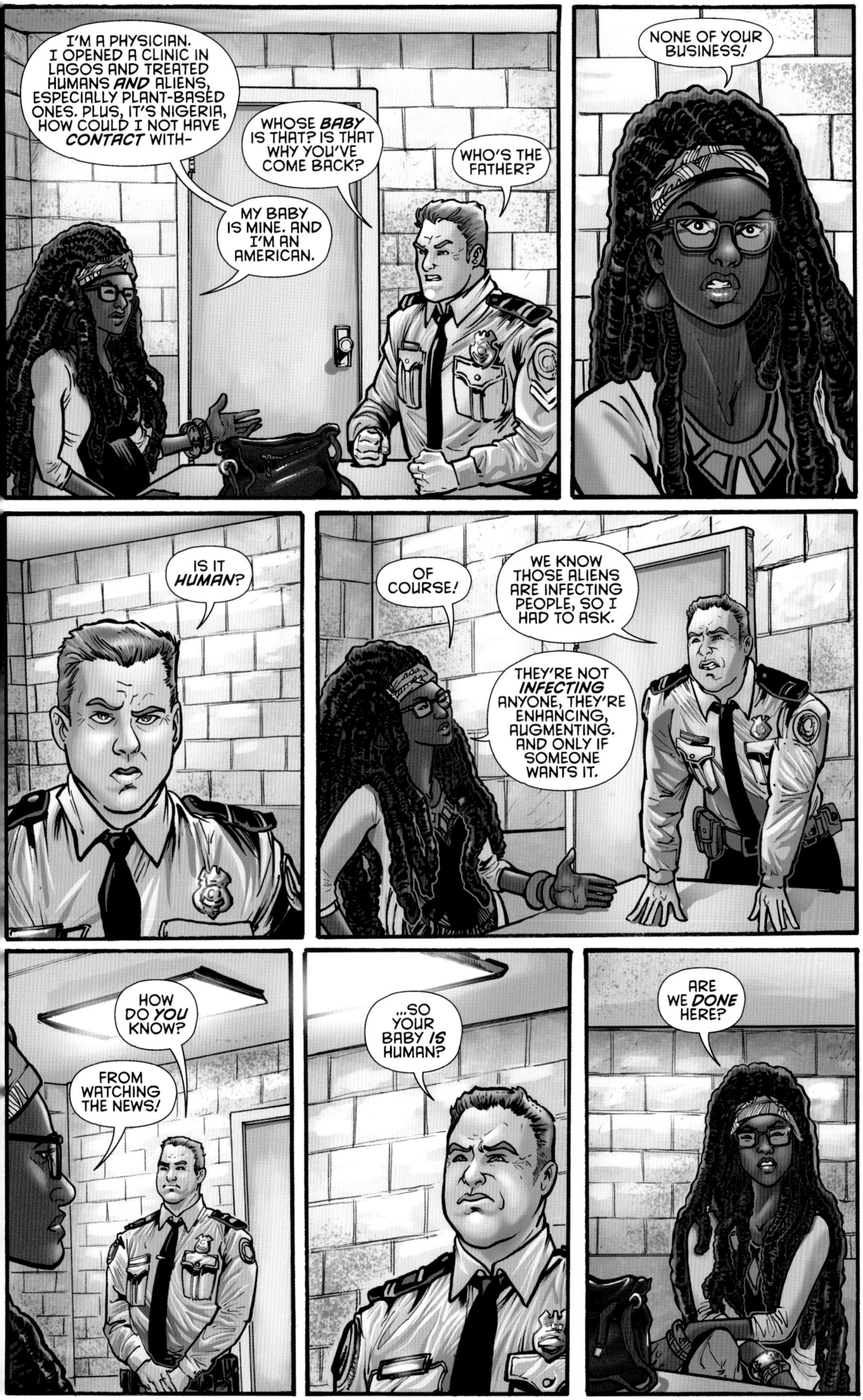
I'M A PHYSICIAN. I OPENED A CLINIC IN LAGOS AND TREATED HUMANS *AND* ALIENS, ESPECIALLY PLANT-BASED ONES. PLUS, IT'S NIGERIA, HOW COULD I NOT HAVE *CONTACT* WITH-
WHOSE *BABY* IS THAT? IS THAT WHY YOU'VE COME BACK?
MY BABY IS MINE. AND I'M AN AMERICAN.
WHO'S THE FATHER?
NONE OF YOUR BUSINESS!
IS IT *HUMAN*?
OF COURSE!
WE KNOW THOSE ALIENS ARE INFECTING PEOPLE, SO I HAD TO ASK.
THEY'RE NOT *INFECTING* ANYONE, THEY'RE ENHANCING, AUGMENTING. AND ONLY IF SOMEONE WANTS IT.
HOW DO *YOU* KNOW?
FROM WATCHING THE NEWS!
...SO YOUR BABY *IS* HUMAN?
ARE WE *DONE* HERE?

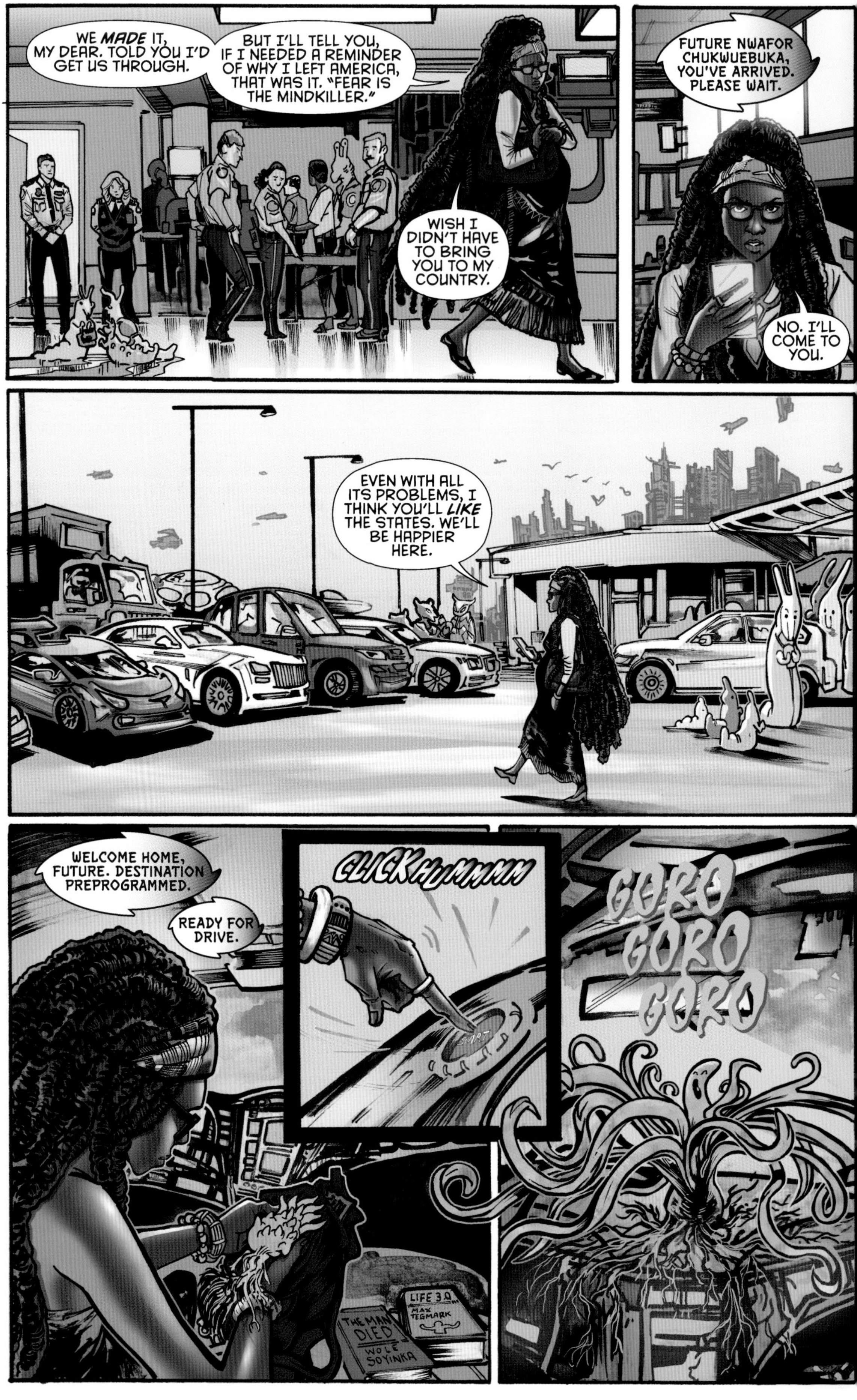
WE MADE IT, MY DEAR. TOLD YOU I'D GET US THROUGH.
BUT I'LL TELL YOU, IF I NEEDED A REMINDER OF WHY I LEFT AMERICA, THAT WAS IT. "FEAR IS THE MINDKILLER."
WISH I DIDN'T HAVE TO BRING YOU TO MY COUNTRY.
FUTURE NWAFOR CHUKWUEBUKA, YOU'VE ARRIVED. PLEASE WAIT.
NO. I'LL COME TO YOU.
EVEN WITH ALL ITS PROBLEMS, I THINK YOU'LL LIKE THE STATES. WE'LL BE HAPPIER HERE.
WELCOME HOME, FUTURE. DESTINATION PREPROGRAMMED.
READY FOR DRIVE.
CLICK HUMMMM
GORO GORO GORO
THE MAN DIED
WOLE SOYINKA
LIFE 3.0
MAX TEGMARK

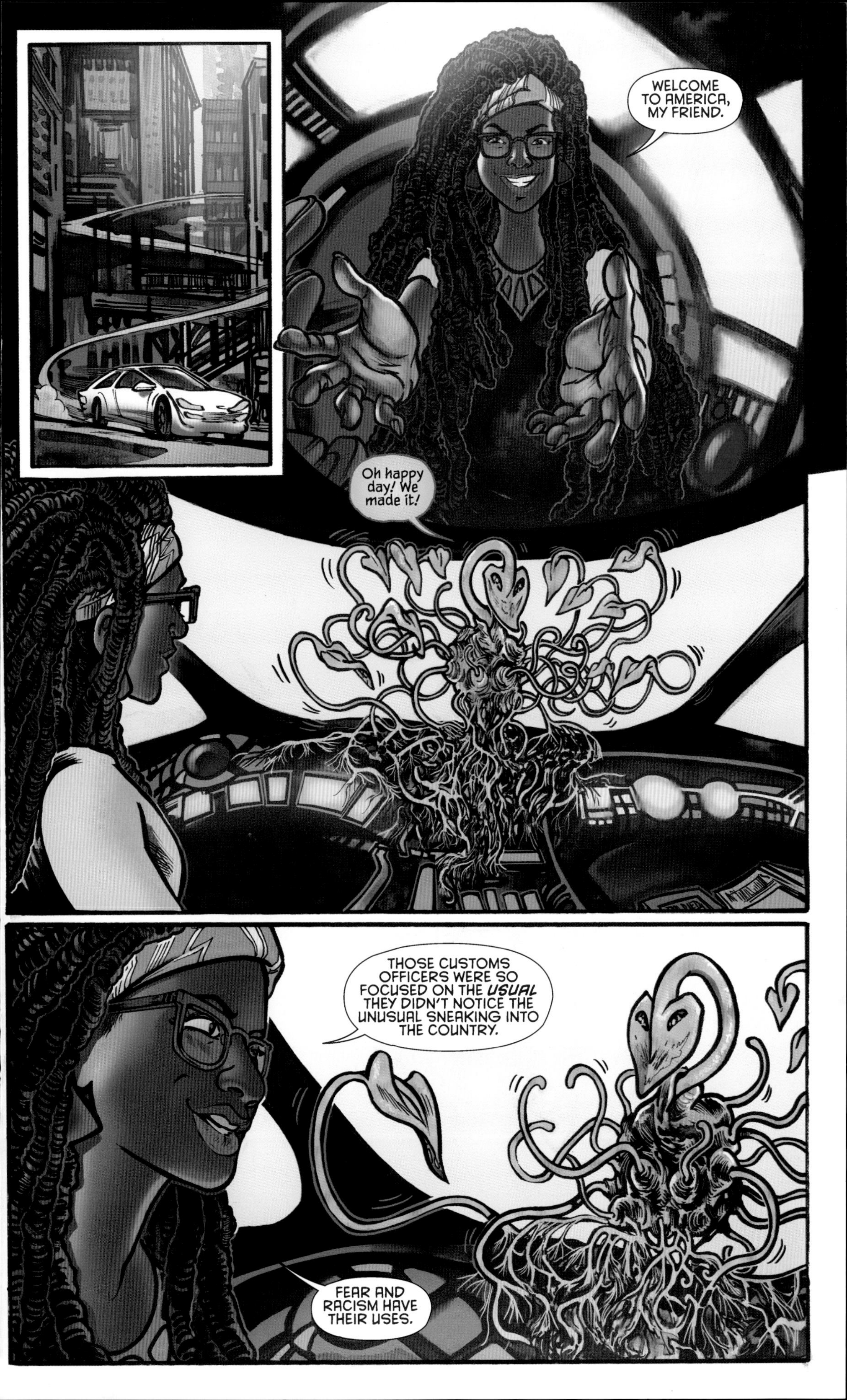
WELCOME TO AMERICA, MY FRIEND.
Oh happy day! We made it!
THOSE CUSTOMS OFFICERS WERE SO FOCUSED ON THE *USUAL* THEY DIDN'T NOTICE THE UNUSUAL SNEAKING INTO THE COUNTRY.
FEAR AND RACISM HAVE THEIR USES.

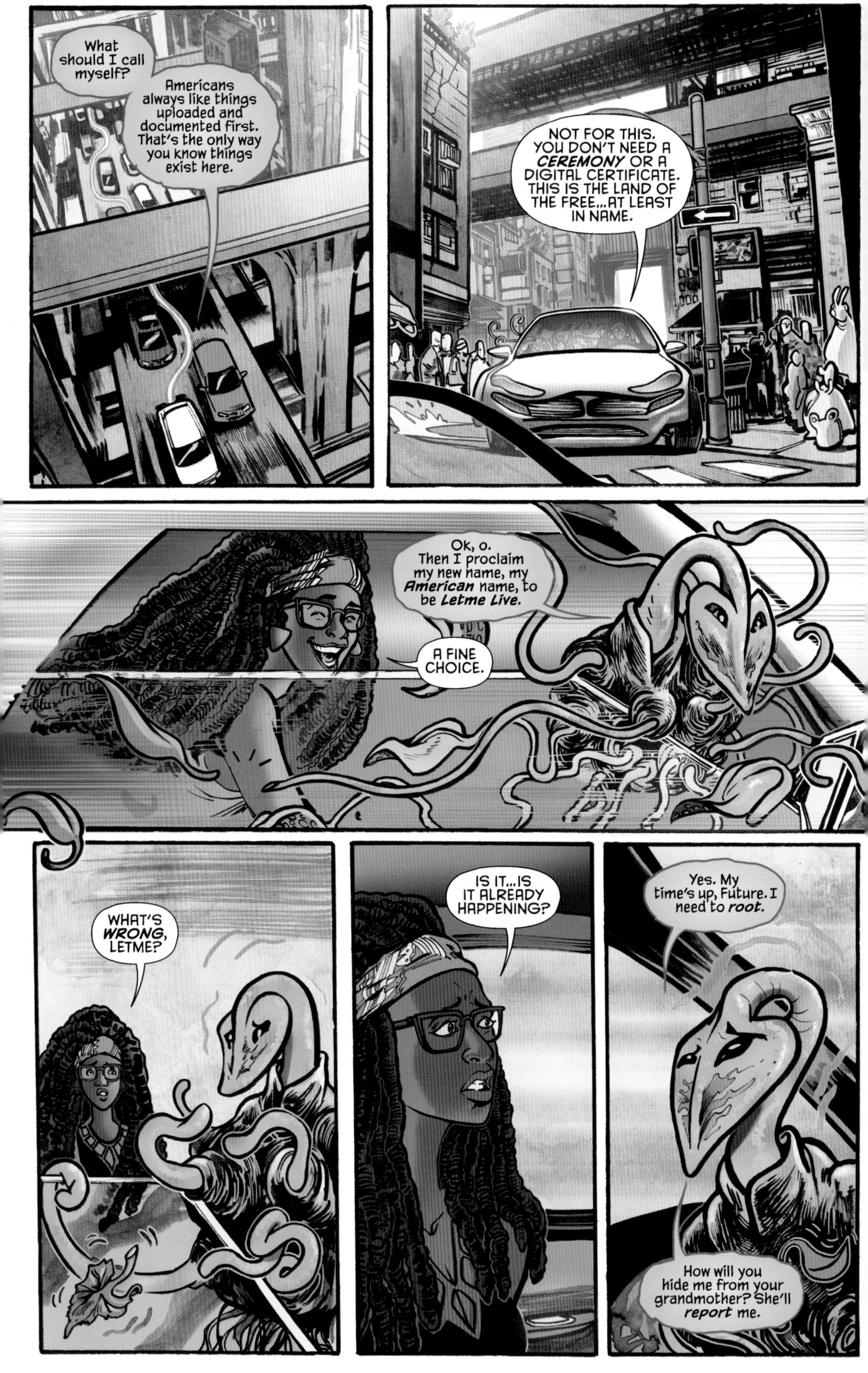
What should I call myself?
Americans always like things uploaded and documented first. That's the only way you know things exist here.
NOT FOR THIS. YOU DON'T NEED A *CEREMONY* OR A DIGITAL CERTIFICATE. THIS IS THE LAND OF THE FREE...AT LEAST IN NAME.
Ok, o. Then I proclaim my new name, my *American* name, to be *Letme Live.*
A FINE CHOICE.
WHAT'S *WRONG*, LETME?
IS IT...IS IT ALREADY HAPPENING?
Yes. My time's up, Future. I need to *root.*
How will you hide me from your grandmother? She'll *report* me.

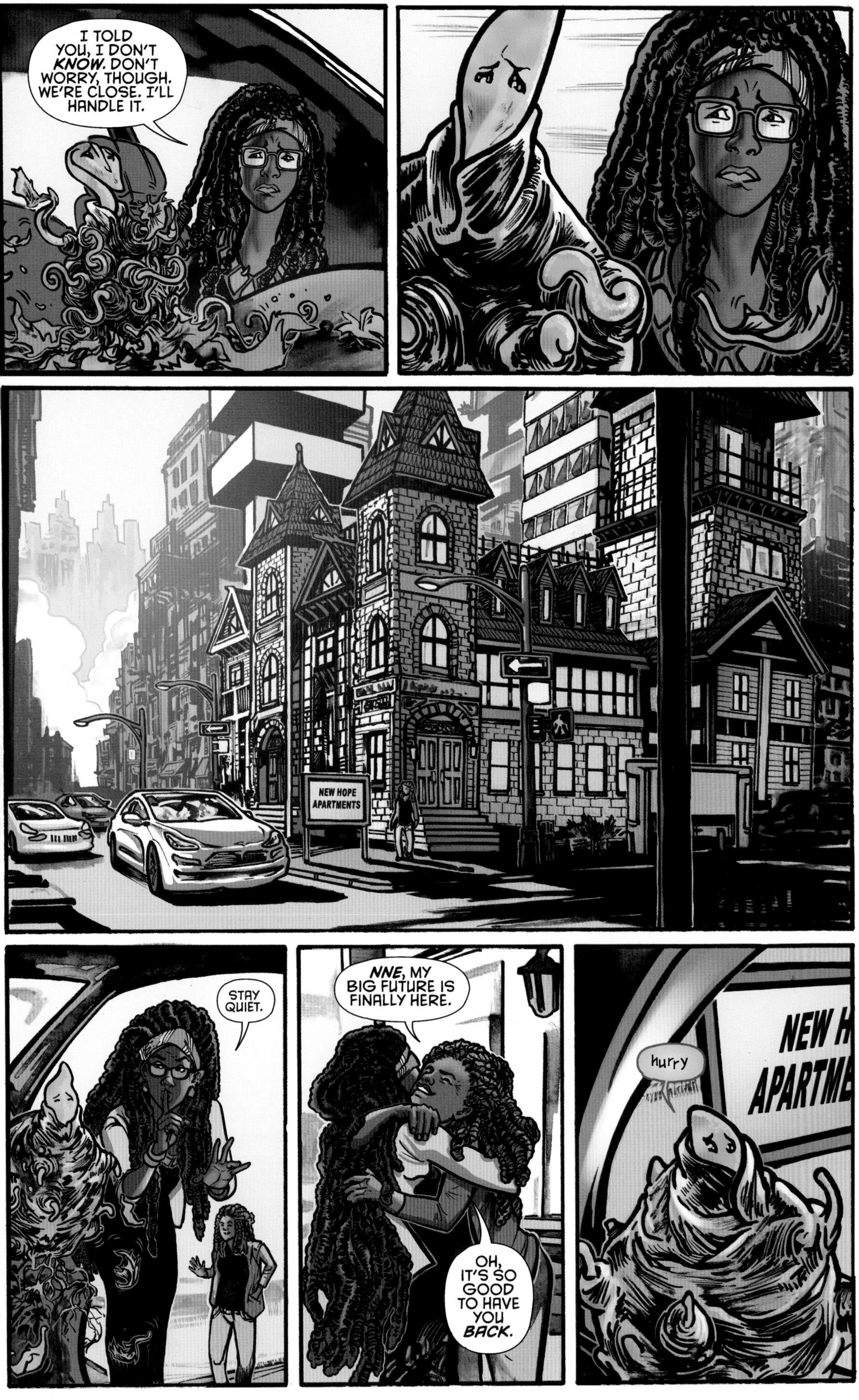
I TOLD YOU, I DON'T KNOW. DON'T WORRY, THOUGH. WE'RE CLOSE. I'LL HANDLE IT.
NEW HOPE APARTMENTS
STAY QUIET.
NNE, MY BIG FUTURE IS FINALLY HERE.
OH, IT'S SO GOOD TO HAVE YOU BACK.
hurry

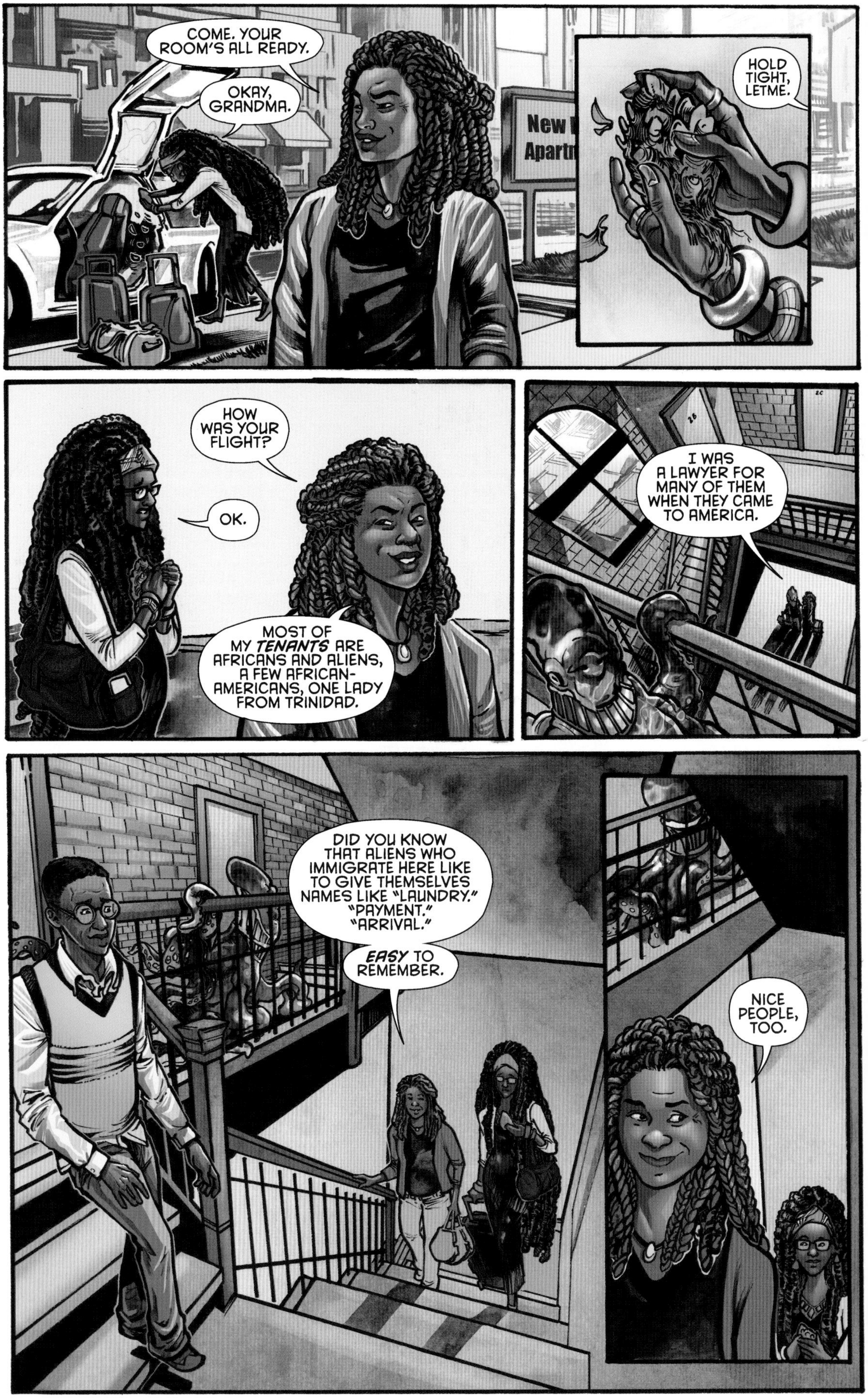
COME. YOUR ROOM'S ALL READY.
OKAY, GRANDMA.
HOLD TIGHT, LETME.
HOW WAS YOUR FLIGHT?
OK.
MOST OF MY *TENANTS* ARE AFRICANS AND ALIENS, A FEW AFRICAN-AMERICANS, ONE LADY FROM TRINIDAD.
I WAS A LAWYER FOR MANY OF THEM WHEN THEY CAME TO AMERICA.
DID YOU KNOW THAT ALIENS WHO IMMIGRATE HERE LIKE TO GIVE THEMSELVES NAMES LIKE "LAUNDRY." "PAYMENT." "ARRIVAL."
EASY TO REMEMBER.
NICE PEOPLE, TOO.

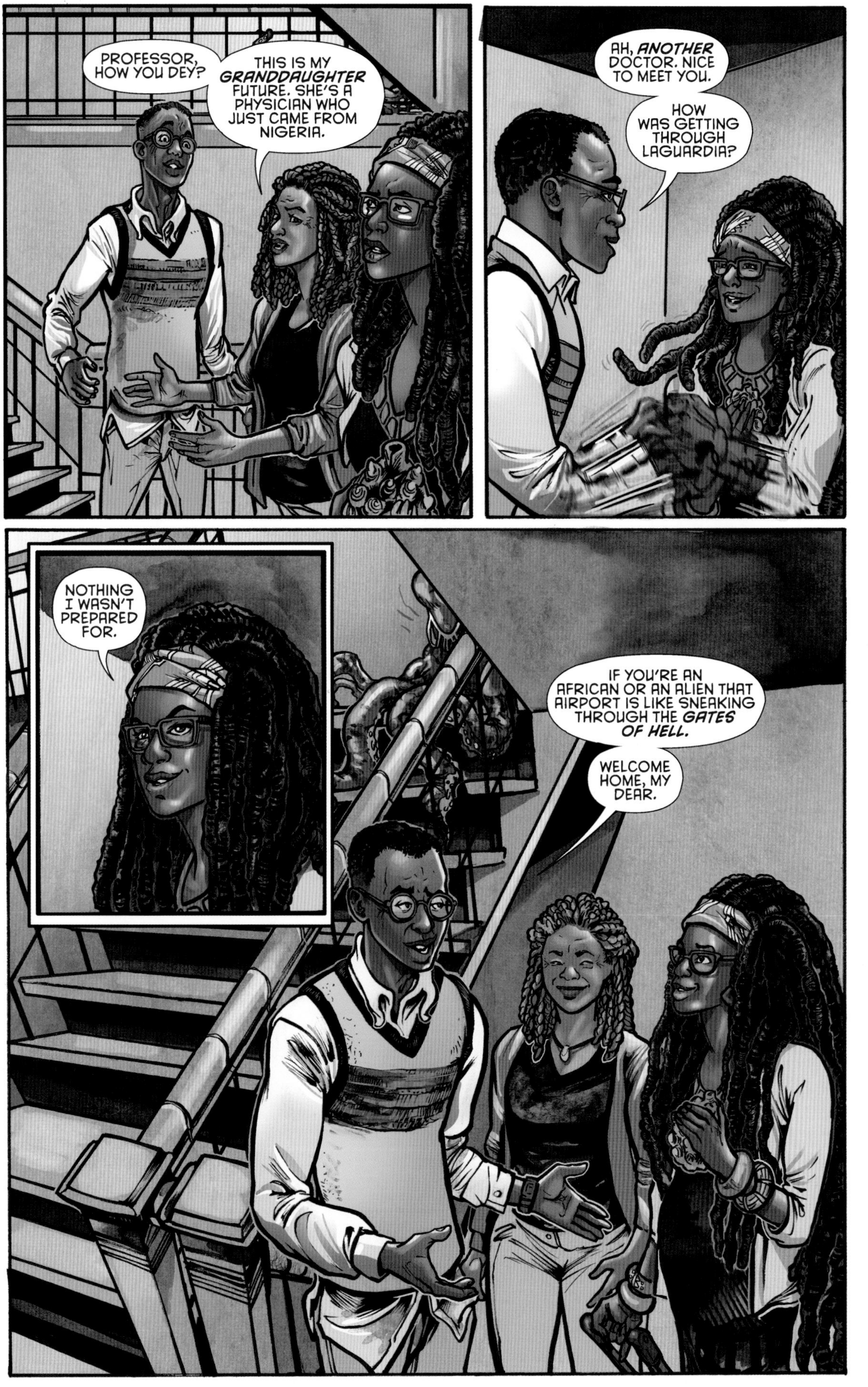
PROFESSOR, HOW YOU DEY?
THIS IS MY GRANDDAUGHTER FUTURE. SHE'S A PHYSICIAN WHO JUST CAME FROM NIGERIA.
AH, ANOTHER DOCTOR. NICE TO MEET YOU.
HOW WAS GETTING THROUGH LAGUARDIA?
NOTHING I WASN'T PREPARED FOR.
IF YOU'RE AN AFRICAN OR AN ALIEN THAT AIRPORT IS LIKE SNEAKING THROUGH THE GATES OF HELL.
WELCOME HOME, MY DEAR.

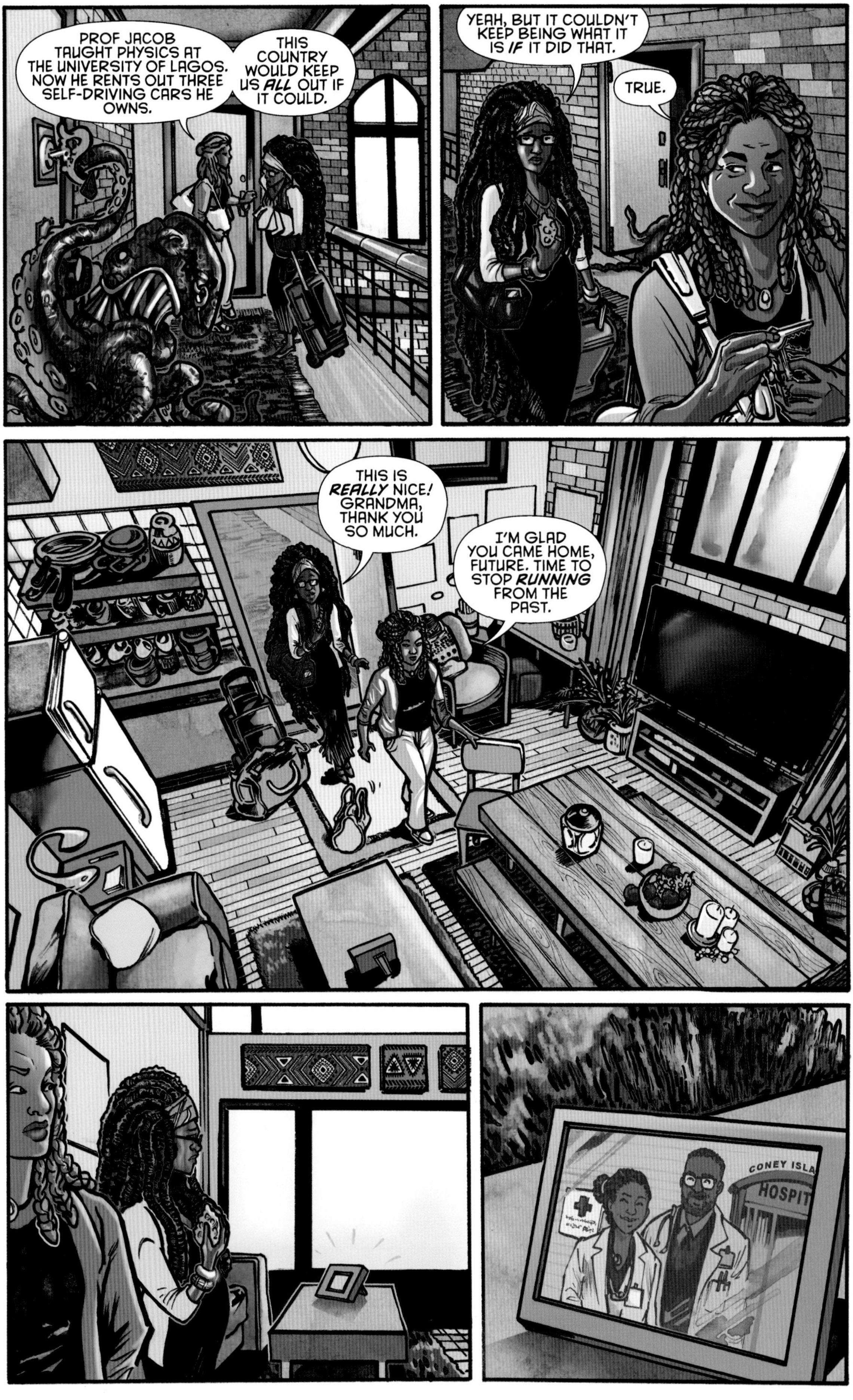

PROF JACOB TAUGHT PHYSICS AT THE UNIVERSITY OF LAGOS. NOW HE RENTS OUT THREE SELF-DRIVING CARS HE OWNS.
THIS COUNTRY WOULD KEEP US *ALL* OUT IF IT COULD.
YEAH, BUT IT COULDN'T KEEP BEING WHAT IT IS *IF* IT DID THAT.
TRUE.
THIS IS *REALLY* NICE! GRANDMA, THANK YOU SO MUCH.
I'M GLAD YOU CAME HOME, FUTURE. TIME TO STOP *RUNNING* FROM THE PAST.
CONEY ISLA
HOSPIT

THEY REBUILT CONEY ISLAND HOSPITAL, FUTURE.

THAT DOESN'T BRING THEM *BACK*, THOUGH. DOES IT.

I DIDN'T SAY IT DID. NOTHING WILL EVER BRING YOUR *PARENTS* BACK.

I WAS JUST POINTING IT OUT.

THERE'S *STILL* HOPE, FUTURE. I'M SO SO SO GLAD YOU'VE COME BACK.

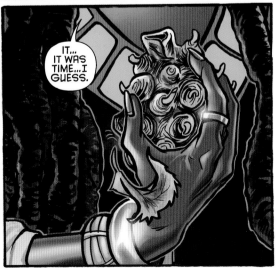

IT... IT WAS TIME...I GUESS.

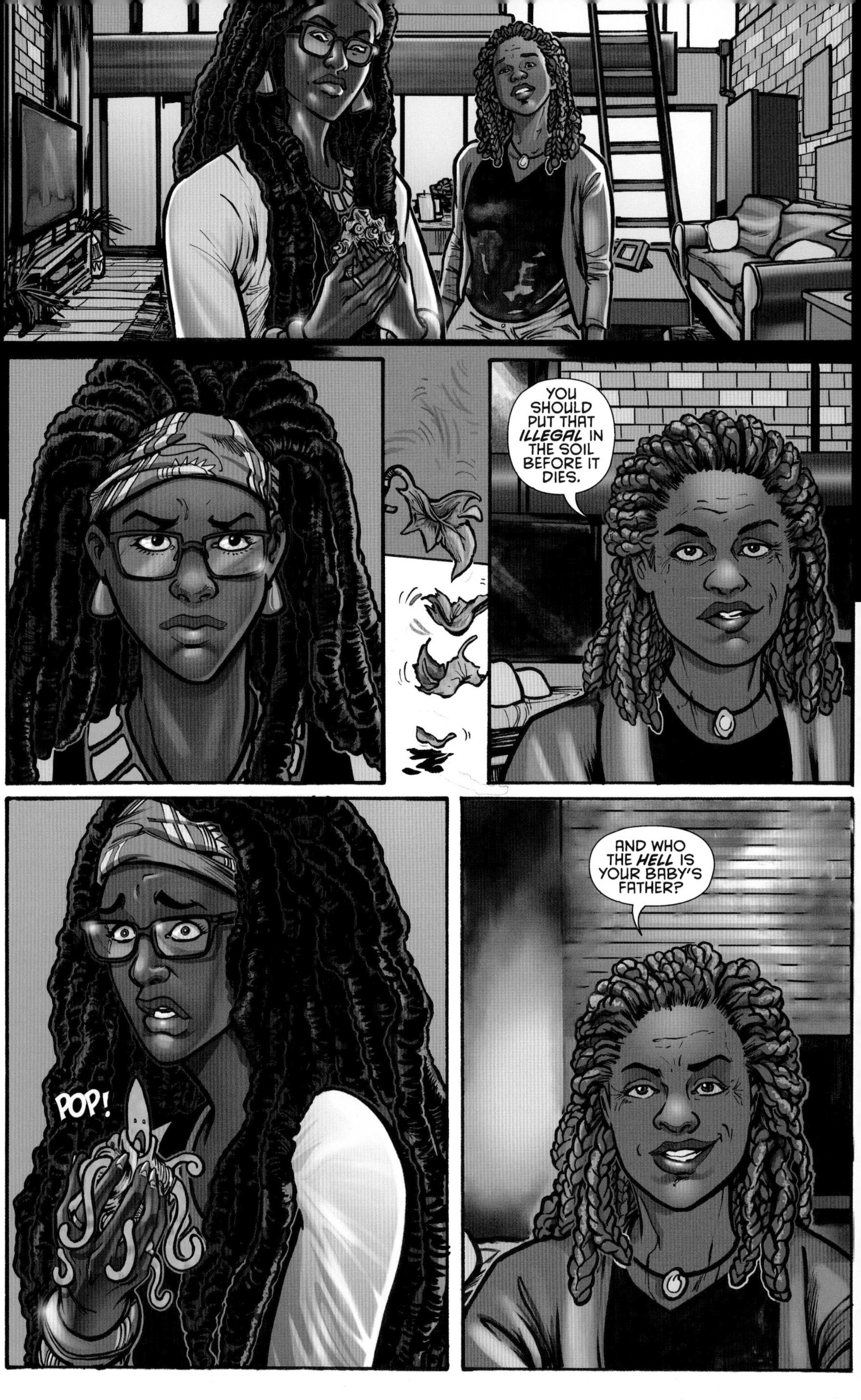
YOU SHOULD PUT THAT ILLEGAL IN THE SOIL BEFORE IT DIES.
POP!
AND WHO THE HELL IS YOUR BABY'S FATHER?

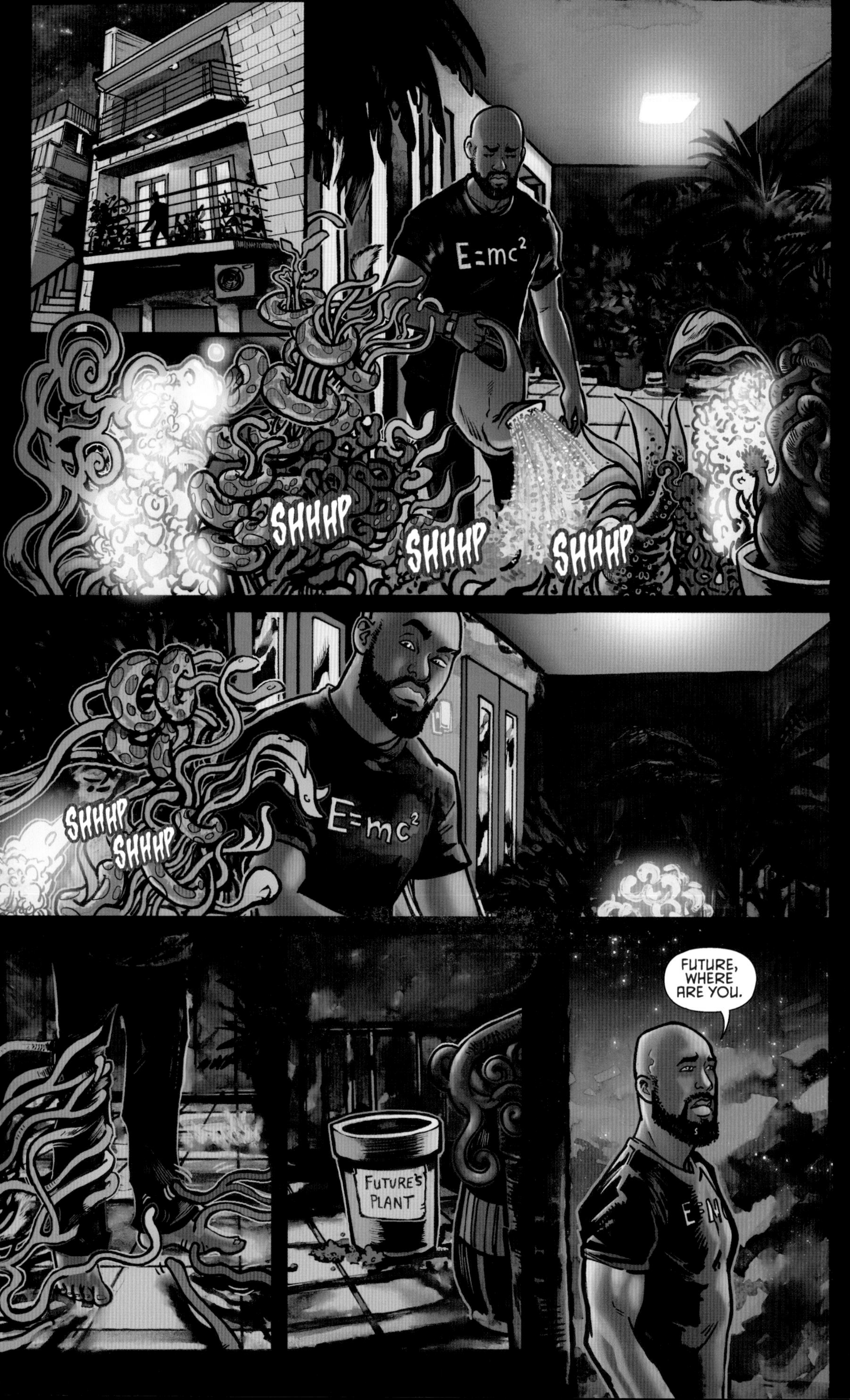
E=mc²
SHHHP
SHHHP
SHHHP
E=mc²
SHHHP
SHHHP
FUTURE'S PLANT
FUTURE, WHERE ARE YOU.

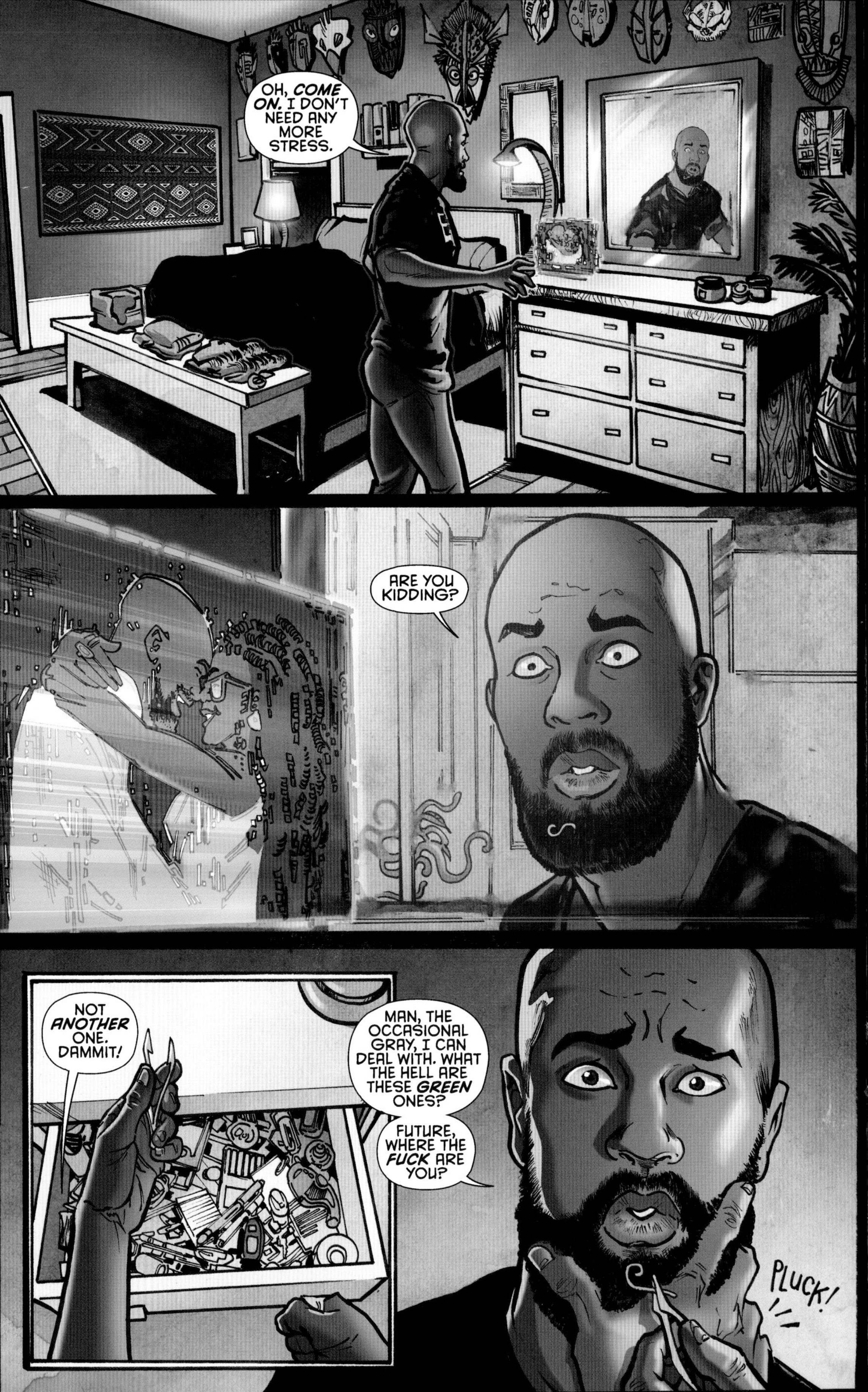
OH, COME ON. I DON'T NEED ANY MORE STRESS.
ARE YOU KIDDING?
NOT ANOTHER ONE. DAMMIT!
MAN, THE OCCASIONAL GRAY, I CAN DEAL WITH. WHAT THE HELL ARE THESE GREEN ONES?
FUTURE, WHERE THE FUCK ARE YOU?
PLUCK!

CHAPTER 2

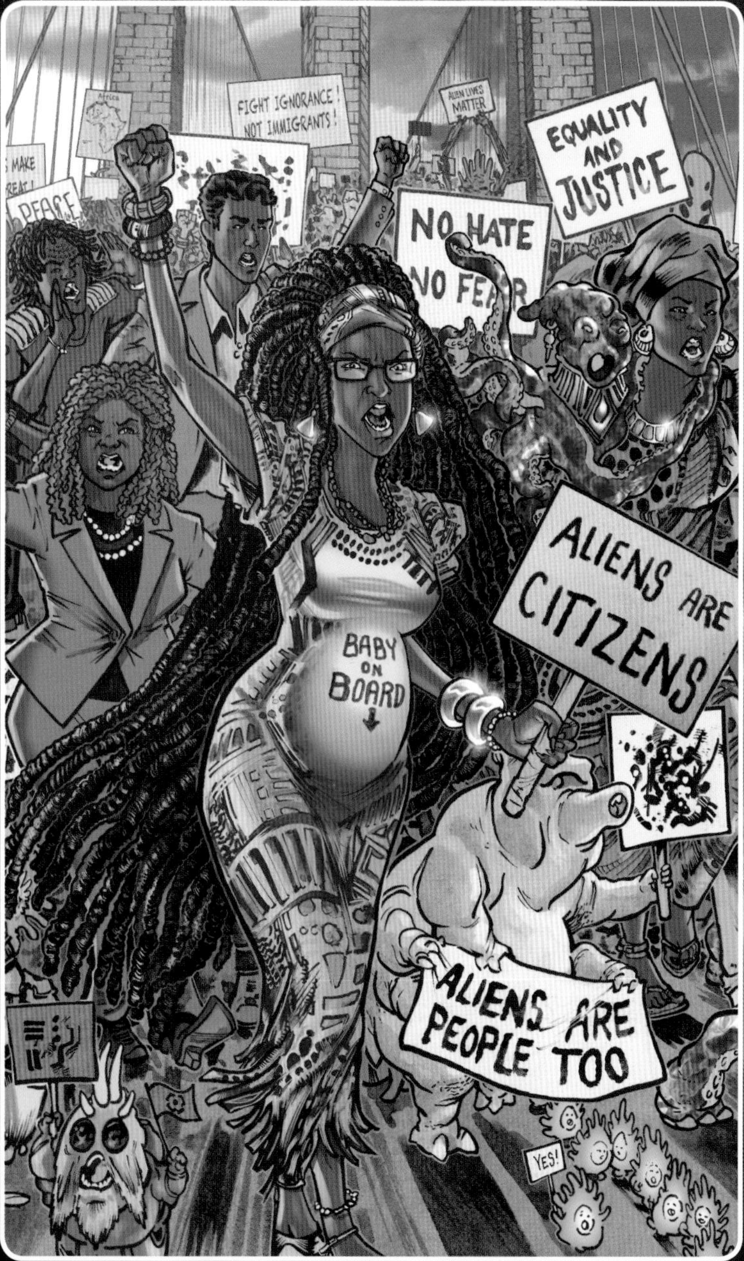
FIGHT IGNORANCE!
NOT IMMIGRANTS!
ALIEN LIVES MATTER
EQUALITY AND JUSTICE
PEACE
NO HATE
BABY ON BOARD
ALIENS ARE CITIZENS
ALIENS ARE PEOPLE TOO
YES!

THE TRAVEL BAN

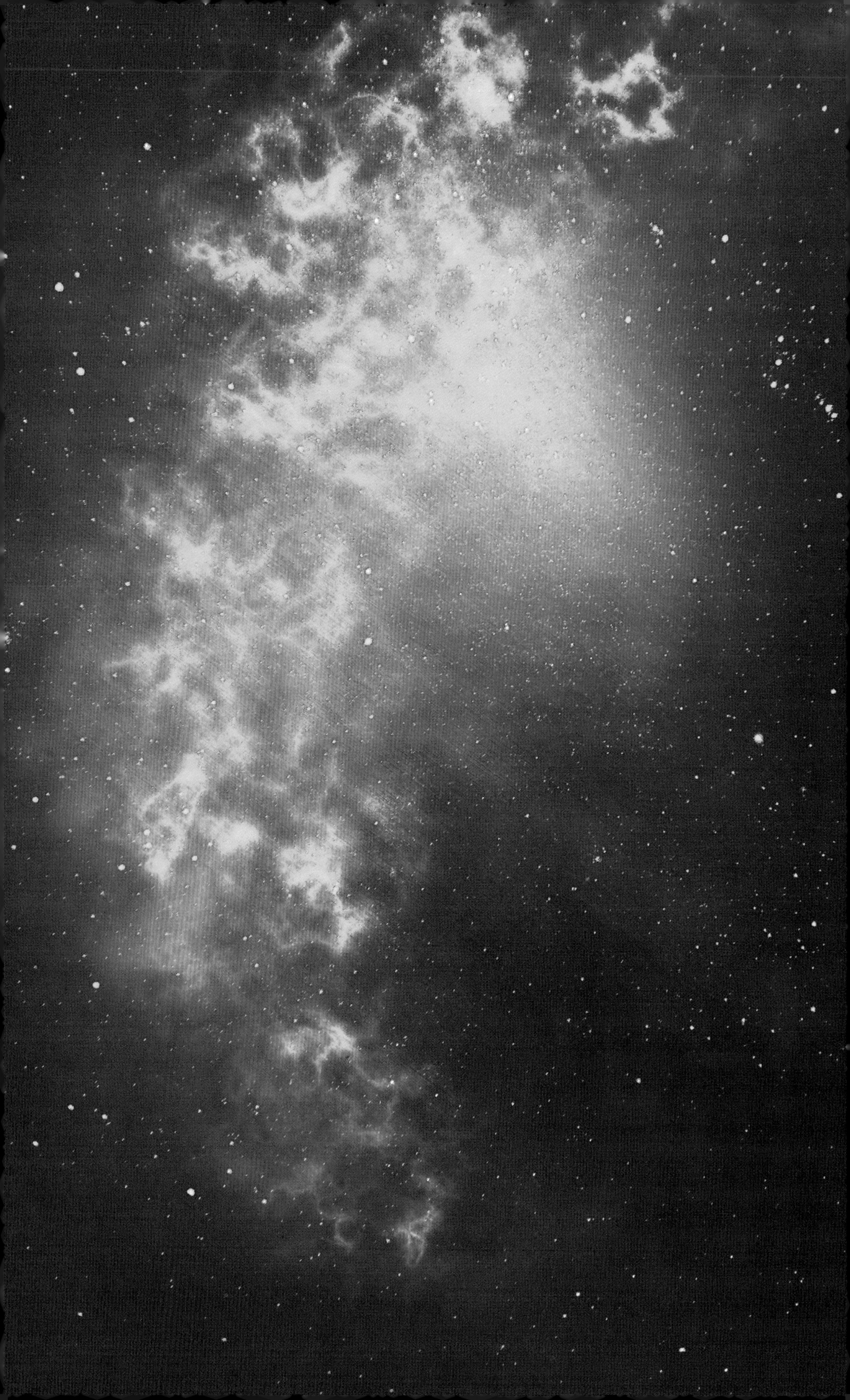

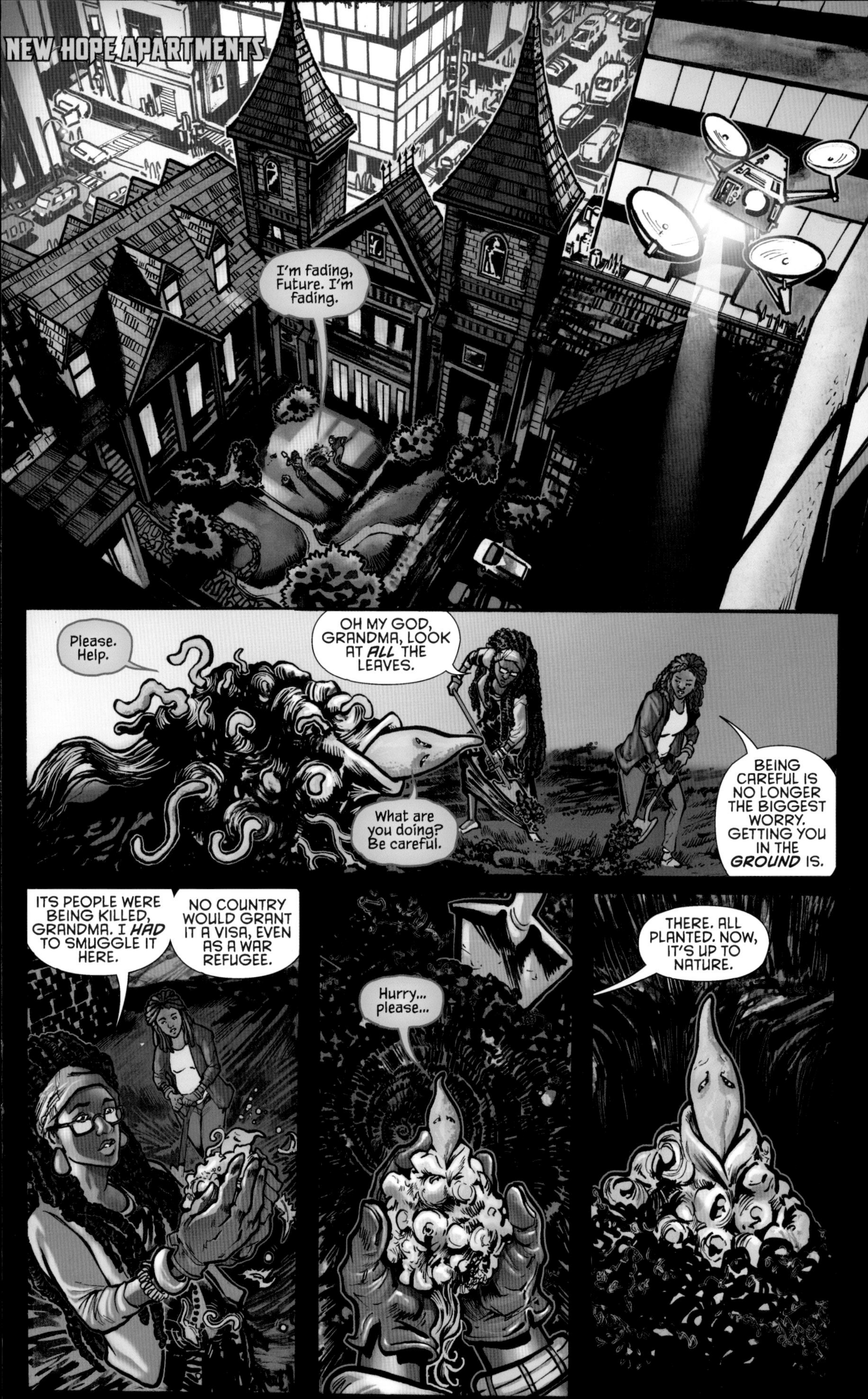
NEW HOPE APARTMENTS
I'm fading, Future. I'm fading.
Please. Help.
OH MY GOD, GRANDMA, LOOK AT *ALL* THE LEAVES.
What are you doing? Be careful.
BEING CAREFUL IS NO LONGER THE BIGGEST WORRY. GETTING YOU IN THE *GROUND* IS.
ITS PEOPLE WERE BEING KILLED, GRANDMA. I *HAD* TO SMUGGLE IT HERE.
NO COUNTRY WOULD GRANT IT A VISA, EVEN AS A WAR REFUGEE.
Hurry... please...
THERE. ALL PLANTED. NOW, IT'S UP TO NATURE.

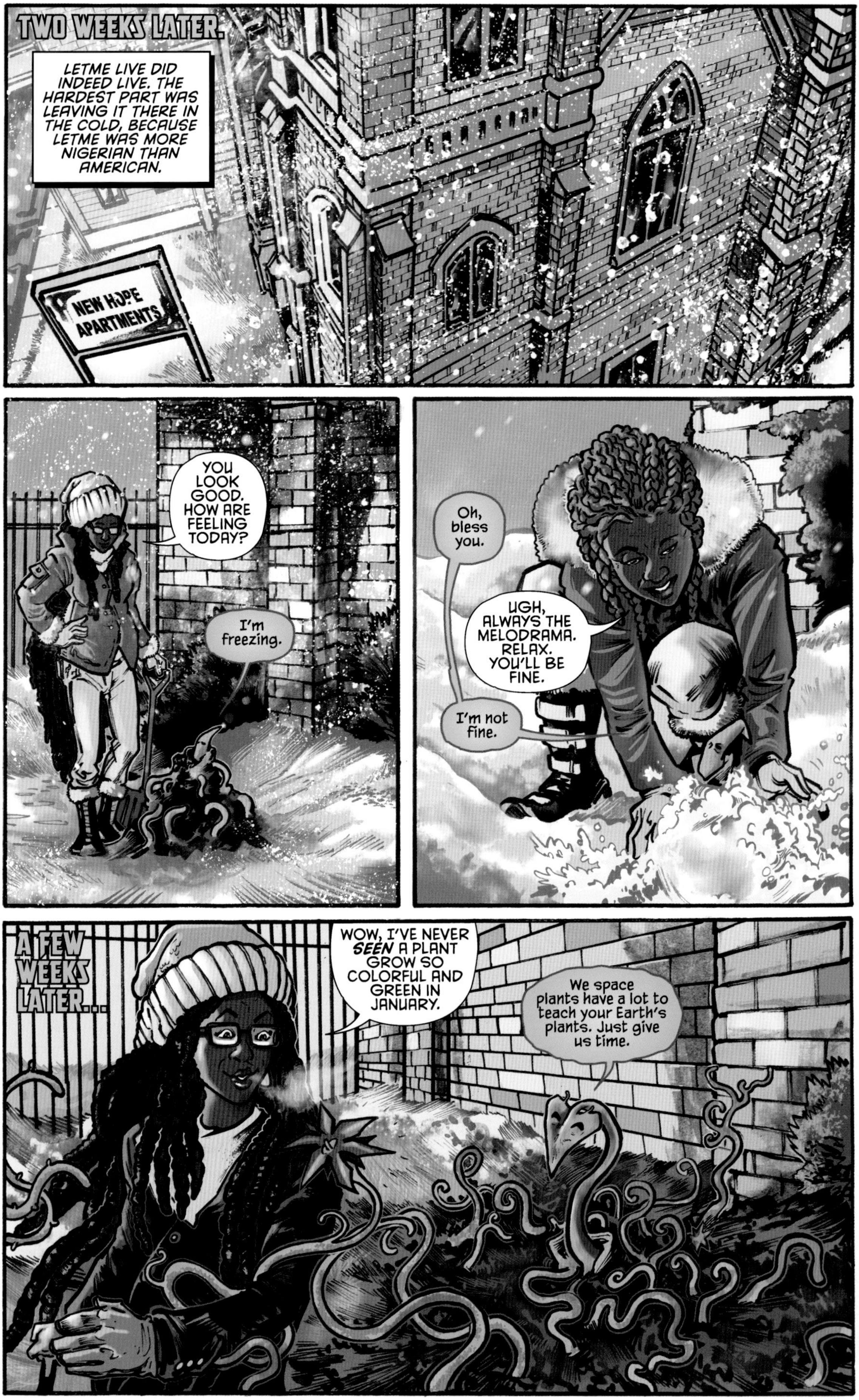
TWO WEEKS LATER.
LETME LIVE DID INDEED LIVE. THE HARDEST PART WAS LEAVING IT THERE IN THE COLD, BECAUSE LETME WAS MORE NIGERIAN THAN AMERICAN.
NEW HOPE APARTMENTS
YOU LOOK GOOD. HOW ARE FEELING TODAY?
I'm freezing.
Oh, bless you.
UGH, ALWAYS THE MELODRAMA. RELAX. YOU'LL BE FINE.
I'm not fine.
A FEW WEEKS LATER...
WOW, I'VE NEVER SEEN A PLANT GROW SO COLORFUL AND GREEN IN JANUARY.
We space plants have a lot to teach your Earth's plants. Just give us time.

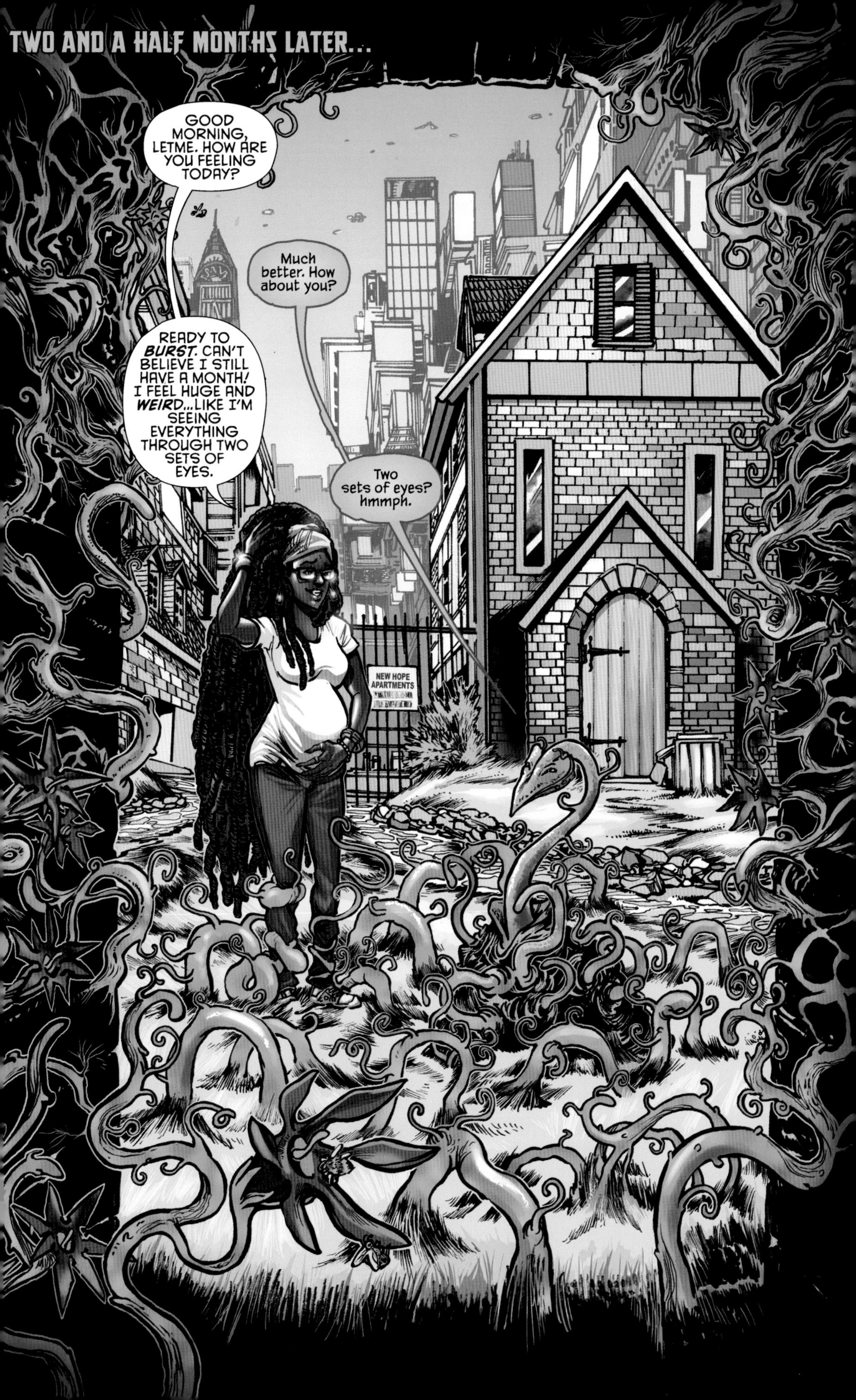
TWO AND A HALF MONTHS LATER...
GOOD MORNING, LETME. HOW ARE YOU FEELING TODAY?
Much better. How about you?
READY TO BURST. CAN'T BELIEVE I STILL HAVE A MONTH! I FEEL HUGE AND WEIRD...LIKE I'M SEEING EVERYTHING THROUGH TWO SETS OF EYES.
Two sets of eyes? hmmph.
NEW HOPE APARTMENTS

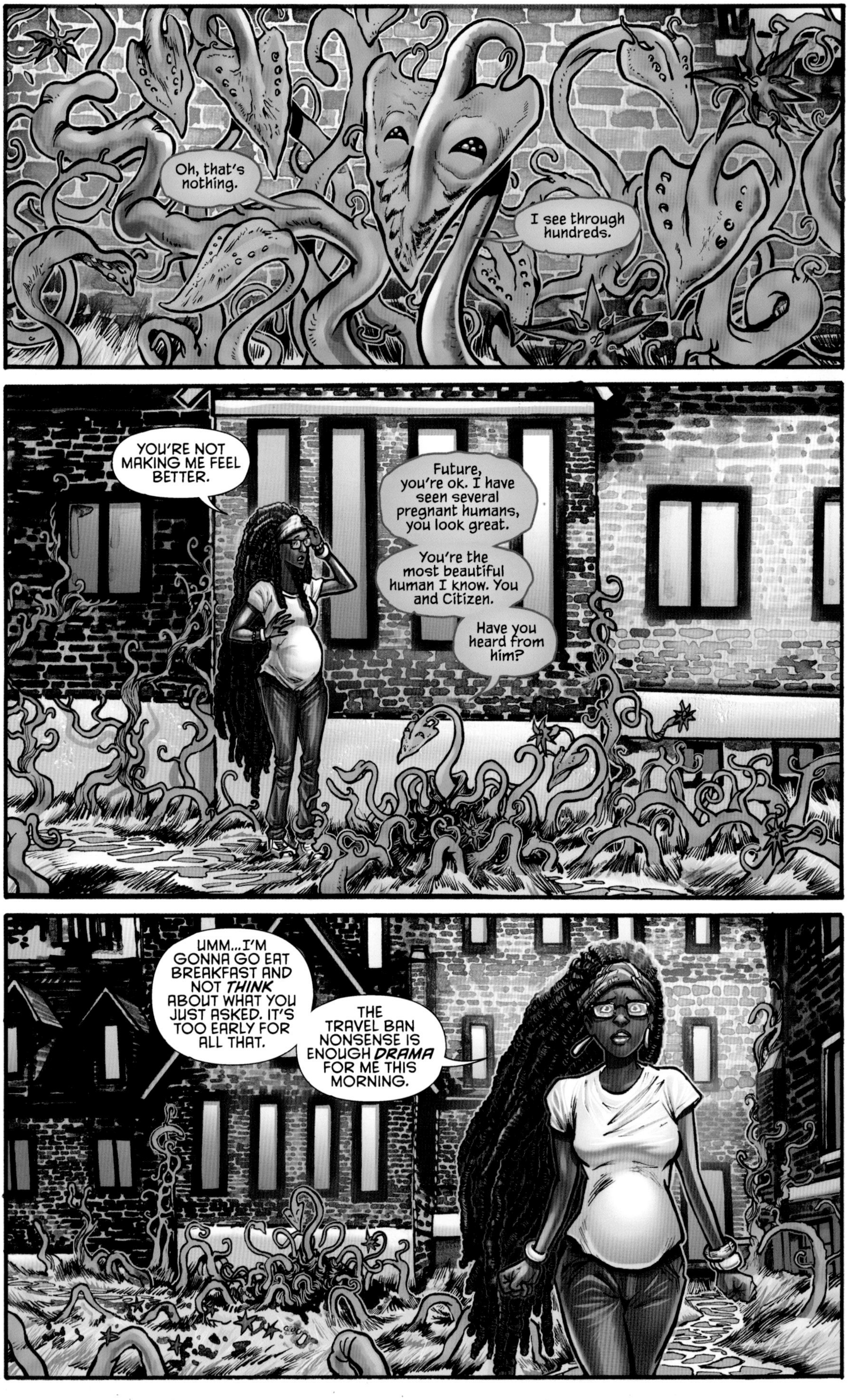
Oh, that's nothing.
I see through hundreds.
YOU'RE NOT MAKING ME FEEL BETTER.
Future, you're ok. I have seen several pregnant humans, you look great.
You're the most beautiful human I know. You and Citizen.
Have you heard from him?
UMM...I'M GONNA GO EAT BREAKFAST AND NOT *THINK* ABOUT WHAT YOU JUST ASKED. IT'S TOO EARLY FOR ALL THAT.
THE TRAVEL BAN NONSENSE IS ENOUGH ***DRAMA*** FOR ME THIS MORNING.

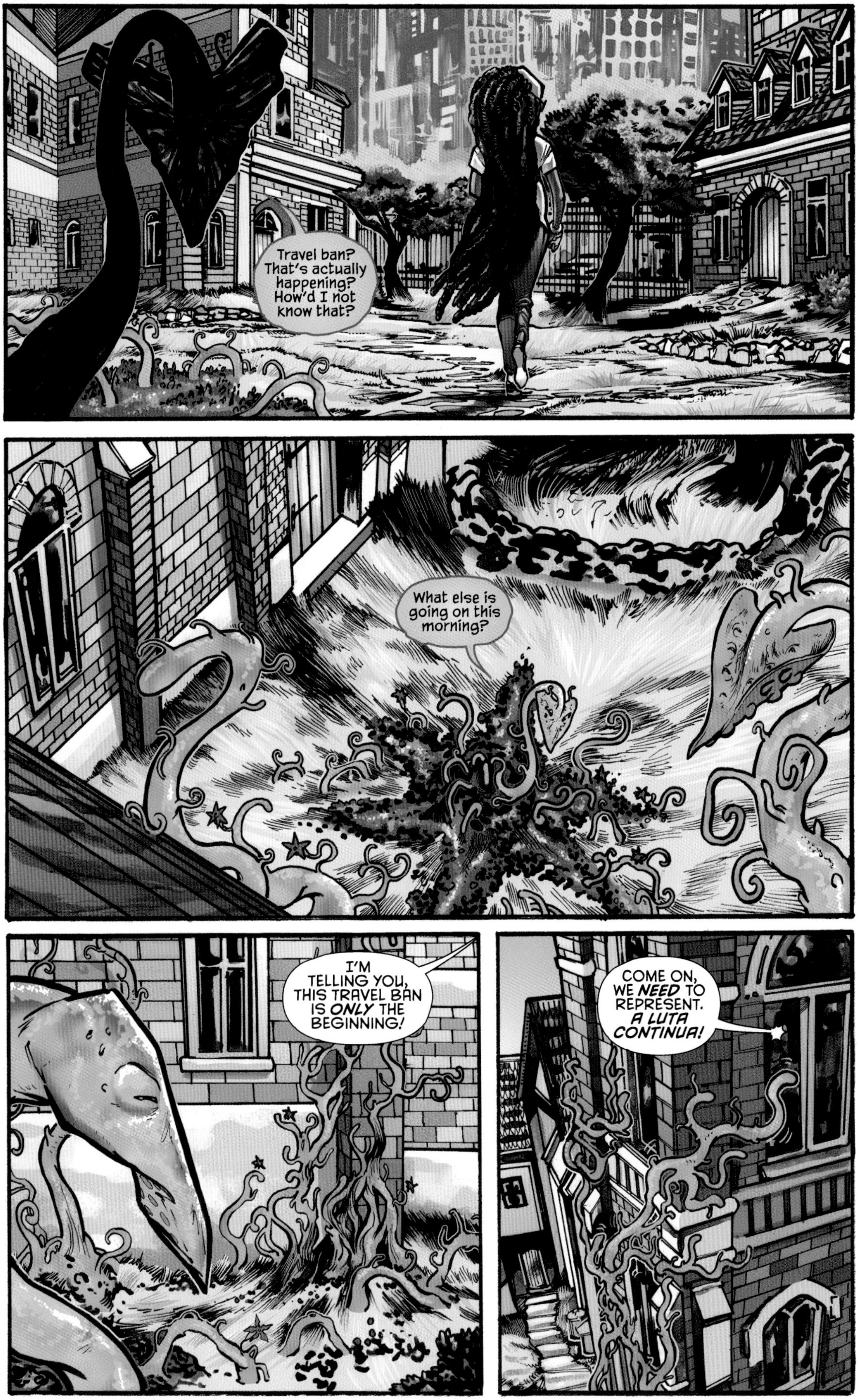
Travel ban? That's actually happening? How'd I not know that?
What else is going on this morning?
I'M TELLING YOU, THIS TRAVEL BAN IS *ONLY* THE BEGINNING!
COME ON, WE *NEED* TO REPRESENT. *A LUTA CONTINUA!*

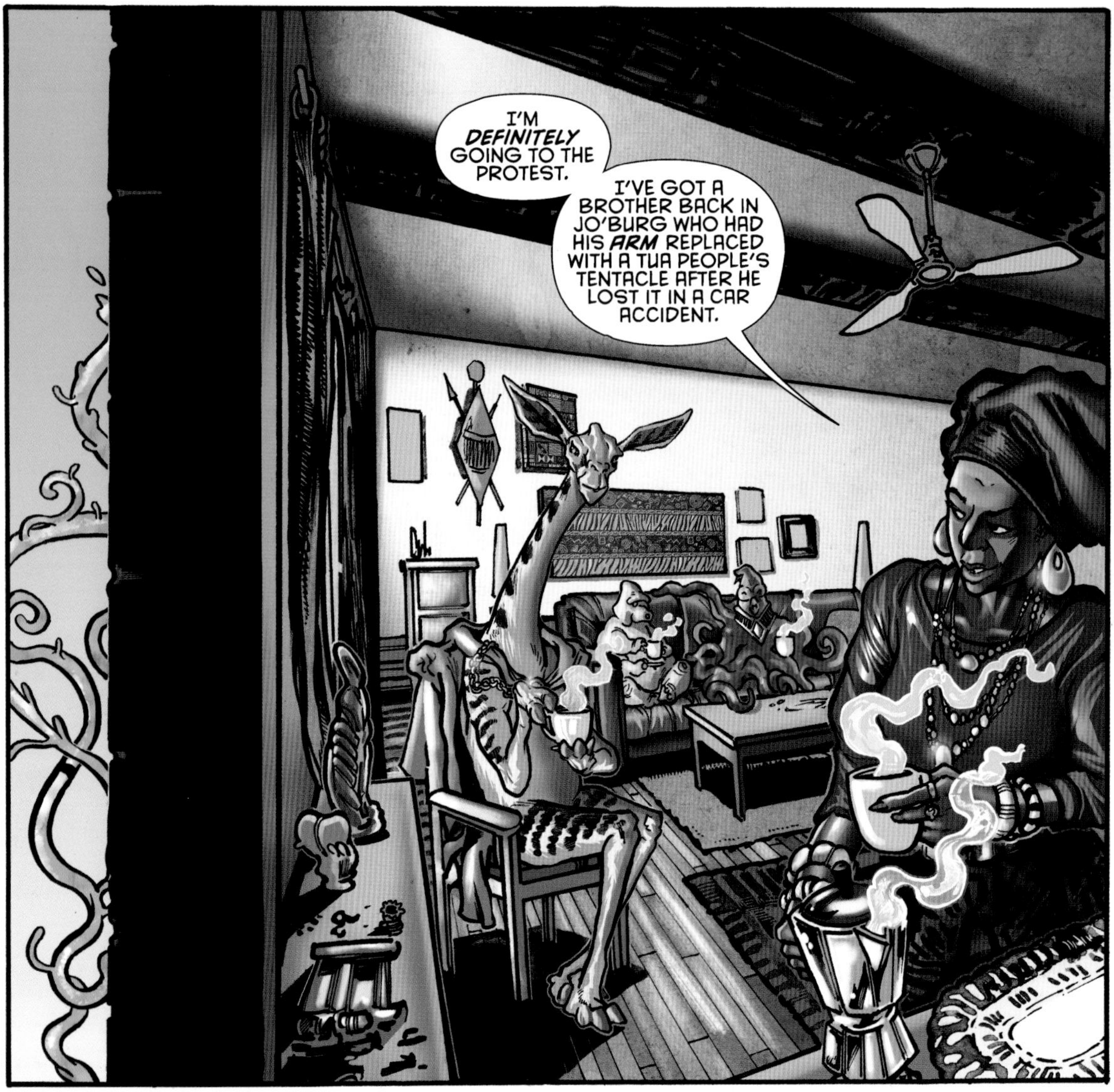
I'M DEFINITELY GOING TO THE PROTEST.
I'VE GOT A BROTHER BACK IN JO'BURG WHO HAD HIS ARM REPLACED WITH A TUA PEOPLE'S TENTACLE AFTER HE LOST IT IN A CAR ACCIDENT.

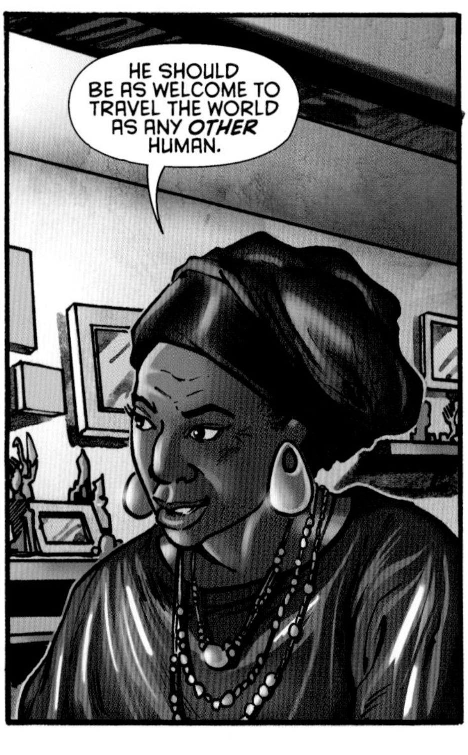
HE SHOULD BE AS WELCOME TO TRAVEL THE WORLD AS ANY OTHER HUMAN.

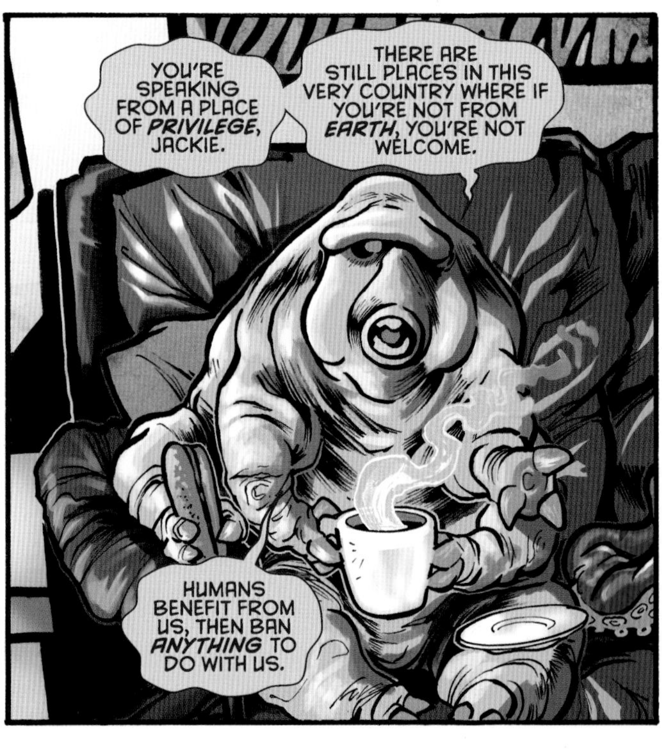
YOU'RE SPEAKING FROM A PLACE OF PRIVILEGE, JACKIE.
THERE ARE STILL PLACES IN THIS VERY COUNTRY WHERE IF YOU'RE NOT FROM EARTH, YOU'RE NOT WELCOME.
HUMANS BENEFIT FROM US, THEN BAN ANYTHING TO DO WITH US.

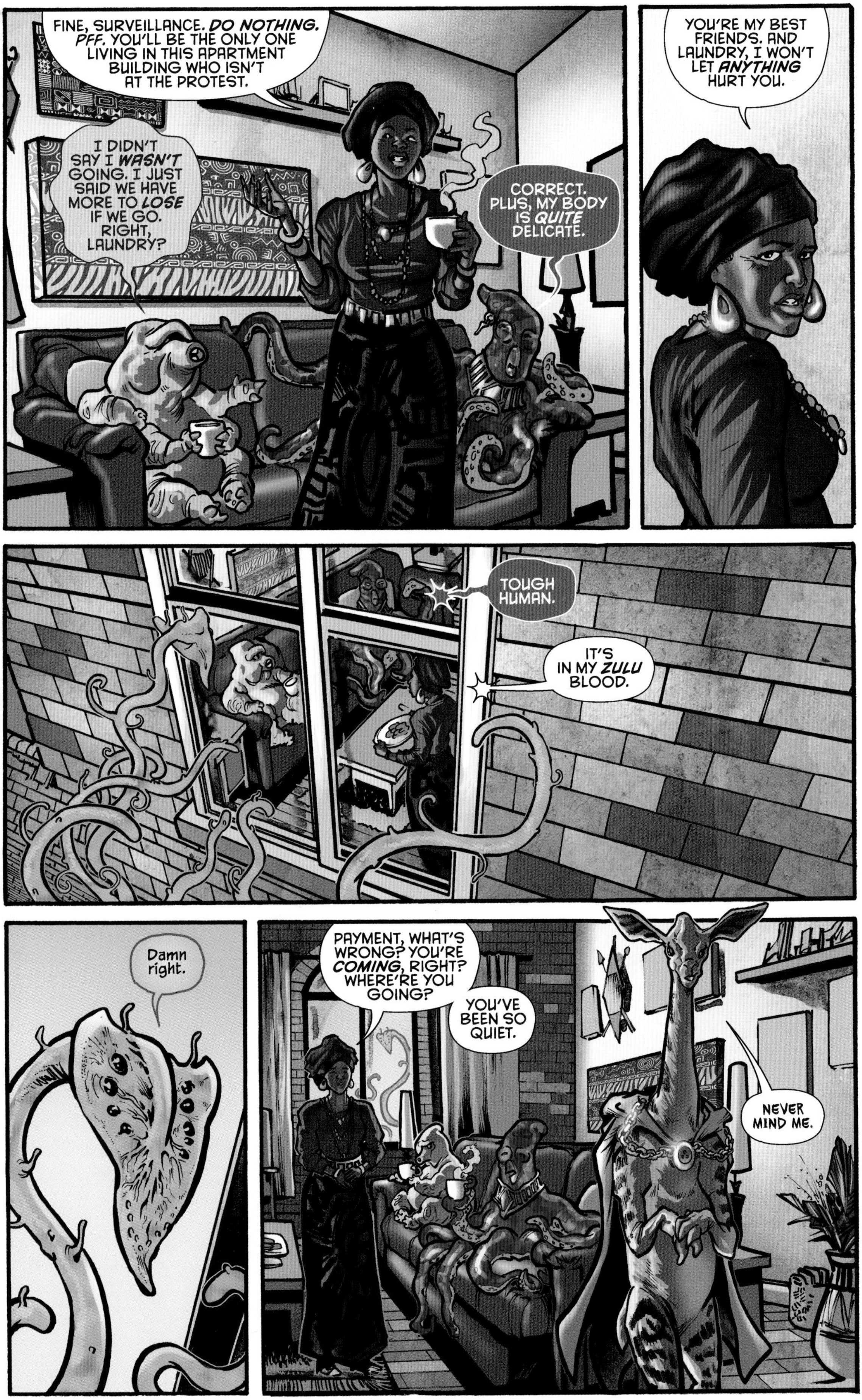
FINE, SURVEILLANCE. DO NOTHING. PFF. YOU'LL BE THE ONLY ONE LIVING IN THIS APARTMENT BUILDING WHO ISN'T AT THE PROTEST.
I DIDN'T SAY I WASN'T GOING. I JUST SAID WE HAVE MORE TO LOSE IF WE GO. RIGHT, LAUNDRY?
CORRECT. PLUS, MY BODY IS QUITE DELICATE.
YOU'RE MY BEST FRIENDS. AND LAUNDRY, I WON'T LET ANYTHING HURT YOU.
TOUGH HUMAN.
IT'S IN MY ZULU BLOOD.
Damn right.
PAYMENT, WHAT'S WRONG? YOU'RE COMING, RIGHT? WHERE'RE YOU GOING?
YOU'VE BEEN SO QUIET.
NEVER MIND ME.

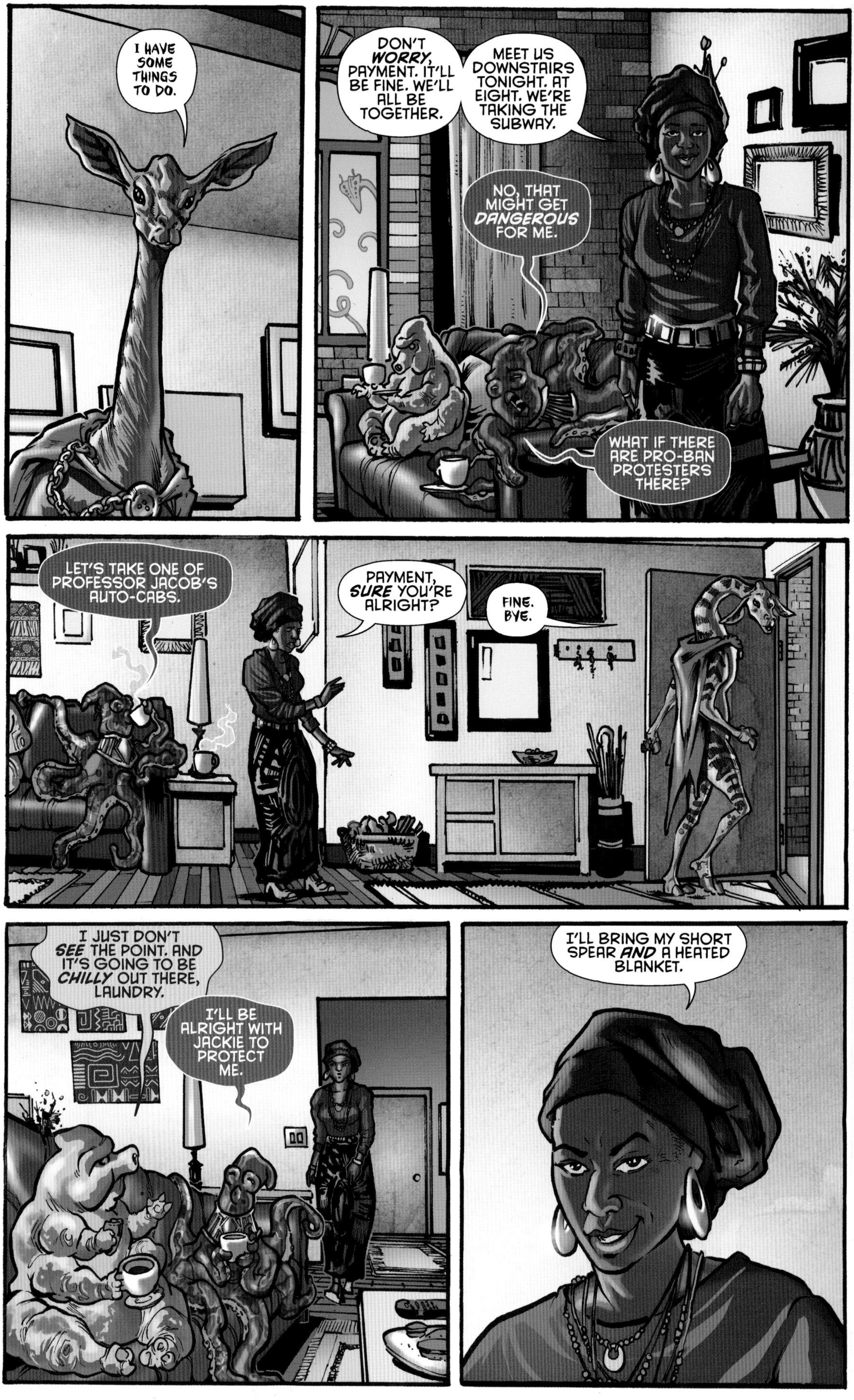
I HAVE SOME THINGS TO DO.
DON'T WORRY, PAYMENT. IT'LL BE FINE. WE'LL ALL BE TOGETHER.
MEET US DOWNSTAIRS TONIGHT. AT EIGHT. WE'RE TAKING THE SUBWAY.
NO, THAT MIGHT GET DANGEROUS FOR ME.
WHAT IF THERE ARE PRO-BAN PROTESTERS THERE?
LET'S TAKE ONE OF PROFESSOR JACOB'S AUTO-CABS.
PAYMENT, SURE YOU'RE ALRIGHT?
FINE. BYE.
I JUST DON'T SEE THE POINT. AND IT'S GOING TO BE CHILLY OUT THERE, LAUNDRY.
I'LL BE ALRIGHT WITH JACKIE TO PROTECT ME.
I'LL BRING MY SHORT SPEAR AND A HEATED BLANKET.

FINALLY.

WELCOME HOME, PAYMENT. ARE YOU STILL GOING TO THE PROTEST?

AM I GOING?

NO HATE

NO BAN

ALL PEOPLE ARE PEOPLE

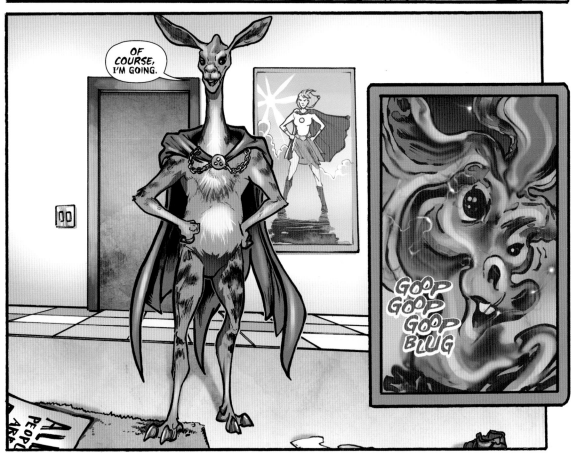

OF COURSE, I'M GOING.

GOOP GOOP GOOP BLUG

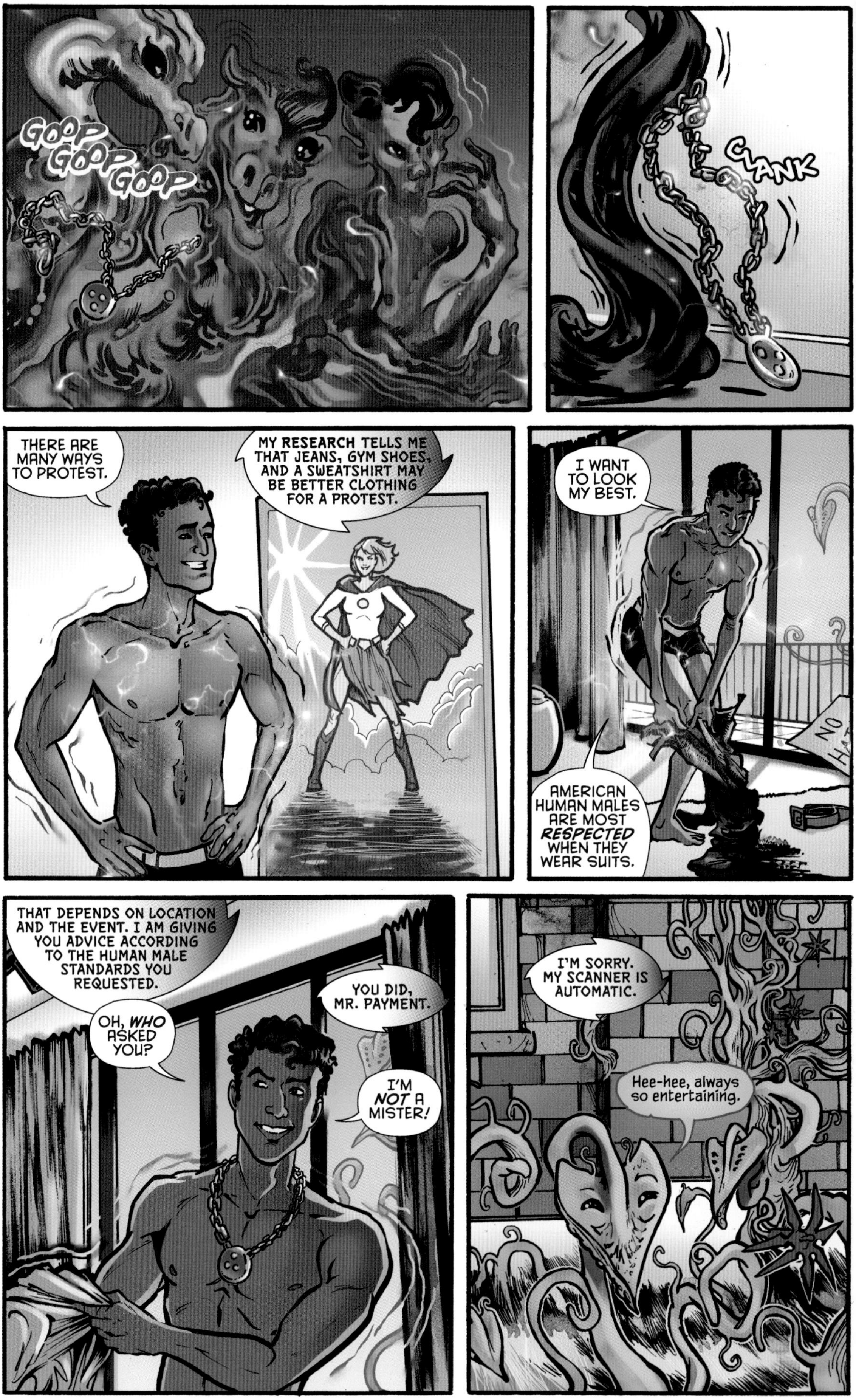
GOOP GOOP GOOP
CLANK
THERE ARE MANY WAYS TO PROTEST.
MY RESEARCH TELLS ME THAT JEANS, GYM SHOES, AND A SWEATSHIRT MAY BE BETTER CLOTHING FOR A PROTEST.
I WANT TO LOOK MY BEST.
AMERICAN HUMAN MALES ARE MOST RESPECTED WHEN THEY WEAR SUITS.
THAT DEPENDS ON LOCATION AND THE EVENT. I AM GIVING YOU ADVICE ACCORDING TO THE HUMAN MALE STANDARDS YOU REQUESTED.
OH, WHO ASKED YOU?
YOU DID, MR. PAYMENT.
I'M NOT A MISTER!
I'M SORRY. MY SCANNER IS AUTOMATIC.
Hee-hee, always so entertaining.

KNOK KNOK KNOK

214

HI, GRANDMA.

I'M MAKING SOME *PLANTAIN* AND STEW. I WENT TO THAT NEW LIBRARY/MUSEUM CALLED THE APOTHECARY.

DID YOU KNOW THERE'S AN *AFRICAN* MARKET NEAR THERE?

FOUND EVERYTHING I NEEDED IN *ONE* PLACE! WANT SOME?

YOU WENT TO THE LIBRARY? THE ONE *NEAR* THE... HOSPITAL?

YEAH, FOR SOME RESEARCH. AND I DIDN'T GO PAST THE HOSPITAL... I WENT *INSIDE*. IT'S *HUMAN ONLY* NOW!

AND THERE'S NOTHING ANYWHERE *COMMEMORATING* MOM AND DAD...OR EVEN THE BOMBING ITSELF!

PEOPLE DON'T *WANT* TO REMEMBER, FUTURE.

THEN, WHERE ARE HUMAN BEINGS WITH ALIEN DNA *SUPPOSED* TO GO?

GOOD QUESTION. WE'RE GOING BACKWARDS.

PRINCIPLE OF NEURO BIOLOGY

FUTURE, I *HAVE* TO GO TO LAGUARDIA.

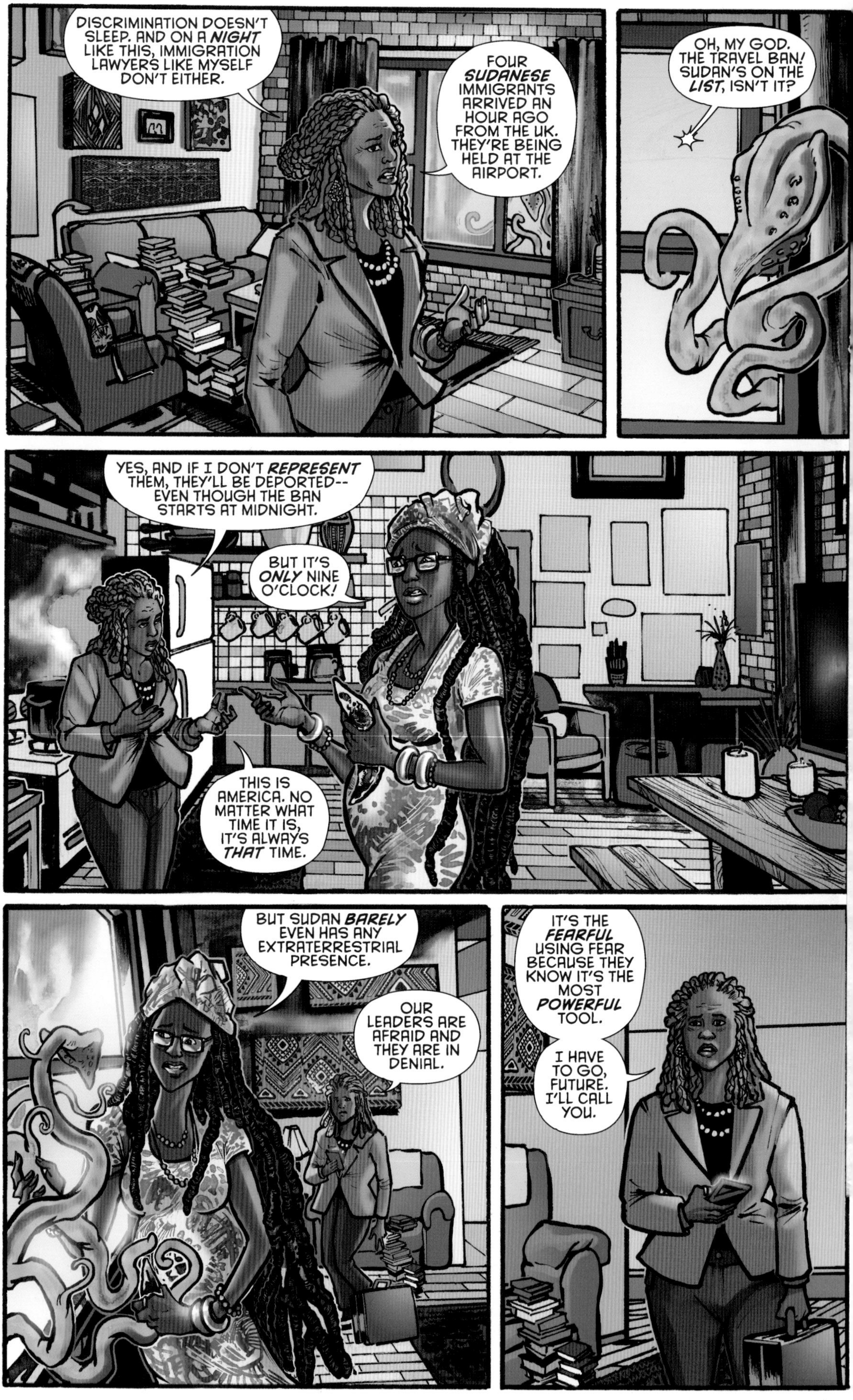
DISCRIMINATION DOESN'T SLEEP. AND ON A *NIGHT* LIKE THIS, IMMIGRATION LAWYERS LIKE MYSELF DON'T EITHER.
FOUR *SUDANESE* IMMIGRANTS ARRIVED AN HOUR AGO FROM THE UK. THEY'RE BEING HELD AT THE AIRPORT.
OH, MY GOD. THE TRAVEL BAN! SUDAN'S ON THE *LIST*, ISN'T IT?
YES, AND IF I DON'T *REPRESENT* THEM, THEY'LL BE DEPORTED-- EVEN THOUGH THE BAN STARTS AT MIDNIGHT.
BUT IT'S *ONLY* NINE O'CLOCK!
THIS IS AMERICA. NO MATTER WHAT TIME IT IS, IT'S ALWAYS *THAT* TIME.
BUT SUDAN *BARELY* EVEN HAS ANY EXTRATERRESTRIAL PRESENCE.
OUR LEADERS ARE AFRAID AND THEY ARE IN DENIAL.
IT'S THE *FEARFUL* USING FEAR BECAUSE THEY KNOW IT'S THE MOST *POWERFUL* TOOL.
I HAVE TO GO, FUTURE. I'LL CALL YOU.

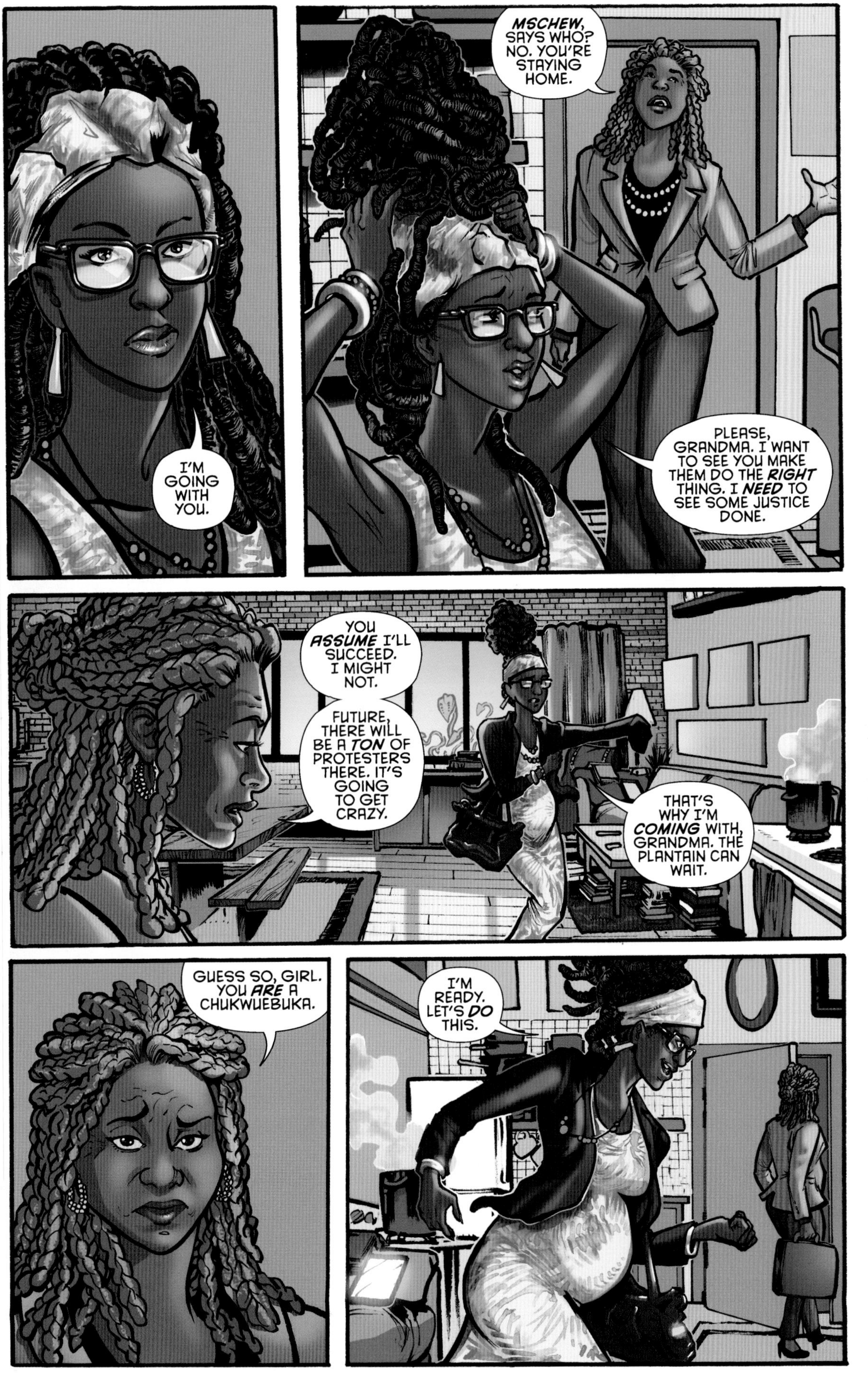
I'M GOING WITH YOU.
MSCHEW, SAYS WHO? NO. YOU'RE STAYING HOME.
PLEASE, GRANDMA. I WANT TO SEE YOU MAKE THEM DO THE RIGHT THING. I NEED TO SEE SOME JUSTICE DONE.
YOU ASSUME I'LL SUCCEED. I MIGHT NOT.
FUTURE, THERE WILL BE A TON OF PROTESTERS THERE. IT'S GOING TO GET CRAZY.
THAT'S WHY I'M COMING WITH, GRANDMA. THE PLANTAIN CAN WAIT.
GUESS SO, GIRL. YOU ARE A CHUKWUEBUKA.
I'M READY. LET'S DO THIS.

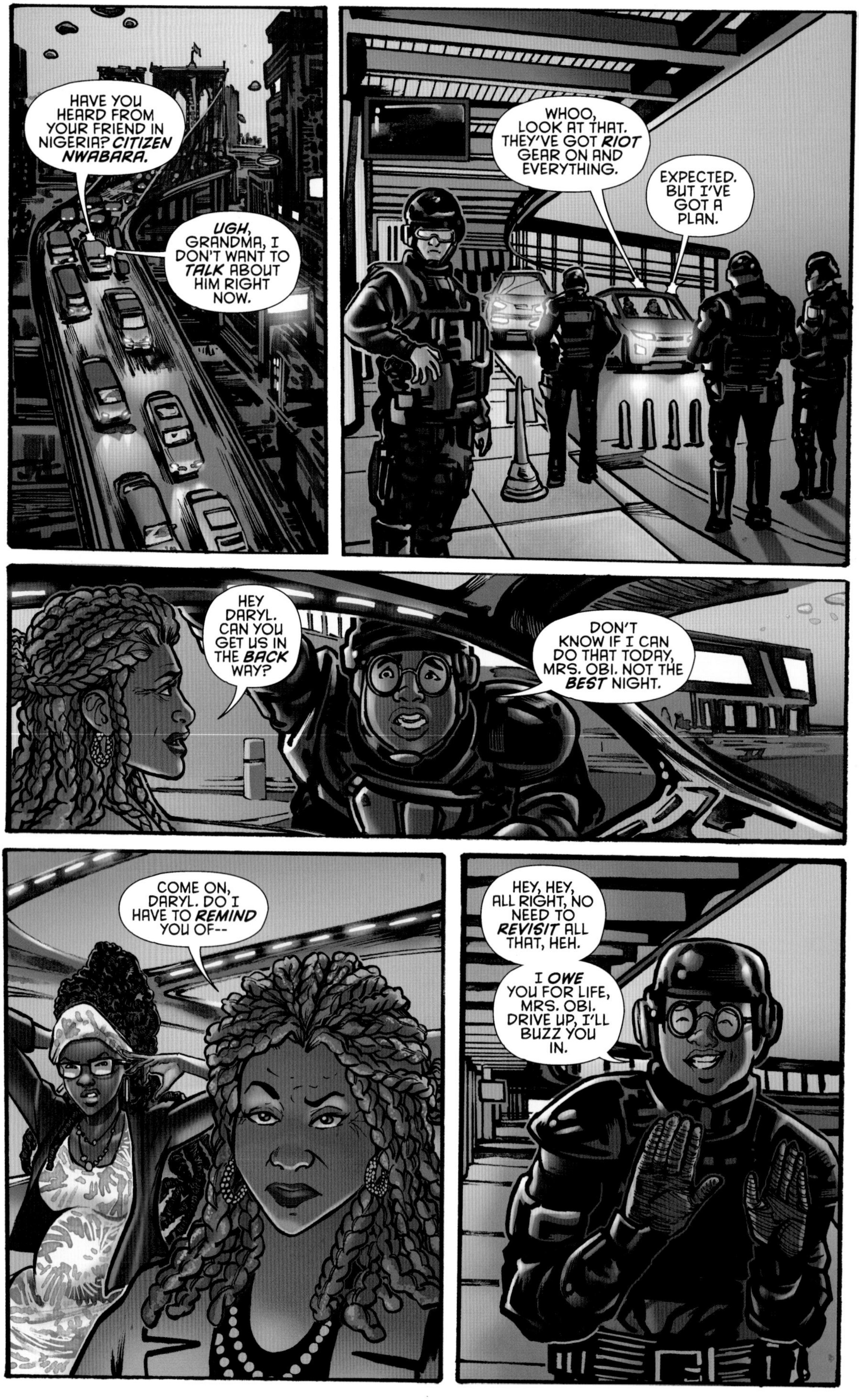
HAVE YOU HEARD FROM YOUR FRIEND IN NIGERIA? *CITIZEN NWABARA.*
UGH, GRANDMA, I DON'T WANT TO *TALK* ABOUT HIM RIGHT NOW.
WHOO, LOOK AT THAT. THEY'VE GOT *RIOT* GEAR ON AND EVERYTHING.
EXPECTED. BUT I'VE GOT A PLAN.
HEY DARYL. CAN YOU GET US IN THE *BACK* WAY?
DON'T KNOW IF I CAN DO THAT TODAY, MRS. OBI. NOT THE *BEST* NIGHT.
COME ON, DARYL. DO I HAVE TO *REMIND* YOU OF--
HEY, HEY, ALL RIGHT, NO NEED TO *REVISIT* ALL THAT, HEH.
I *OWE* YOU FOR LIFE, MRS. OBI. DRIVE UP, I'LL BUZZ YOU IN.

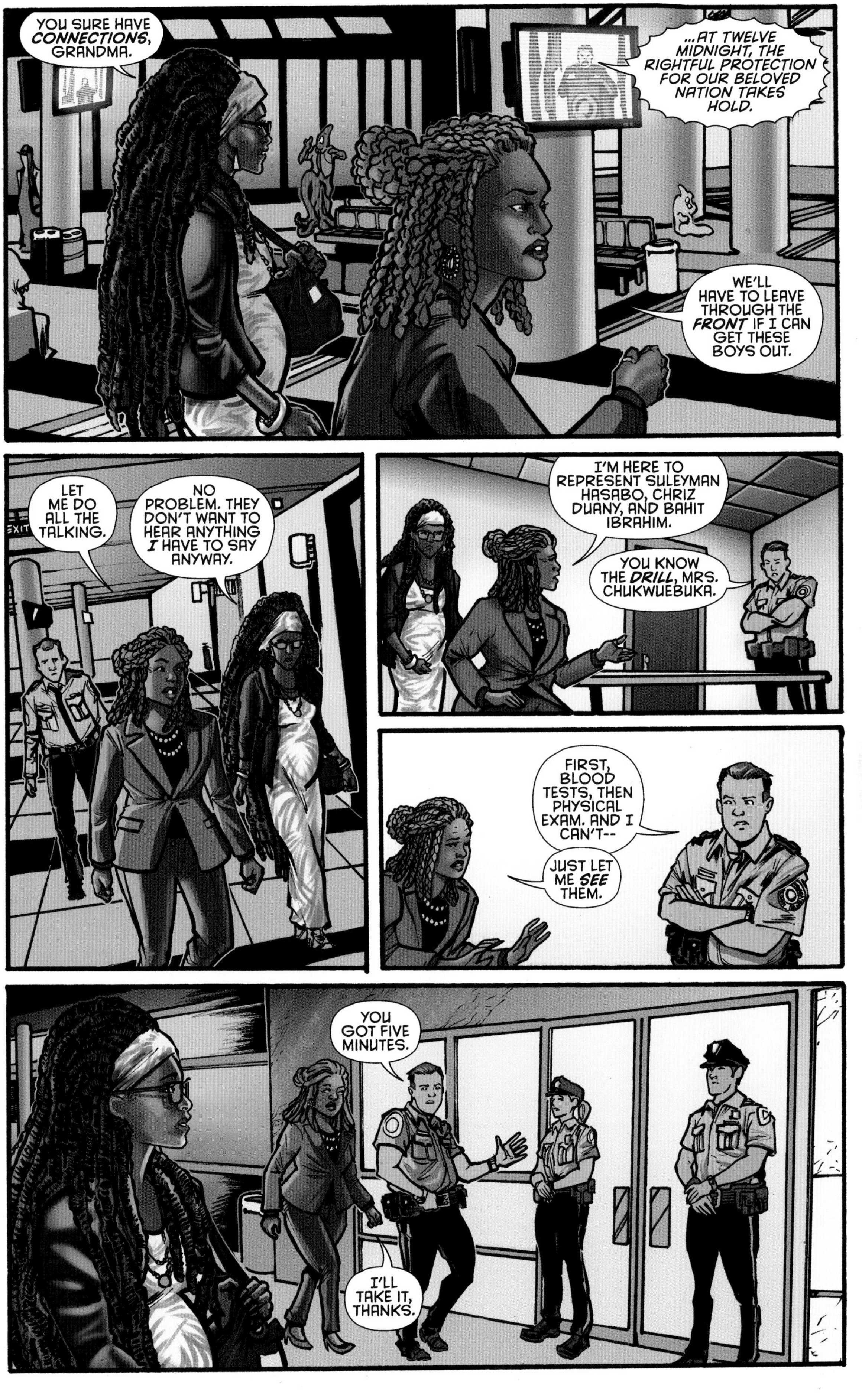
YOU SURE HAVE CONNECTIONS, GRANDMA.
...AT TWELVE MIDNIGHT, THE RIGHTFUL PROTECTION FOR OUR BELOVED NATION TAKES HOLD.
WE'LL HAVE TO LEAVE THROUGH THE FRONT IF I CAN GET THESE BOYS OUT.
LET ME DO ALL THE TALKING.
NO PROBLEM. THEY DON'T WANT TO HEAR ANYTHING I HAVE TO SAY ANYWAY.
EXIT
I'M HERE TO REPRESENT SULEYMAN HASABO, CHRIZ DUANY, AND BAHIT IBRAHIM.
YOU KNOW THE DRILL, MRS. CHUKWUEBUKA.
FIRST, BLOOD TESTS, THEN PHYSICAL EXAM. AND I CAN'T--
JUST LET ME SEE THEM.
YOU GOT FIVE MINUTES.
I'LL TAKE IT, THANKS.

OH, I HOPE MRS. CHUKWUEBUKA COMES SOON. WHAT IF SHE *DOESN'T* COME AT ALL?

DON'T START, SULEYMAN. SHE'LL COME.

BUT WHAT IS *ALL* THIS? WE FOLLOWED THE SUDAN LEAVER'S GUIDE.

WE SMILED AT EVERYONE. WE CAN SPEAK GOOD PROPER ENGLISH.

WHAT'D WE DO WRONG?

TSA NOTICE

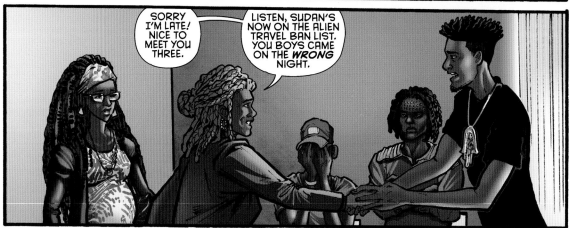

SORRY I'M LATE! NICE TO MEET YOU THREE.

LISTEN, SUDAN'S NOW ON THE ALIEN TRAVEL BAN LIST. YOU BOYS CAME ON THE *WRONG* NIGHT.

BUT WE DON'T *HAVE* ALIEN BLOOD! WE ARE *JUST* HUMAN BEINGS.

WE'RE HERE FOR UNIVERSITY.

I KNOW. *THEY* KNOW.

IT ISN'T ABOUT YOU THREE, IT'S ABOUT FEAR. IT'S *ALWAYS* BEEN ABOUT FEAR.

BUT *WHY* US?

WE'RE JUST HERE TO LEARN.

YEAH, THAT'S THEIR PROBLEM WITH US.

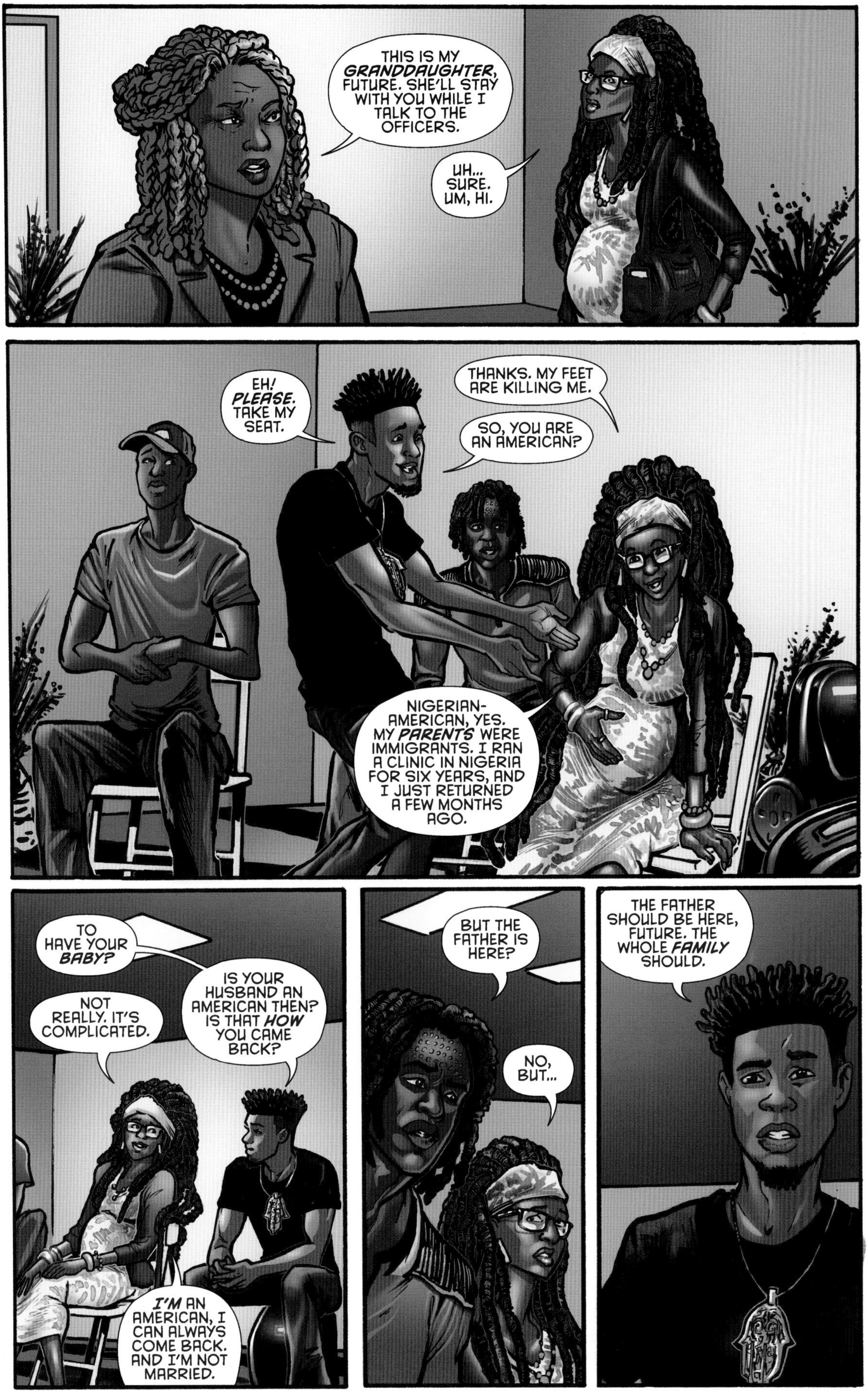
THIS IS MY *GRANDDAUGHTER*, FUTURE. SHE'LL STAY WITH YOU WHILE I TALK TO THE OFFICERS.
UH... SURE. UM, HI.
EH! *PLEASE*. TAKE MY SEAT.
THANKS. MY FEET ARE KILLING ME.
SO, YOU ARE AN AMERICAN?
NIGERIAN-AMERICAN, YES. MY *PARENTS* WERE IMMIGRANTS. I RAN A CLINIC IN NIGERIA FOR SIX YEARS, AND I JUST RETURNED A FEW MONTHS AGO.
TO HAVE YOUR *BABY?*
NOT REALLY. IT'S COMPLICATED.
IS YOUR HUSBAND AN AMERICAN THEN? IS THAT *HOW* YOU CAME BACK?
I'M AN AMERICAN, I CAN ALWAYS COME BACK. AND I'M NOT MARRIED.
BUT THE FATHER IS HERE?
NO, BUT...
THE FATHER SHOULD BE HERE, FUTURE. THE WHOLE *FAMILY* SHOULD.

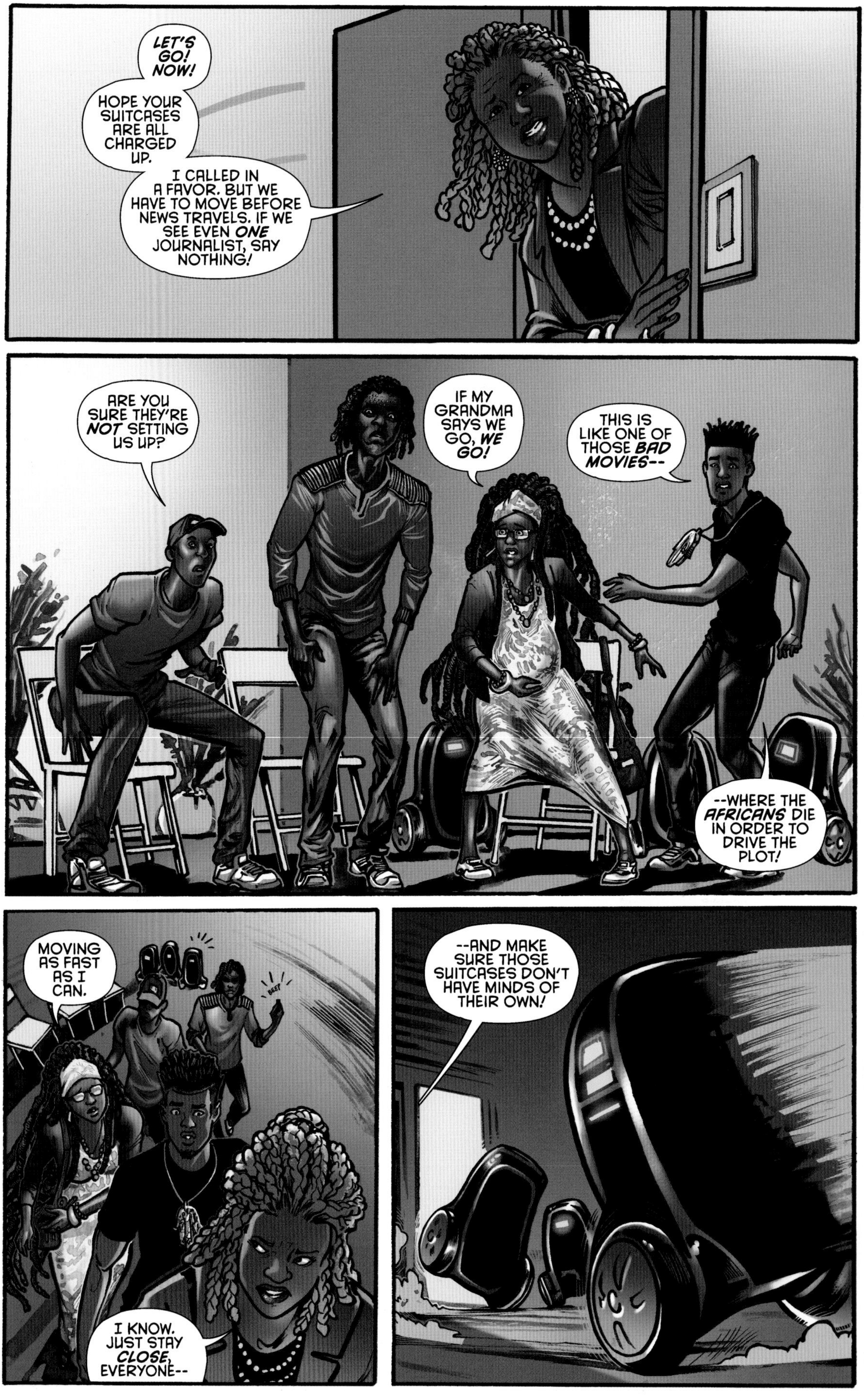
LET'S GO! NOW!
HOPE YOUR SUITCASES ARE ALL CHARGED UP.
I CALLED IN A FAVOR. BUT WE HAVE TO MOVE BEFORE NEWS TRAVELS. IF WE SEE EVEN ONE JOURNALIST, SAY NOTHING!
ARE YOU SURE THEY'RE NOT SETTING US UP?
IF MY GRANDMA SAYS WE GO, WE GO!
THIS IS LIKE ONE OF THOSE BAD MOVIES--
--WHERE THE AFRICANS DIE IN ORDER TO DRIVE THE PLOT!
MOVING AS FAST AS I CAN.
I KNOW. JUST STAY CLOSE, EVERYONE--
--AND MAKE SURE THOSE SUITCASES DON'T HAVE MINDS OF THEIR OWN!

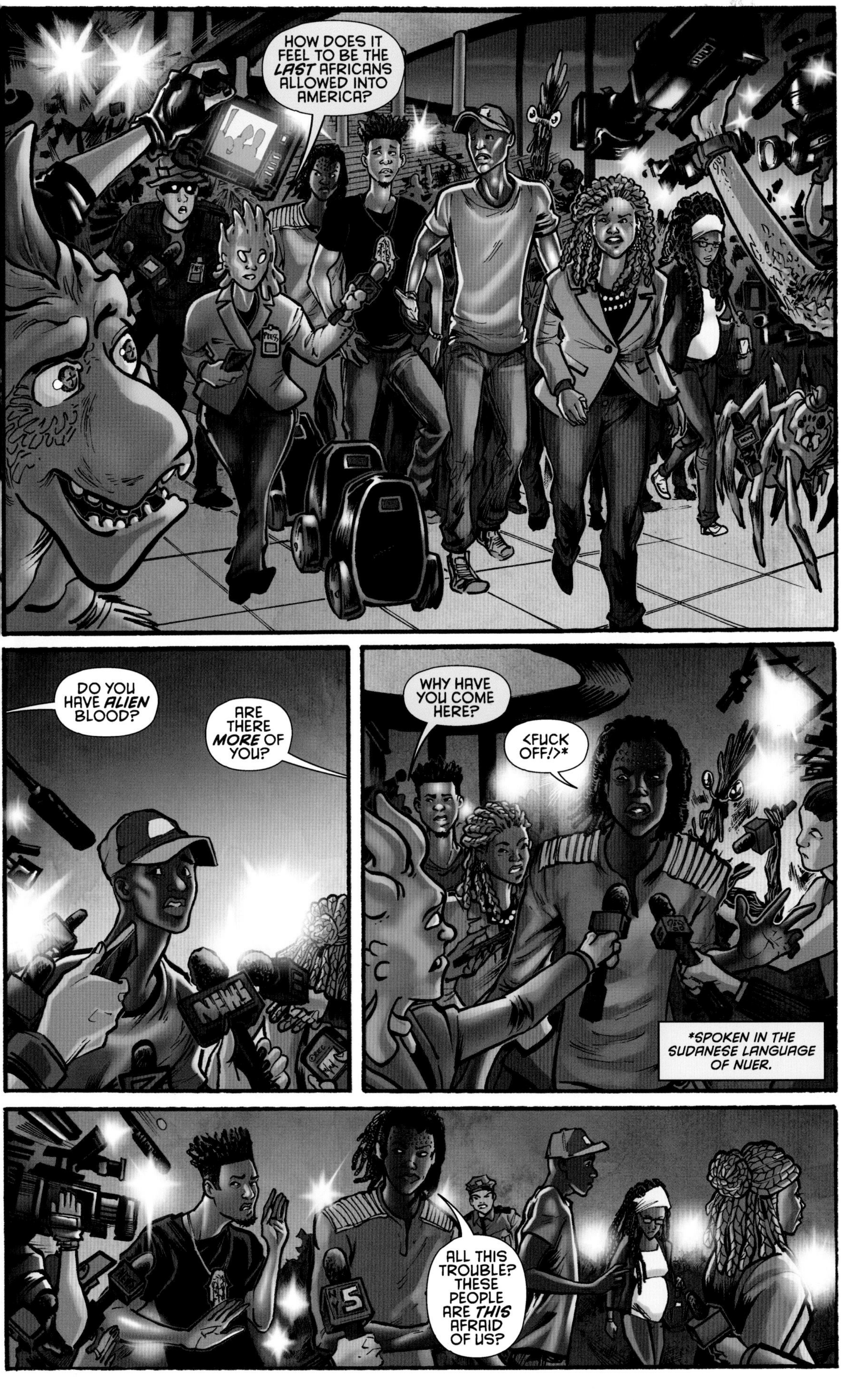
HOW DOES IT FEEL TO BE THE *LAST* AFRICANS ALLOWED INTO AMERICA?
DO YOU HAVE *ALIEN* BLOOD?
ARE THERE *MORE* OF YOU?
NEWS
WHY HAVE YOU COME HERE?
<FUCK OFF!>*
*SPOKEN IN THE SUDANESE LANGUAGE OF NUER.
ALL THIS TROUBLE? THESE PEOPLE ARE *THIS* AFRAID OF US?

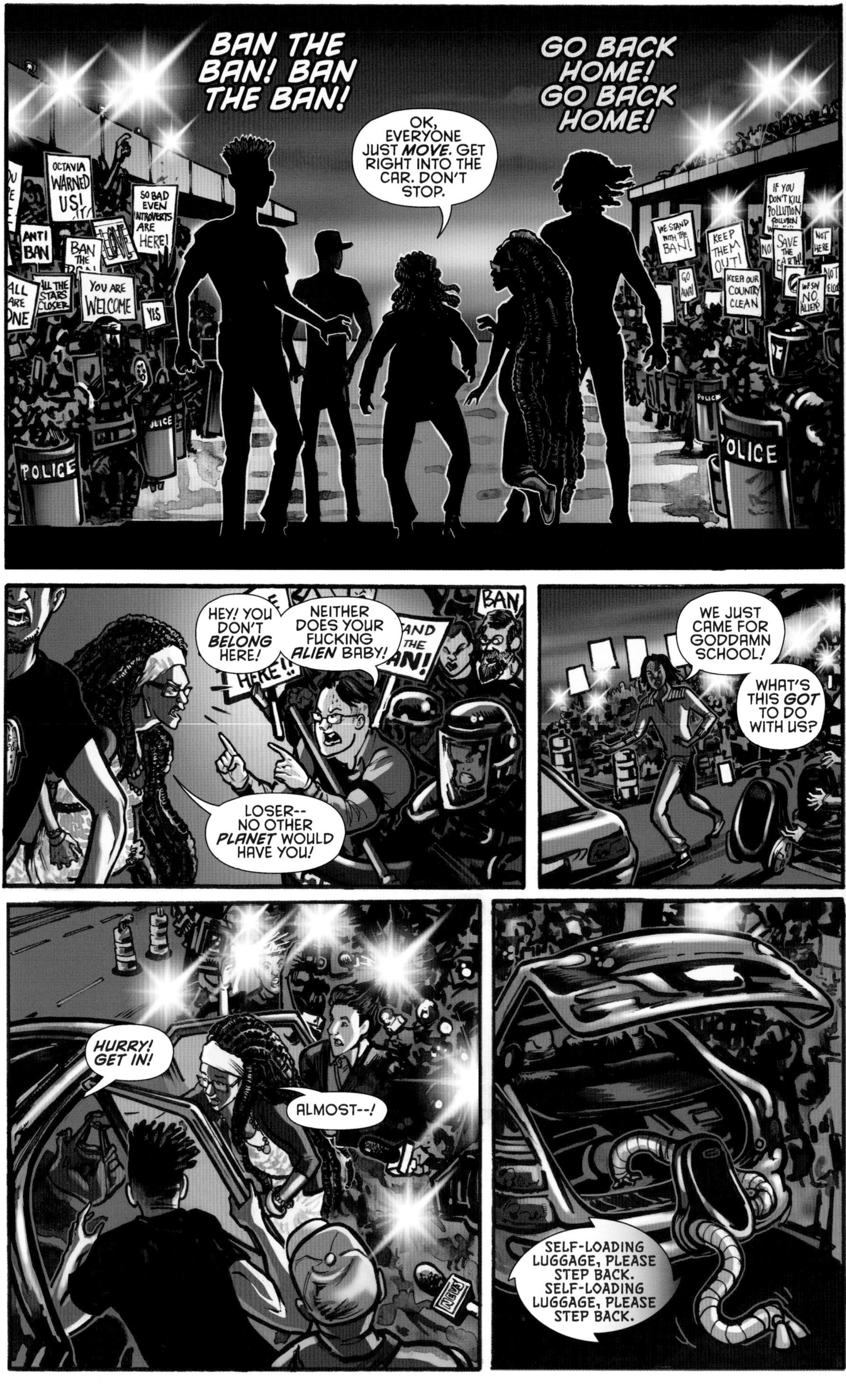
BAN THE BAN! BAN THE BAN!
GO BACK HOME! GO BACK HOME!
OK, EVERYONE JUST MOVE. GET RIGHT INTO THE CAR. DON'T STOP.
OCTAVIA WARNED US!
SO BAD EVEN INTROVERTS ARE HERE!
ANTI BAN
ALL THE STARS CLOSER
YOU ARE WELCOME
WE STAND WITH THE BAN!
KEEP THEM OUT!
KEEP OUR COUNTRY CLEAN
GO AWAY!
NOT HERE
POLICE
HEY! YOU DON'T BELONG HERE!
NEITHER DOES YOUR FUCKING ALIEN BABY!
LOSER-- NO OTHER PLANET WOULD HAVE YOU!
WE JUST CAME FOR GODDAMN SCHOOL!
WHAT'S THIS GOT TO DO WITH US?
HURRY! GET IN!
ALMOST--!
SELF-LOADING LUGGAGE, PLEASE STEP BACK. SELF-LOADING LUGGAGE, PLEASE STEP BACK.

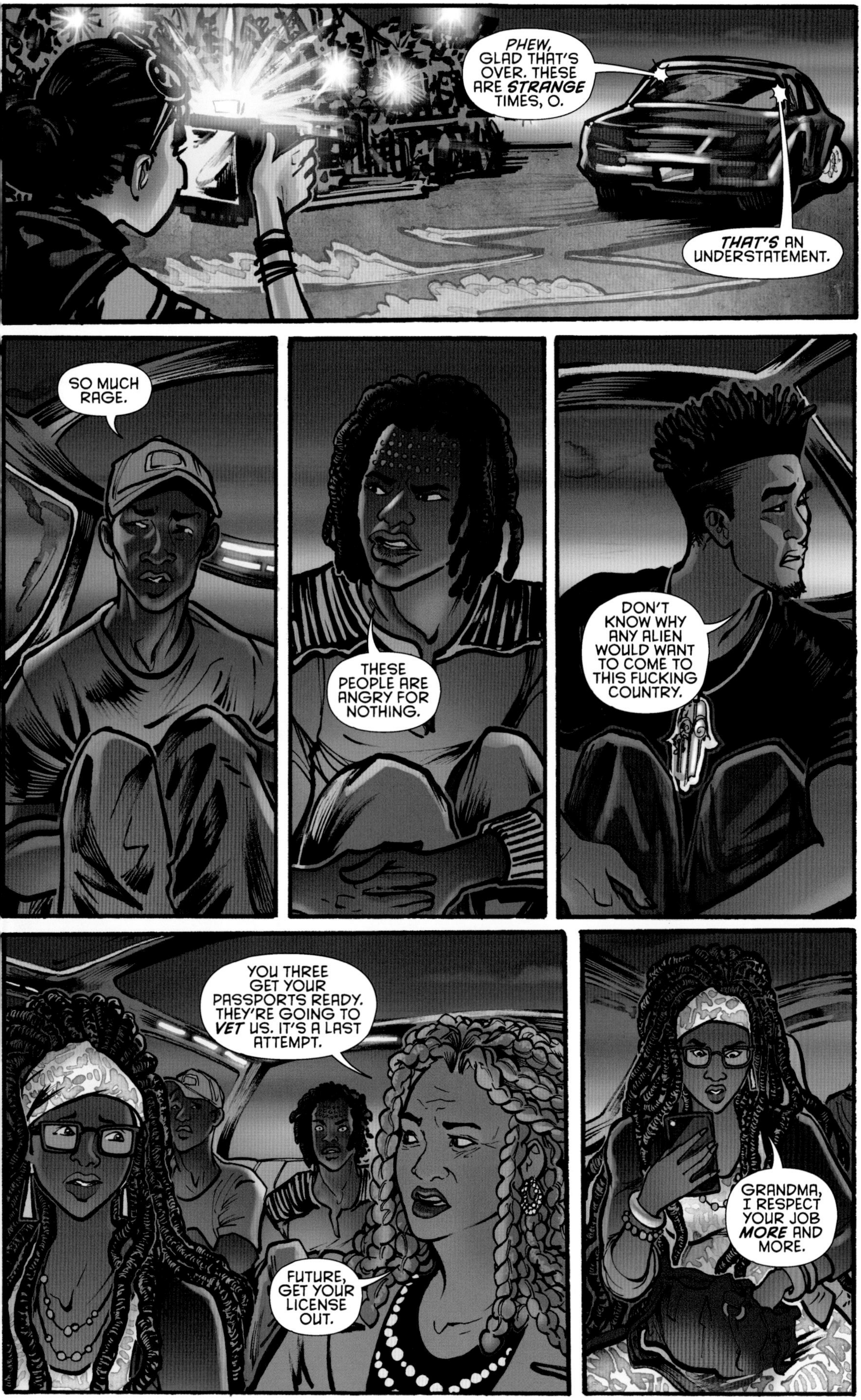
PHEW, GLAD THAT'S OVER. THESE ARE STRANGE TIMES, O.
THAT'S AN UNDERSTATEMENT.
SO MUCH RAGE.
THESE PEOPLE ARE ANGRY FOR NOTHING.
DON'T KNOW WHY ANY ALIEN WOULD WANT TO COME TO THIS FUCKING COUNTRY.
YOU THREE GET YOUR PASSPORTS READY. THEY'RE GOING TO VET US. IT'S A LAST ATTEMPT.
FUTURE, GET YOUR LICENSE OUT.
GRANDMA, I RESPECT YOUR JOB MORE AND MORE.

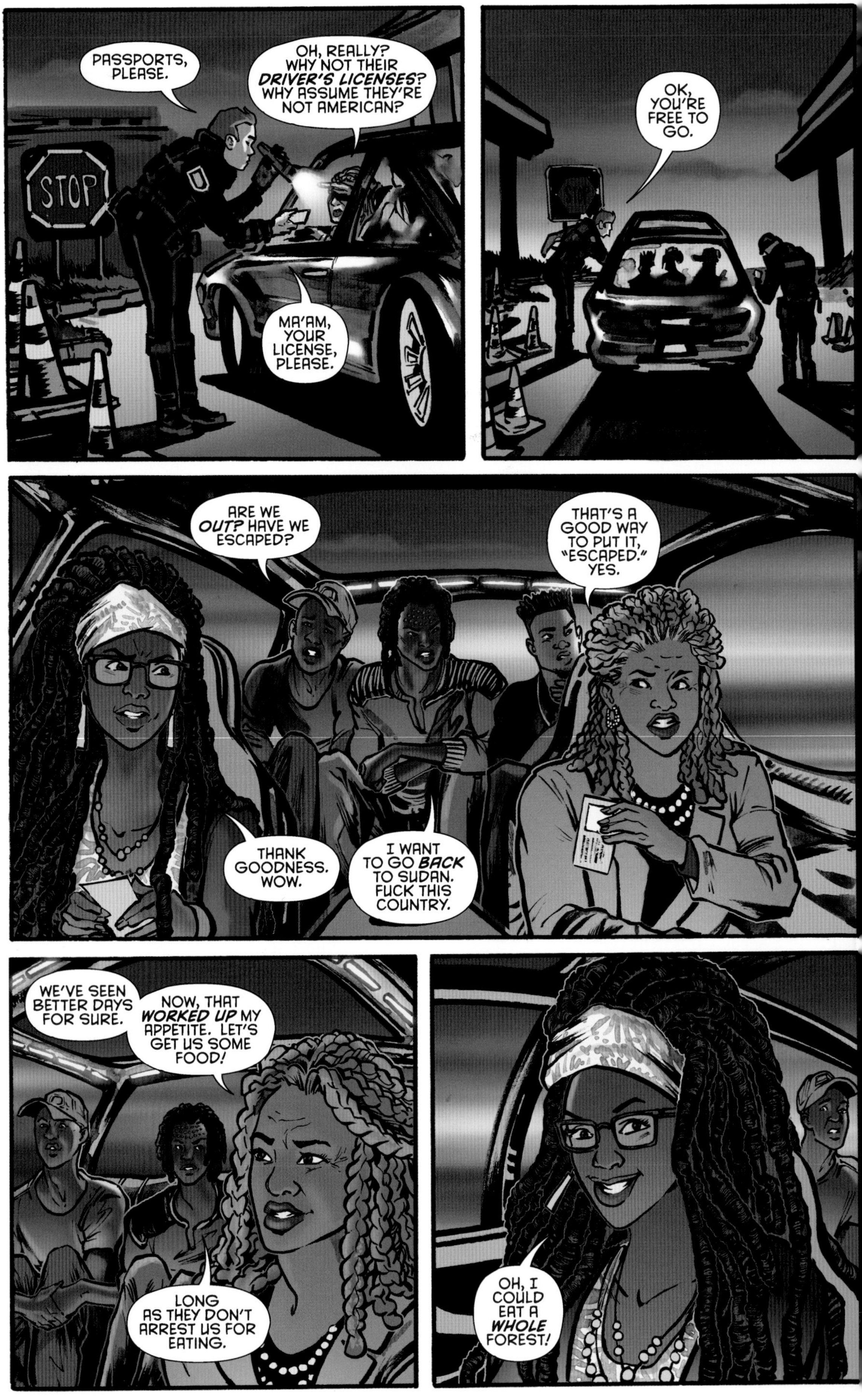
PASSPORTS, PLEASE.
OH, REALLY? WHY NOT THEIR DRIVER'S LICENSES? WHY ASSUME THEY'RE NOT AMERICAN?
MA'AM, YOUR LICENSE, PLEASE.
OK, YOU'RE FREE TO GO.
ARE WE OUT? HAVE WE ESCAPED?
THAT'S A GOOD WAY TO PUT IT, "ESCAPED." YES.
THANK GOODNESS. WOW.
I WANT TO GO BACK TO SUDAN. FUCK THIS COUNTRY.
WE'VE SEEN BETTER DAYS FOR SURE.
NOW, THAT WORKED UP MY APPETITE. LET'S GET US SOME FOOD!
LONG AS THEY DON'T ARREST US FOR EATING.
OH, I COULD EAT A WHOLE FOREST!

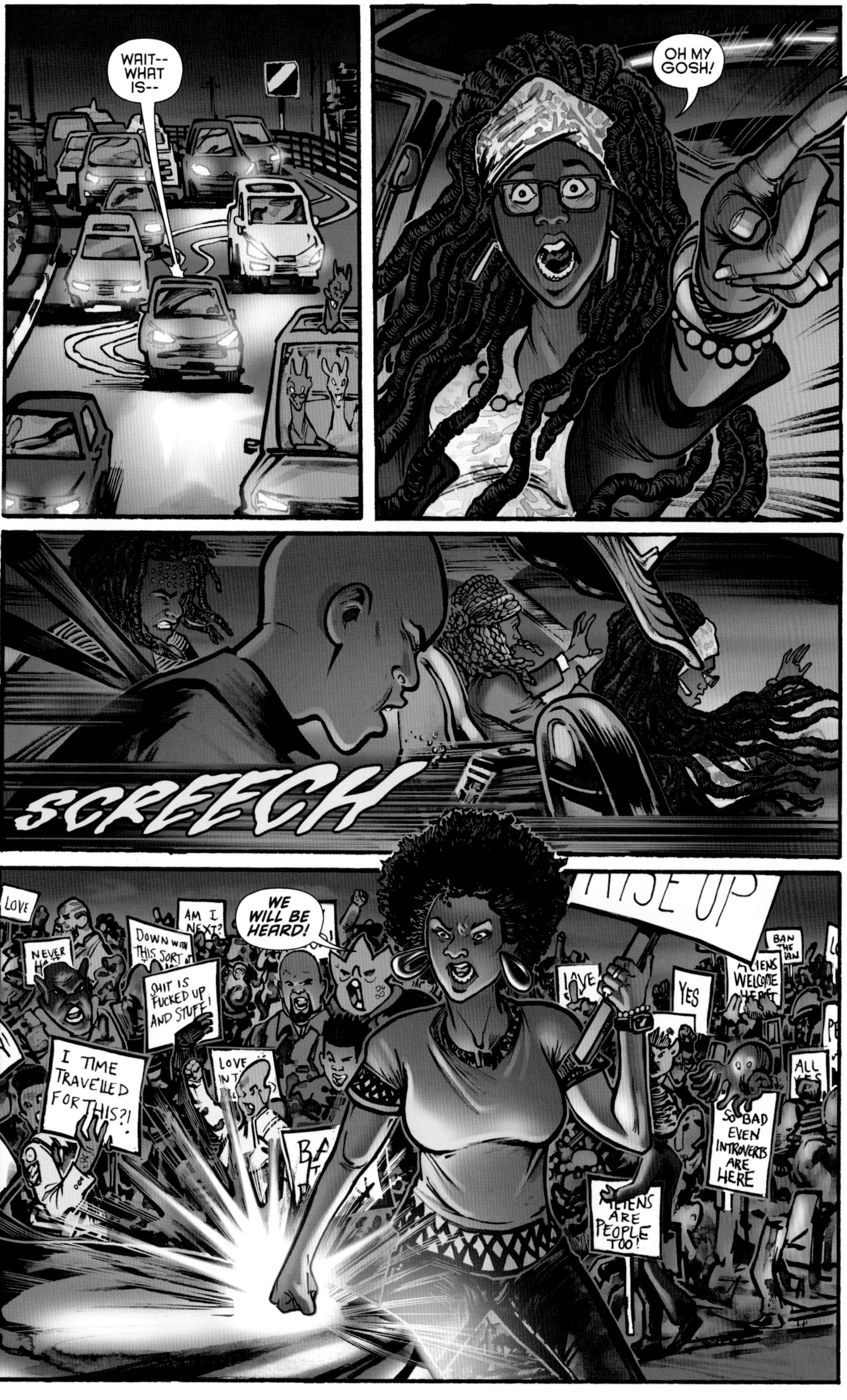
WAIT-- WHAT IS--
OH MY GOSH!
SCREECH
WE WILL BE HEARD!
LOVE
AM I NEXT?
DOWN WITH THIS SORT
NEVER
SHIT IS FUCKED UP AND STUFF!
I TIME TRAVELLED FOR THIS?!
YES
SO BAD EVEN INTROVERTS ARE HERE
ARE PEOPLE TOO!

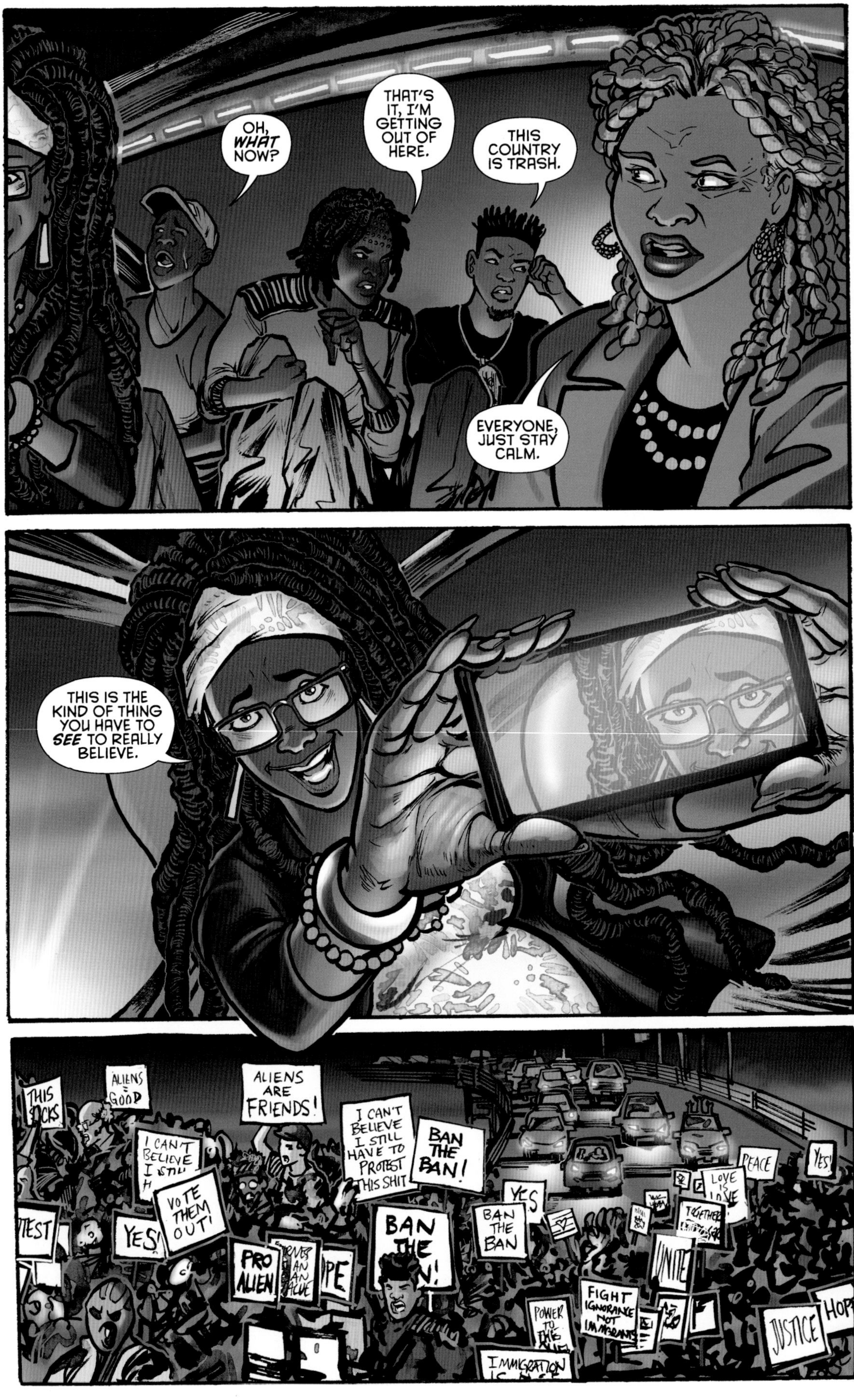
OH, *WHAT* NOW?
THAT'S IT, I'M GETTING OUT OF HERE.
THIS COUNTRY IS TRASH.
EVERYONE, JUST STAY CALM.
THIS IS THE KIND OF THING YOU HAVE TO *SEE* TO REALLY BELIEVE.
ALIENS = GOOD
ALIENS ARE FRIENDS!
I CAN'T BELIEVE I STILL HAVE TO PROTEST THIS SHIT
BAN THE BAN!
VOTE THEM OUT!
YES!
PRO ALIEN
BAN THE BAN
PEACE
YES!
LOVE IS LOVE
UNITE
FIGHT IGNORANCE NOT IMMIGRANTS
POWER TO THE
JUSTICE

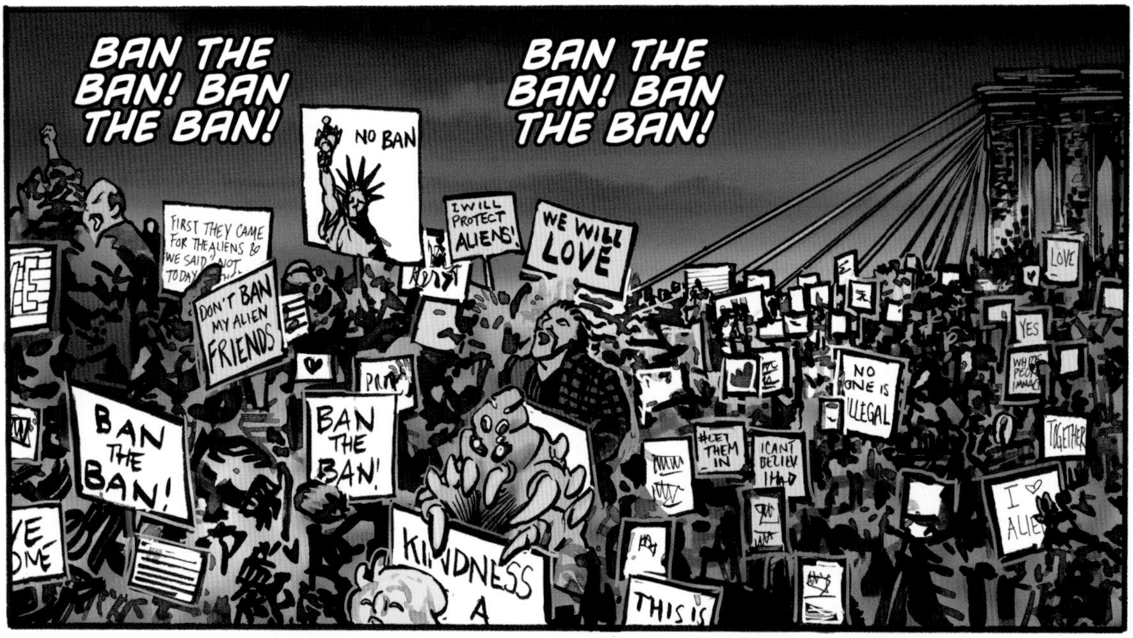
BAN THE BAN! BAN THE BAN!
BAN THE BAN! BAN THE BAN!
NO BAN
FIRST THEY CAME FOR THE ALIENS & WE SAID NOT TODAY
I WILL PROTECT ALIENS!
WE WILL LOVE
DON'T BAN MY ALIEN FRIENDS
BAN THE BAN!
BAN THE BAN!
NO ONE IS ILLEGAL
#LET THEM IN
LOVE
YES
TOGETHER
KINDNESS

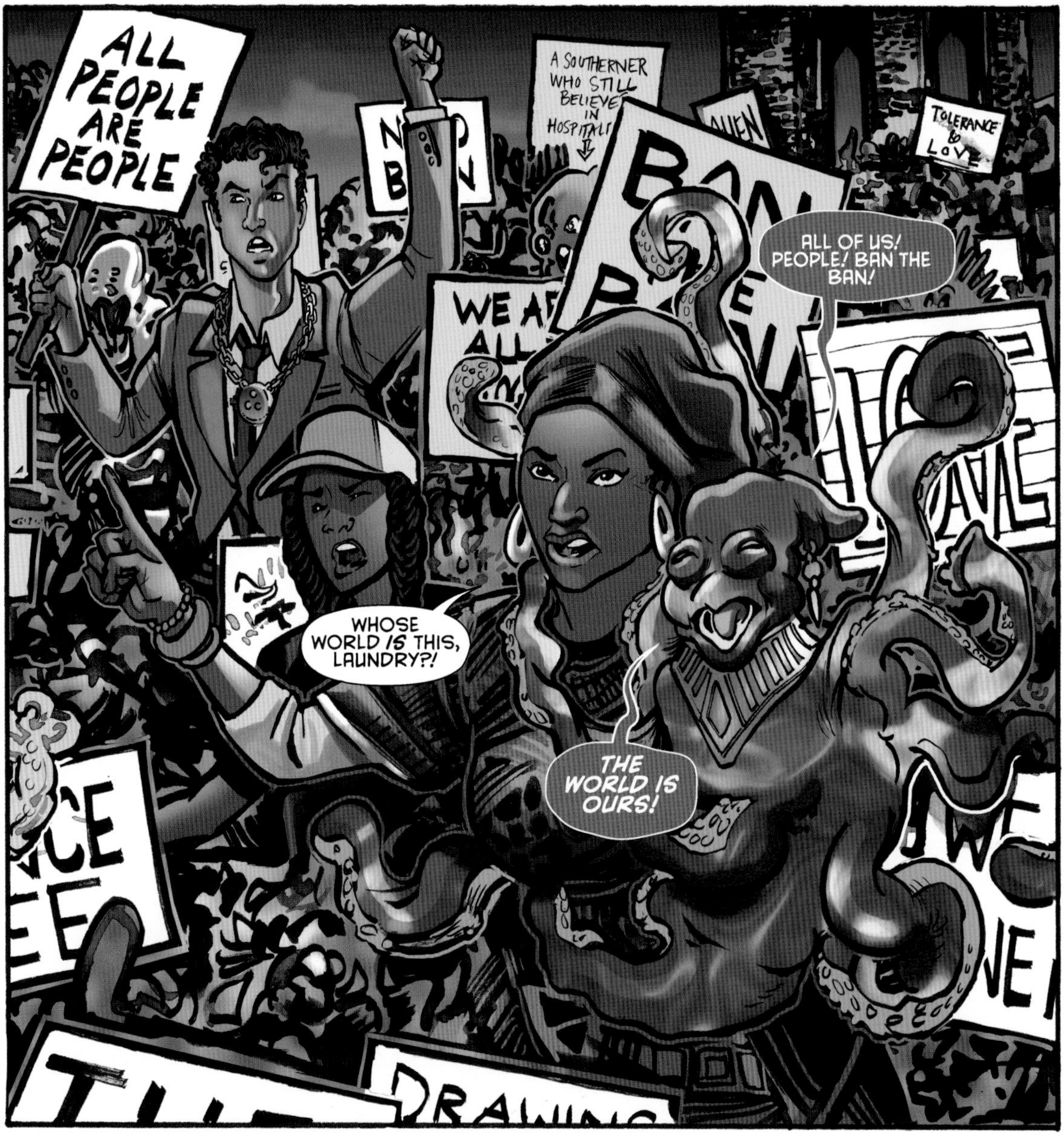
ALL PEOPLE ARE PEOPLE
A SOUTHERNER WHO STILL BELIEVES IN
TOLERANCE & LOVE
WHOSE WORLD IS THIS, LAUNDRY?!
THE WORLD IS OURS!
ALL OF US! PEOPLE! BAN THE BAN!

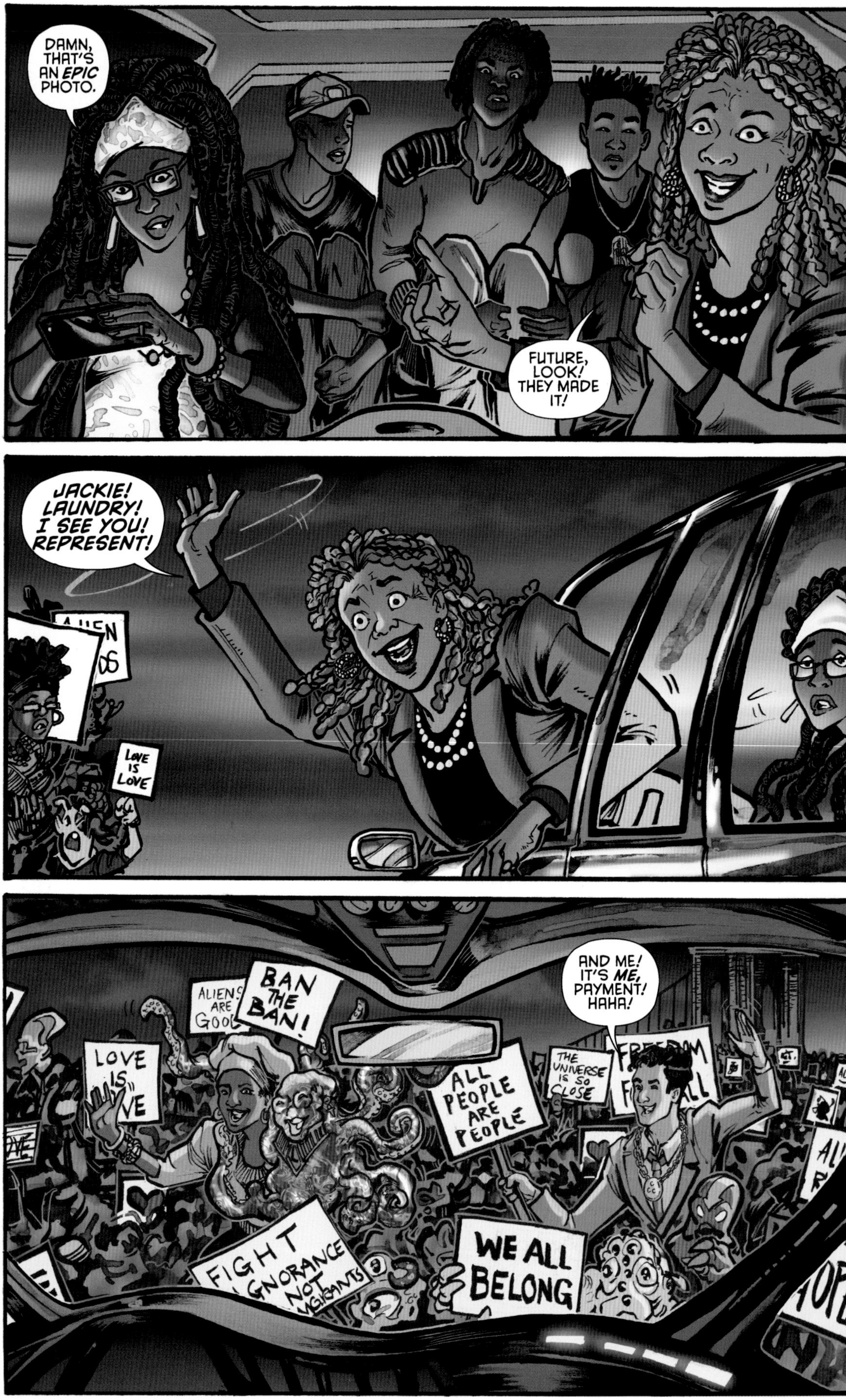
DAMN, THAT'S AN *EPIC* PHOTO.
FUTURE, LOOK! THEY MADE IT!
JACKIE! LAUNDRY! I SEE YOU! REPRESENT!
LOVE IS LOVE
AND ME! IT'S *ME*, PAYMENT! HAHA!
BAN THE BAN!
ALL PEOPLE ARE PEOPLE
THE UNIVERSE IS SO CLOSE
FIGHT
WE ALL BELONG

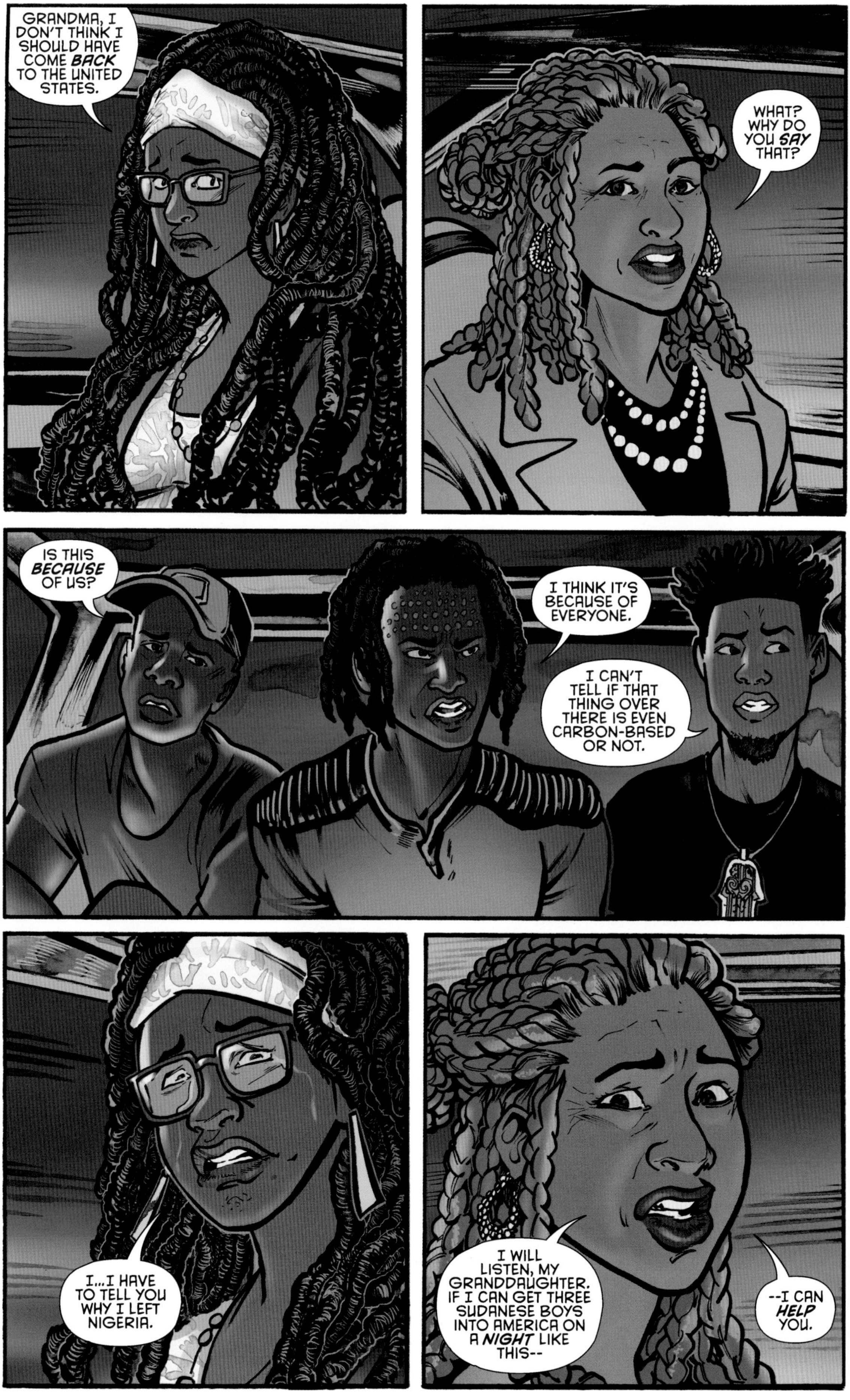
GRANDMA, I DON'T THINK I SHOULD HAVE COME *BACK* TO THE UNITED STATES.
WHAT? WHY DO YOU *SAY* THAT?
IS THIS *BECAUSE* OF US?
I THINK IT'S BECAUSE OF EVERYONE.
I CAN'T TELL IF THAT THING OVER THERE IS EVEN CARBON-BASED OR NOT.
I...I HAVE TO TELL YOU WHY I LEFT NIGERIA.
I WILL LISTEN, MY GRANDDAUGHTER. IF I CAN GET THREE SUDANESE BOYS INTO AMERICA ON A *NIGHT* LIKE THIS--
--I CAN *HELP* YOU.

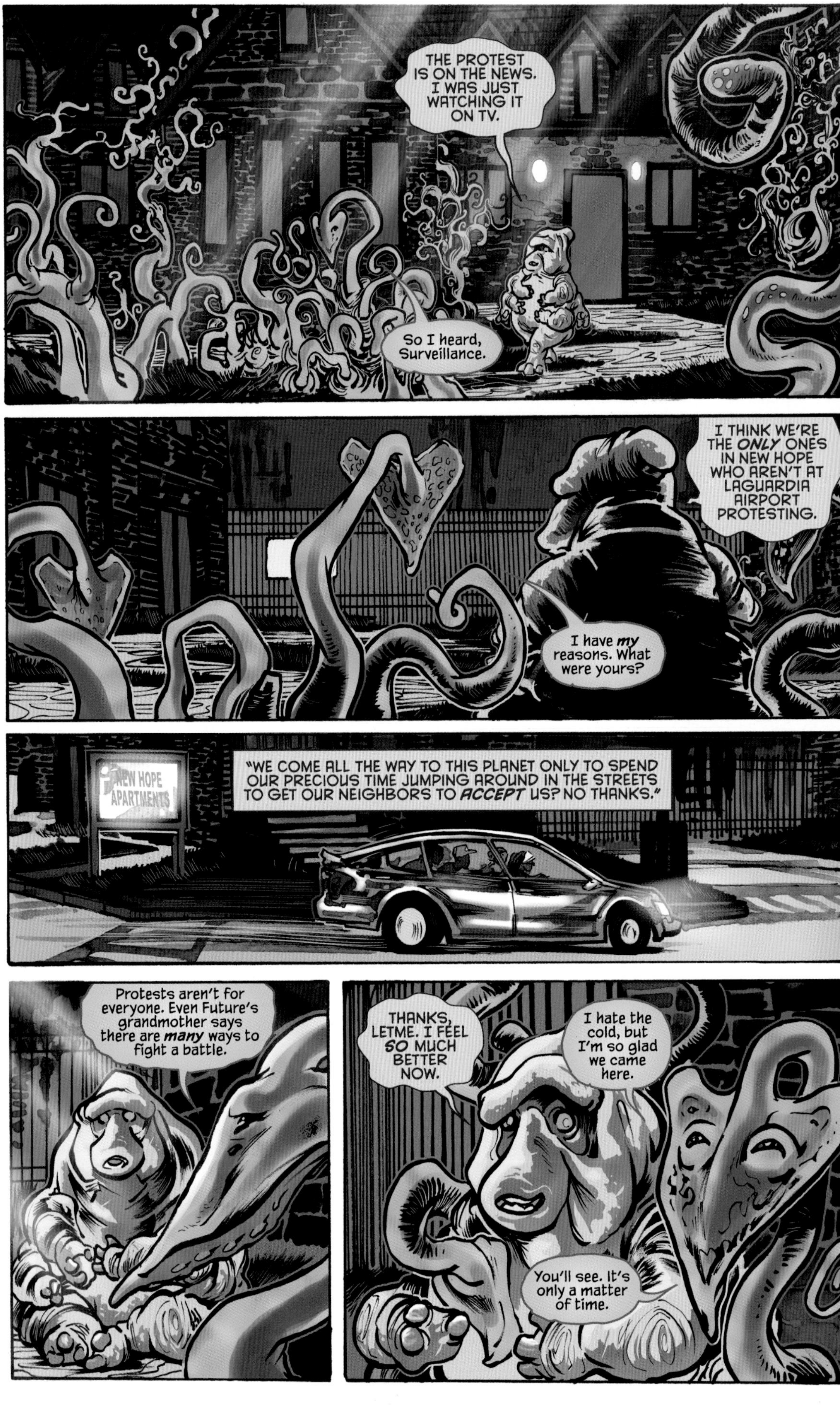
THE PROTEST IS ON THE NEWS. I WAS JUST WATCHING IT ON TV.
So I heard, Surveillance.
I THINK WE'RE THE *ONLY* ONES IN NEW HOPE WHO AREN'T AT LAGUARDIA AIRPORT PROTESTING.
I have *my* reasons. What were yours?
NEW HOPE APARTMENTS
"WE COME ALL THE WAY TO THIS PLANET ONLY TO SPEND OUR PRECIOUS TIME JUMPING AROUND IN THE STREETS TO GET OUR NEIGHBORS TO *ACCEPT* US? NO THANKS."
Protests aren't for everyone. Even Future's grandmother says there are *many* ways to fight a battle.
THANKS, LETME. I FEEL *SO* MUCH BETTER NOW.
I hate the cold, but I'm so glad we came here.
You'll see. It's only a matter of time.

CHAPTER 3

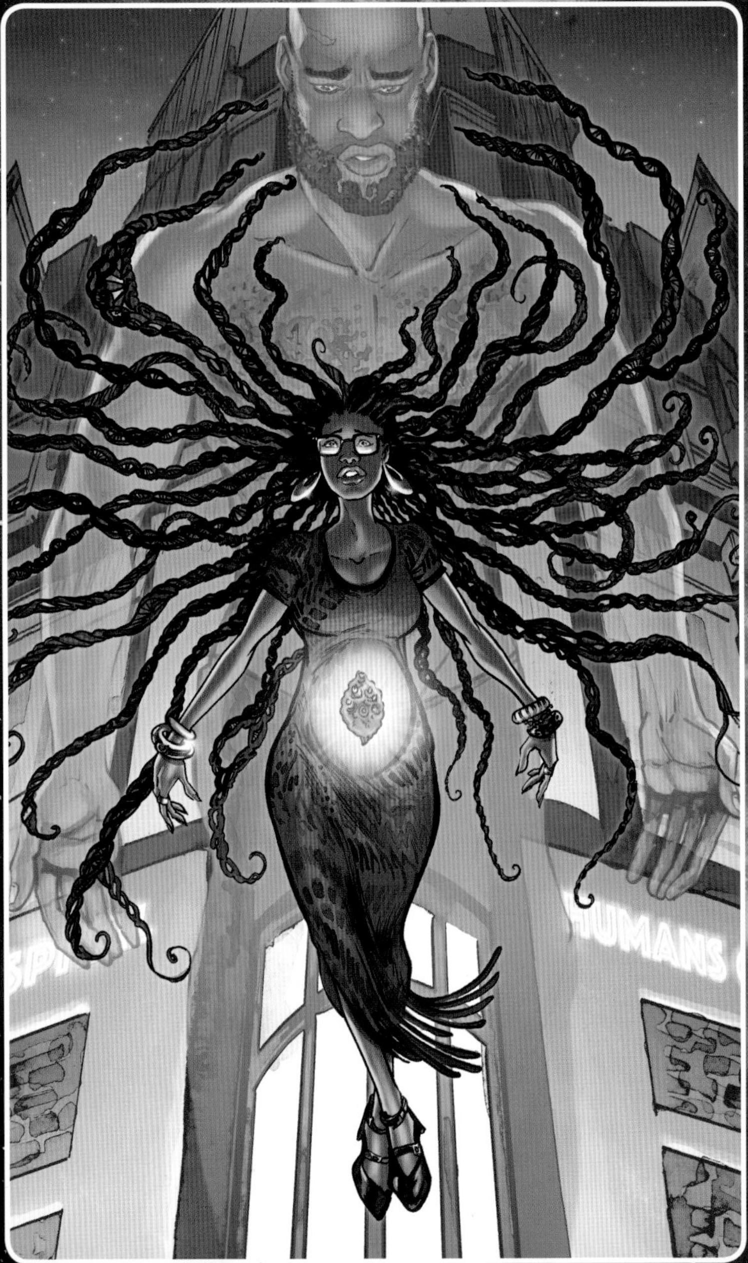
HUMANS

ROOTS

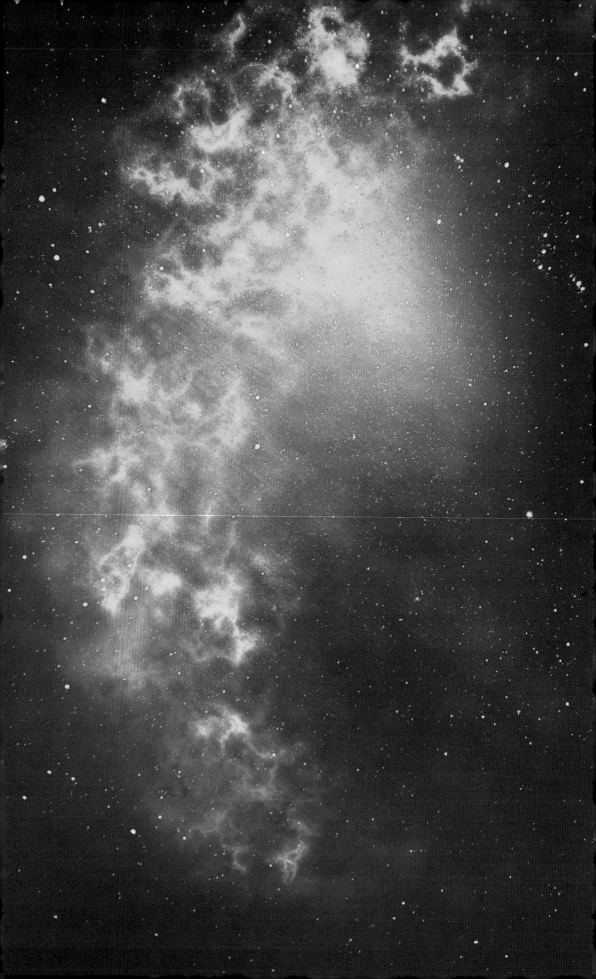

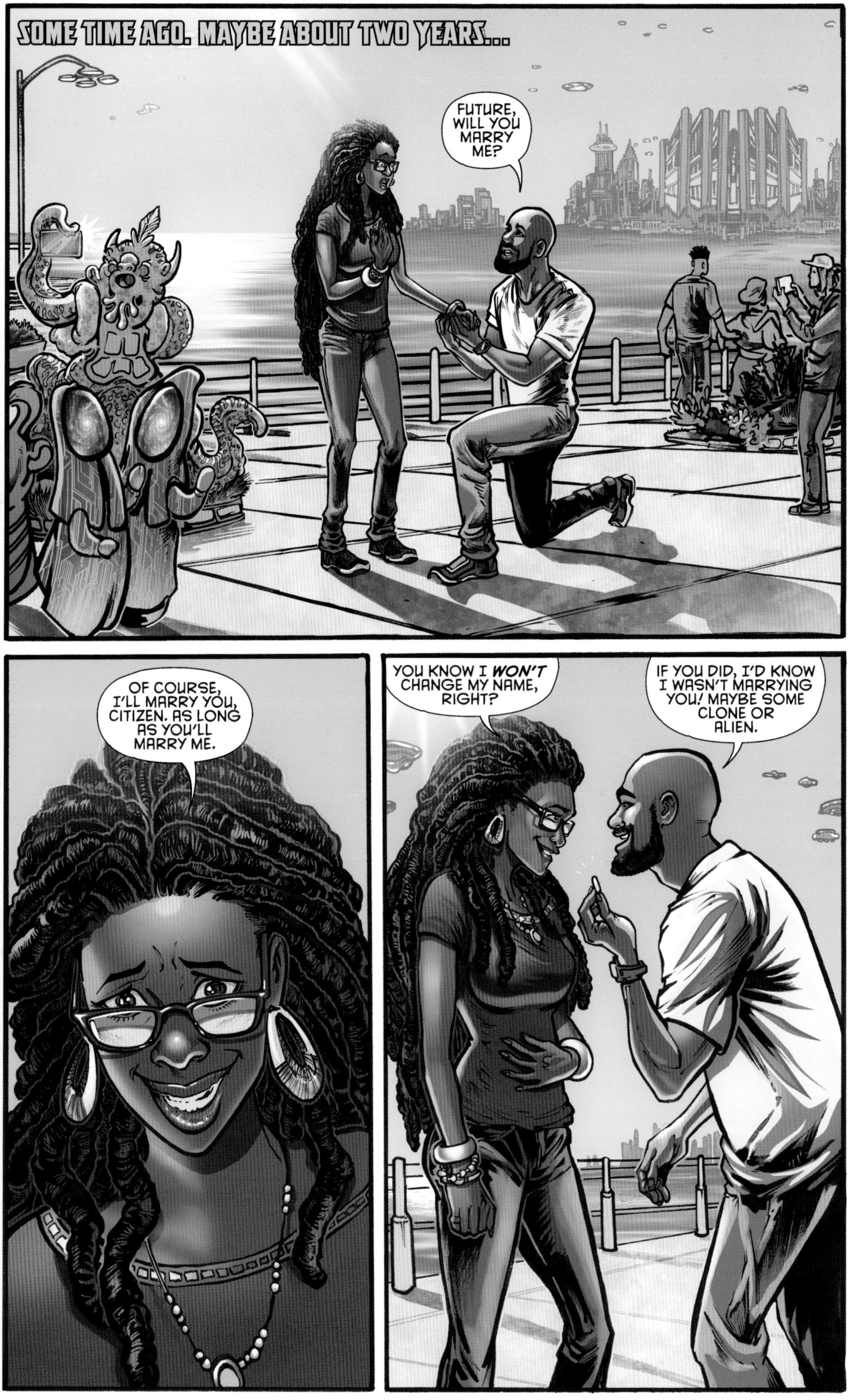
SOME TIME AGO. MAYBE ABOUT TWO YEARS...
FUTURE, WILL YOU MARRY ME?
OF COURSE, I'LL MARRY YOU, CITIZEN. AS LONG AS YOU'LL MARRY ME.
YOU KNOW I *WON'T* CHANGE MY NAME, RIGHT?
IF YOU DID, I'D KNOW I WASN'T MARRYING YOU! MAYBE SOME CLONE OR ALIEN.

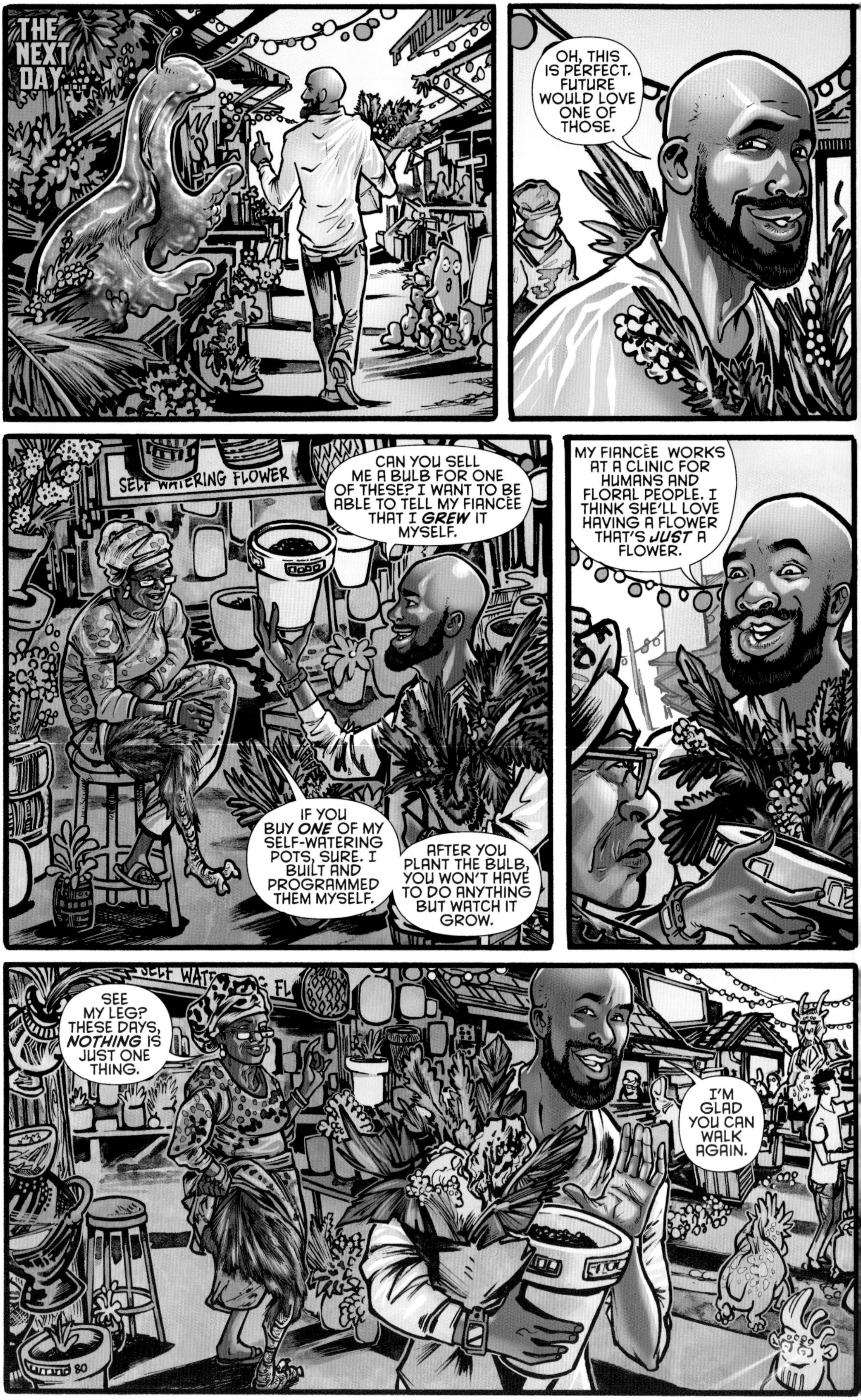
THE NEXT DAY...
OH, THIS IS PERFECT. FUTURE WOULD LOVE ONE OF THOSE.
SELF WATERING FLOWER
CAN YOU SELL ME A BULB FOR ONE OF THESE? I WANT TO BE ABLE TO TELL MY FIANCÉE THAT I *GREW* IT MYSELF.
IF YOU BUY *ONE* OF MY SELF-WATERING POTS, SURE. I BUILT AND PROGRAMMED THEM MYSELF.
AFTER YOU PLANT THE BULB, YOU WON'T HAVE TO DO ANYTHING BUT WATCH IT GROW.
MY FIANCÉE WORKS AT A CLINIC FOR HUMANS AND FLORAL PEOPLE. I THINK SHE'LL LOVE HAVING A FLOWER THAT'S *JUST* A FLOWER.
SEE MY LEG? THESE DAYS, *NOTHING* IS JUST ONE THING.
I'M GLAD YOU CAN WALK AGAIN.

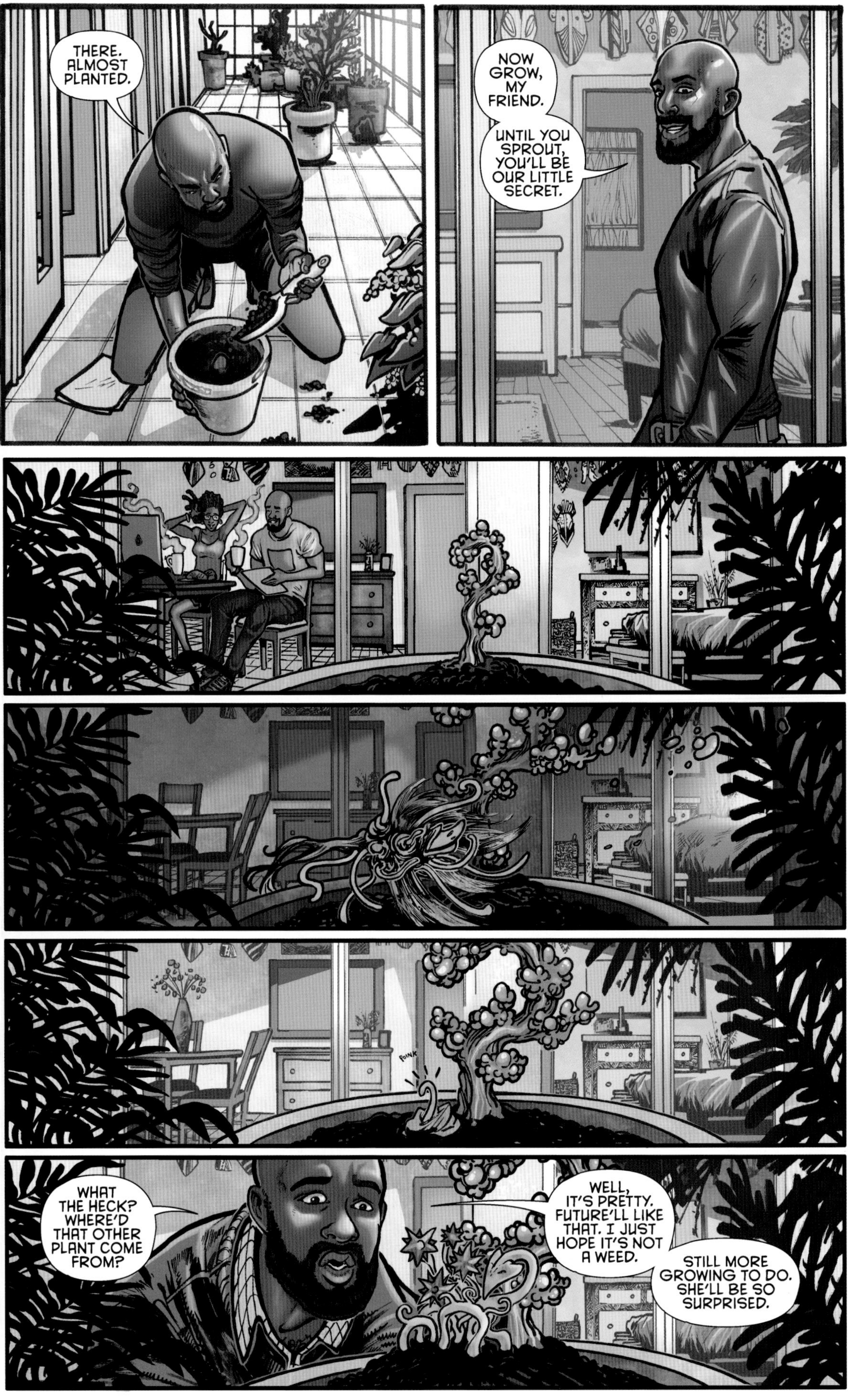
THERE. ALMOST PLANTED.
NOW GROW, MY FRIEND.
UNTIL YOU SPROUT, YOU'LL BE OUR LITTLE SECRET.
POINK
WHAT THE HECK? WHERE'D THAT OTHER PLANT COME FROM?
WELL, IT'S PRETTY. FUTURE'LL LIKE THAT. I JUST HOPE IT'S NOT A WEED.
STILL MORE GROWING TO DO. SHE'LL BE SO SURPRISED.

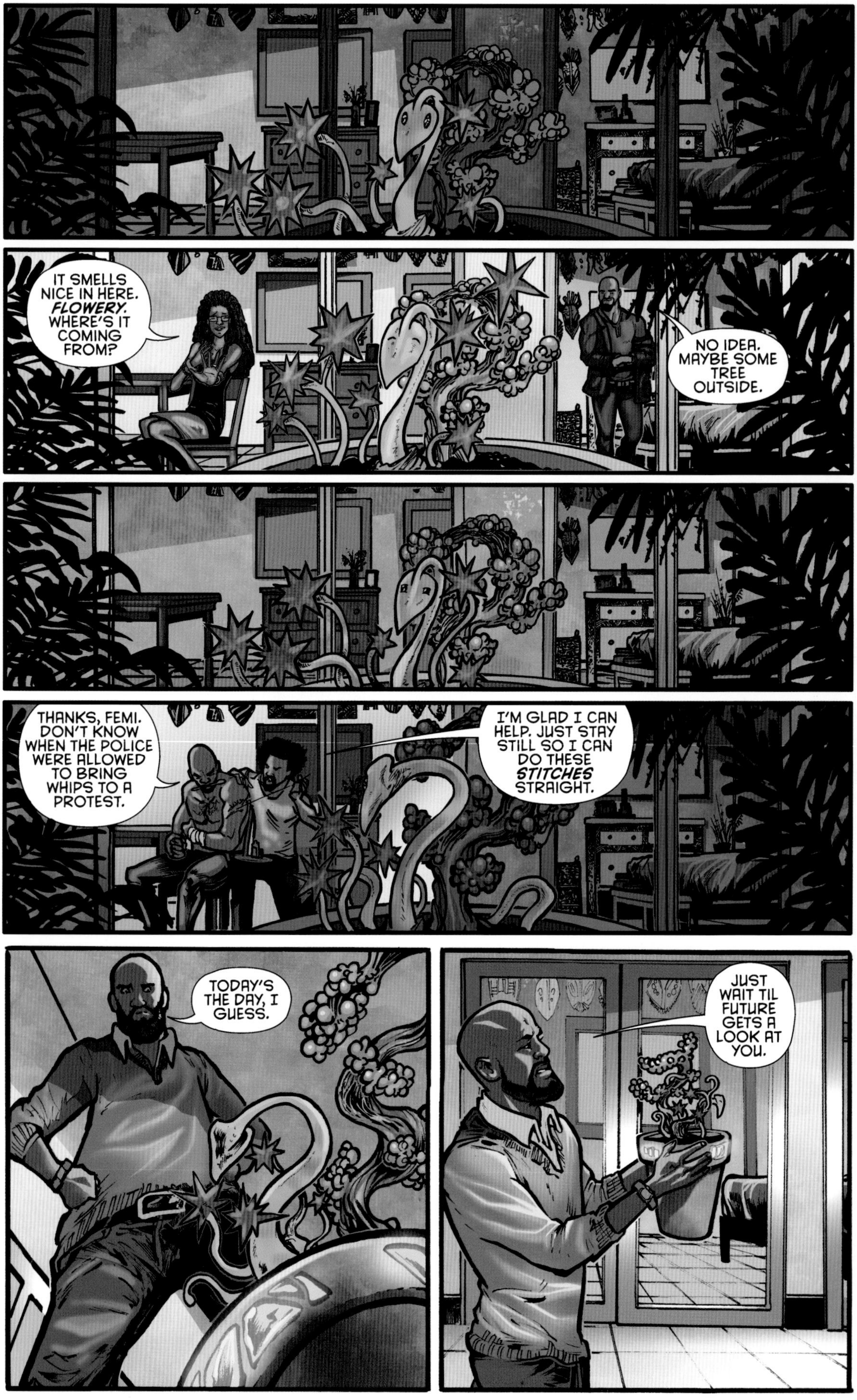
IT SMELLS NICE IN HERE. FLOWERY. WHERE'S IT COMING FROM?
NO IDEA. MAYBE SOME TREE OUTSIDE.
THANKS, FEMI. DON'T KNOW WHEN THE POLICE WERE ALLOWED TO BRING WHIPS TO A PROTEST.
I'M GLAD I CAN HELP. JUST STAY STILL SO I CAN DO THESE STITCHES STRAIGHT.
TODAY'S THE DAY, I GUESS.
JUST WAIT TIL FUTURE GETS A LOOK AT YOU.

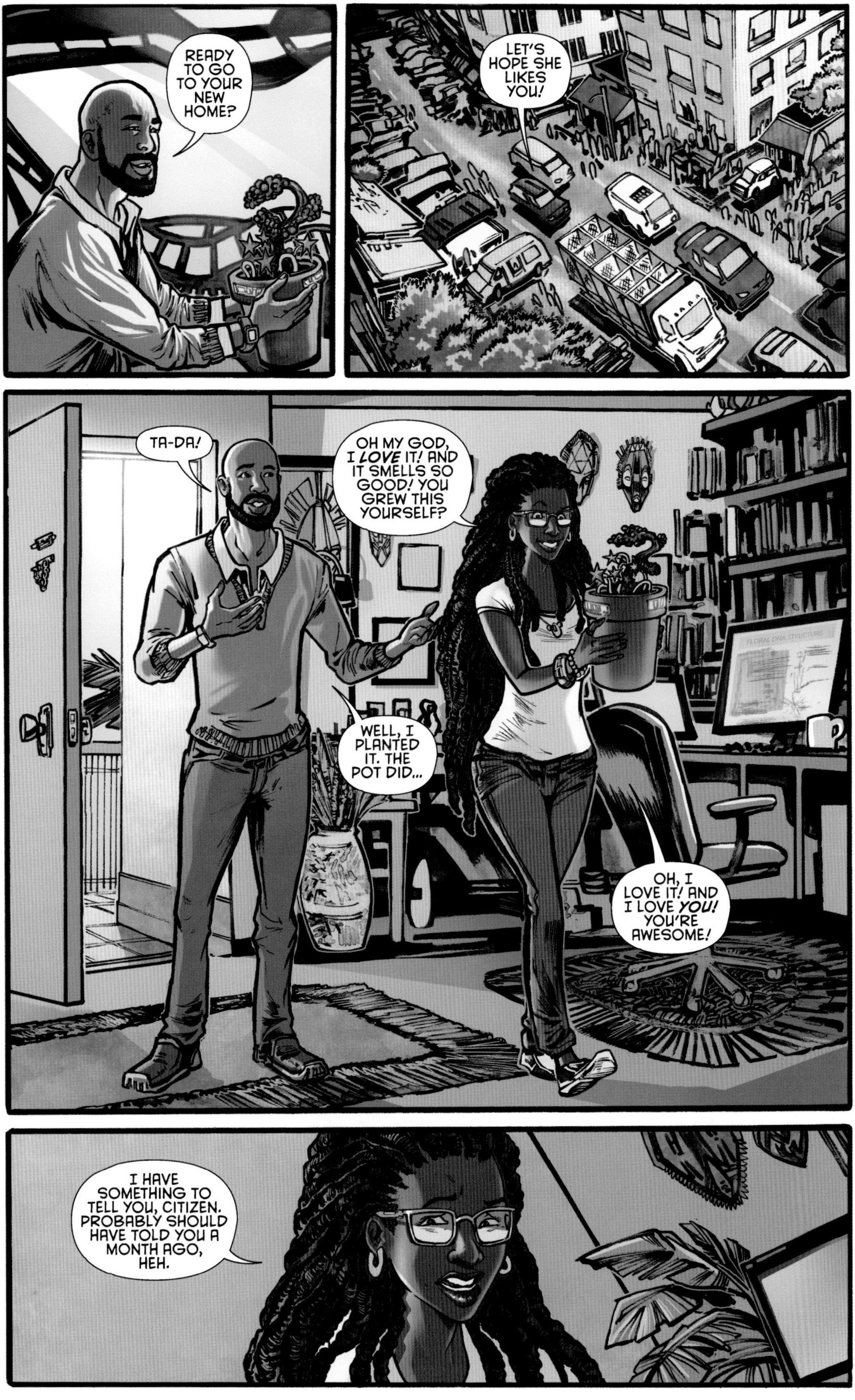
READY TO GO TO YOUR NEW HOME?
LET'S HOPE SHE LIKES YOU!
TA-DA!
OH MY GOD, I LOVE IT! AND IT SMELLS SO GOOD! YOU GREW THIS YOURSELF?
WELL, I PLANTED IT. THE POT DID...
FLORAL DNA STRUCTURE
OH, I LOVE IT! AND I LOVE YOU! YOU'RE AWESOME!
I HAVE SOMETHING TO TELL YOU, CITIZEN. PROBABLY SHOULD HAVE TOLD YOU A MONTH AGO, HEH.

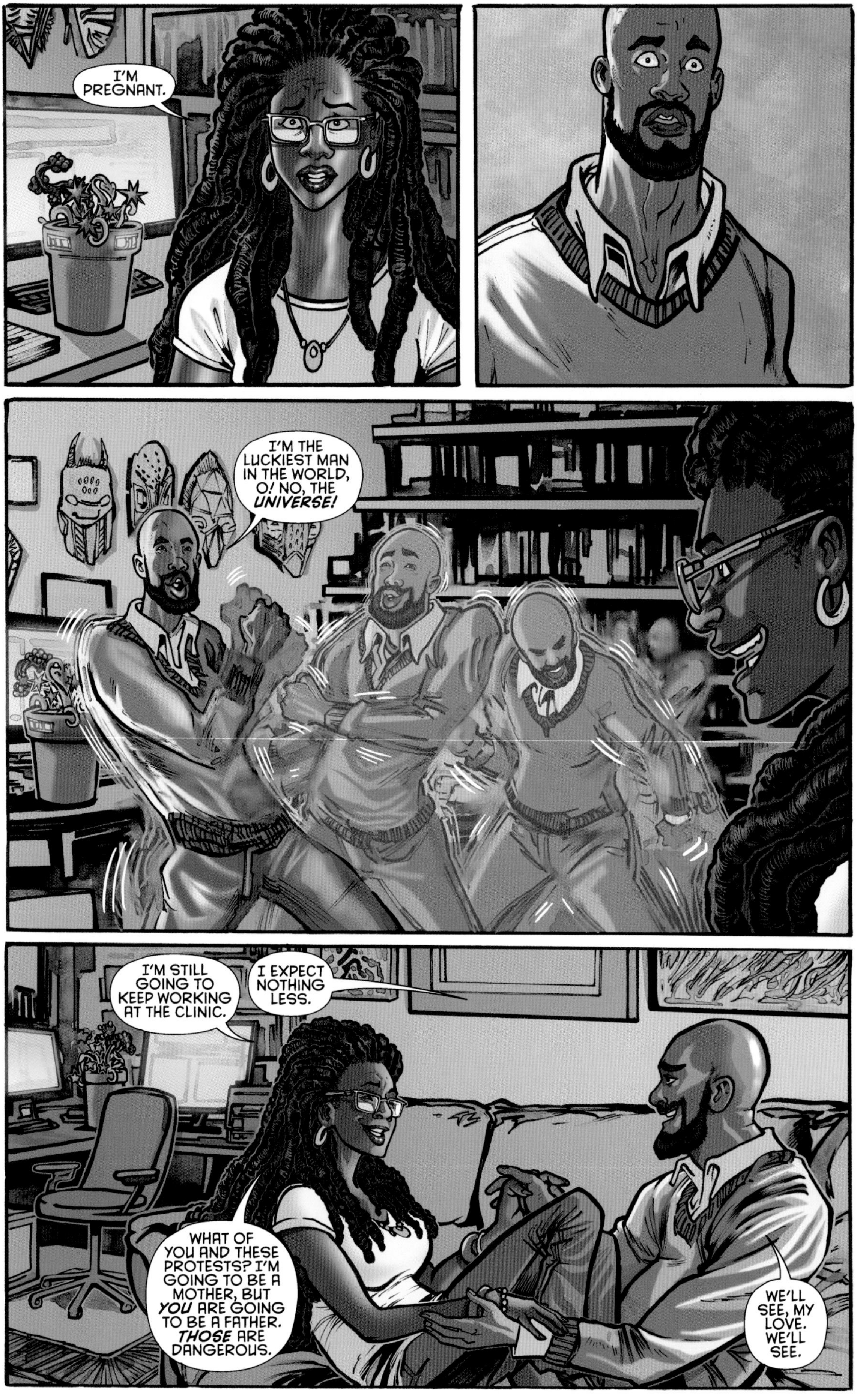
I'M PREGNANT.
I'M THE LUCKIEST MAN IN THE WORLD, O! NO, THE *UNIVERSE!*
I'M STILL GOING TO KEEP WORKING AT THE CLINIC.
I EXPECT NOTHING LESS.
WHAT OF YOU AND THESE PROTESTS? I'M GOING TO BE A MOTHER, BUT *YOU* ARE GOING TO BE A FATHER. *THOSE* ARE DANGEROUS.
WE'LL SEE, MY LOVE. WE'LL SEE.

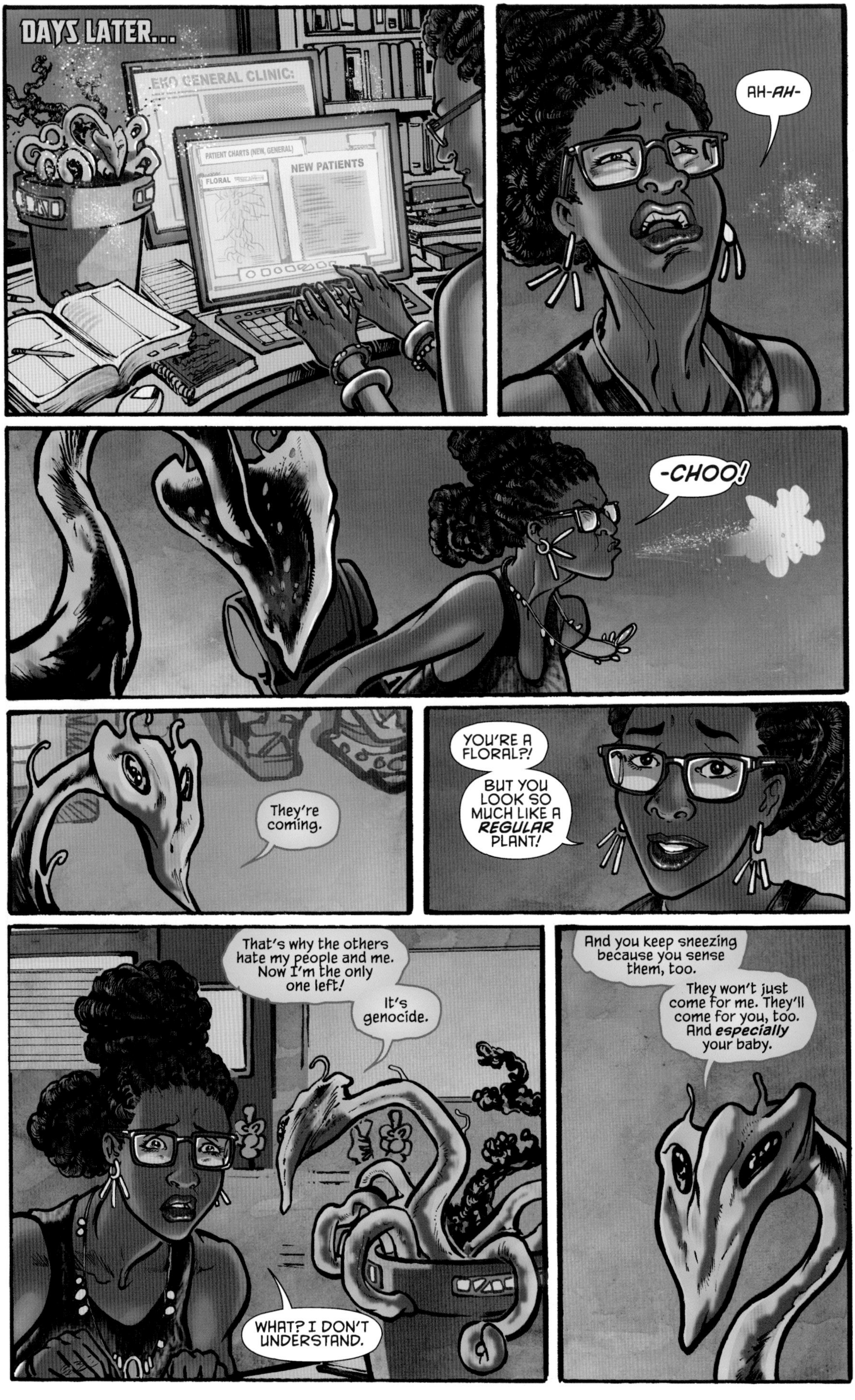
DAYS LATER...
EKO GENERAL CLINIC:
PATIENT CHARTS (NEW, GENERAL)
FLORAL
NEW PATIENTS
AH-*AH*-
-CHOO!
They're coming.
YOU'RE A FLORAL?!
BUT YOU LOOK SO MUCH LIKE A *REGULAR* PLANT!
That's why the others hate my people and me. Now I'm the only one left!
It's genocide.
WHAT? I DON'T UNDERSTAND.
And you keep sneezing because you sense them, too.
They won't just come for me. They'll come for you, too. And *especially* your baby.

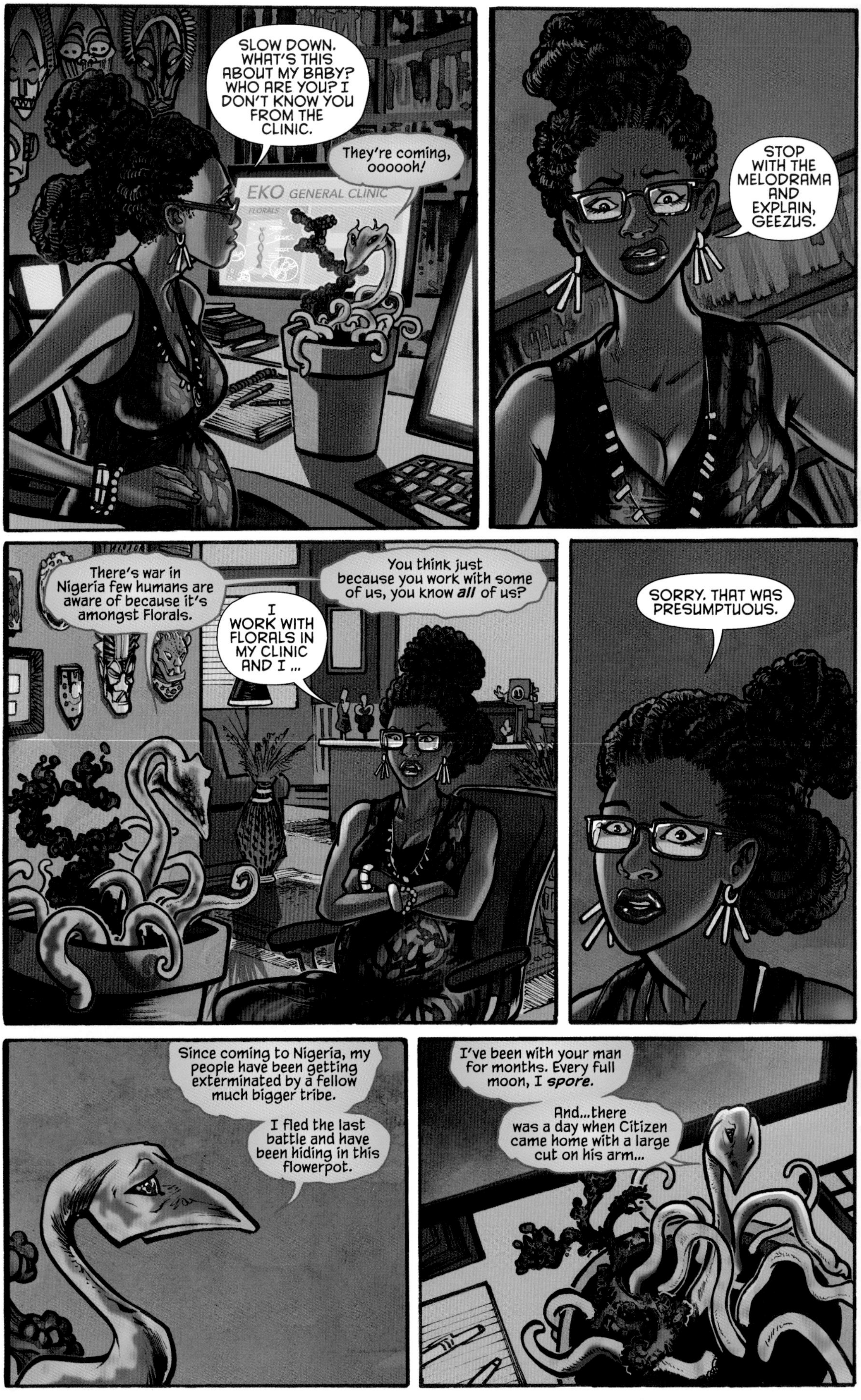
SLOW DOWN. WHAT'S THIS ABOUT MY BABY? WHO ARE YOU? I DON'T KNOW YOU FROM THE CLINIC.
They're coming, oooooh!
EKO GENERAL CLINIC
FLORALS
STOP WITH THE MELODRAMA AND EXPLAIN, GEEZUS.
There's war in Nigeria few humans are aware of because it's amongst Florals.
You think just because you work with some of us, you know *all* of us?
I WORK WITH FLORALS IN MY CLINIC AND I ...
SORRY. THAT WAS PRESUMPTUOUS.
Since coming to Nigeria, my people have been getting exterminated by a fellow much bigger tribe.
I fled the last battle and have been hiding in this flowerpot.
I've been with your man for months. Every full moon, I *spore.*
And...there was a day when Citizen came home with a large cut on his arm...

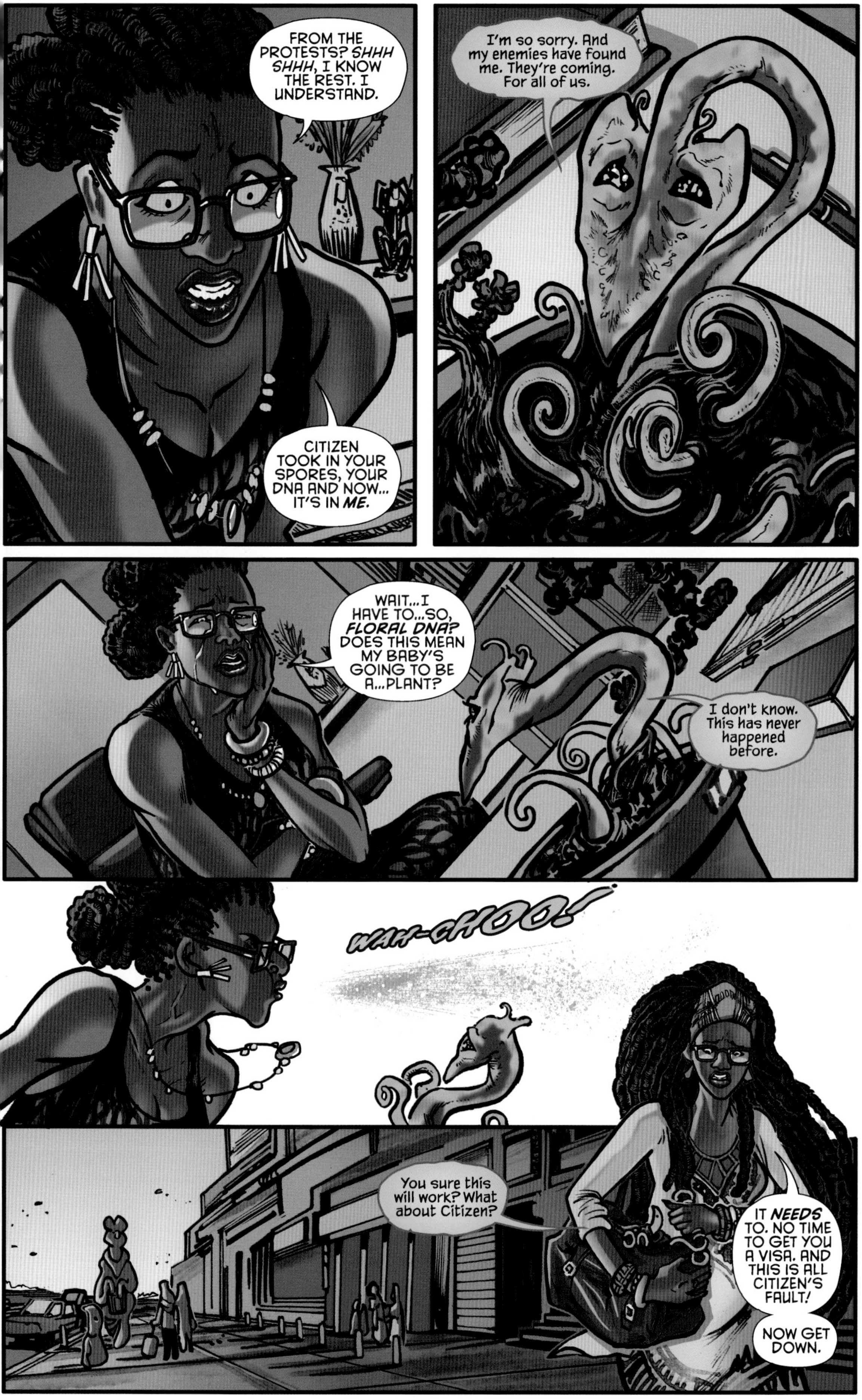
FROM THE PROTESTS? SHHH SHHH, I KNOW THE REST. I UNDERSTAND.
CITIZEN TOOK IN YOUR SPORES, YOUR DNA AND NOW... IT'S IN ME.
I'm so sorry. And my enemies have found me. They're coming. For all of us.
WAIT...I HAVE TO...SO, FLORAL DNA? DOES THIS MEAN MY BABY'S GOING TO BE A...PLANT?
I don't know. This has never happened before.
WAH-CHOO!
You sure this will work? What about Citizen?
IT NEEDS TO. NO TIME TO GET YOU A VISA. AND THIS IS ALL CITIZEN'S FAULT!
NOW GET DOWN.

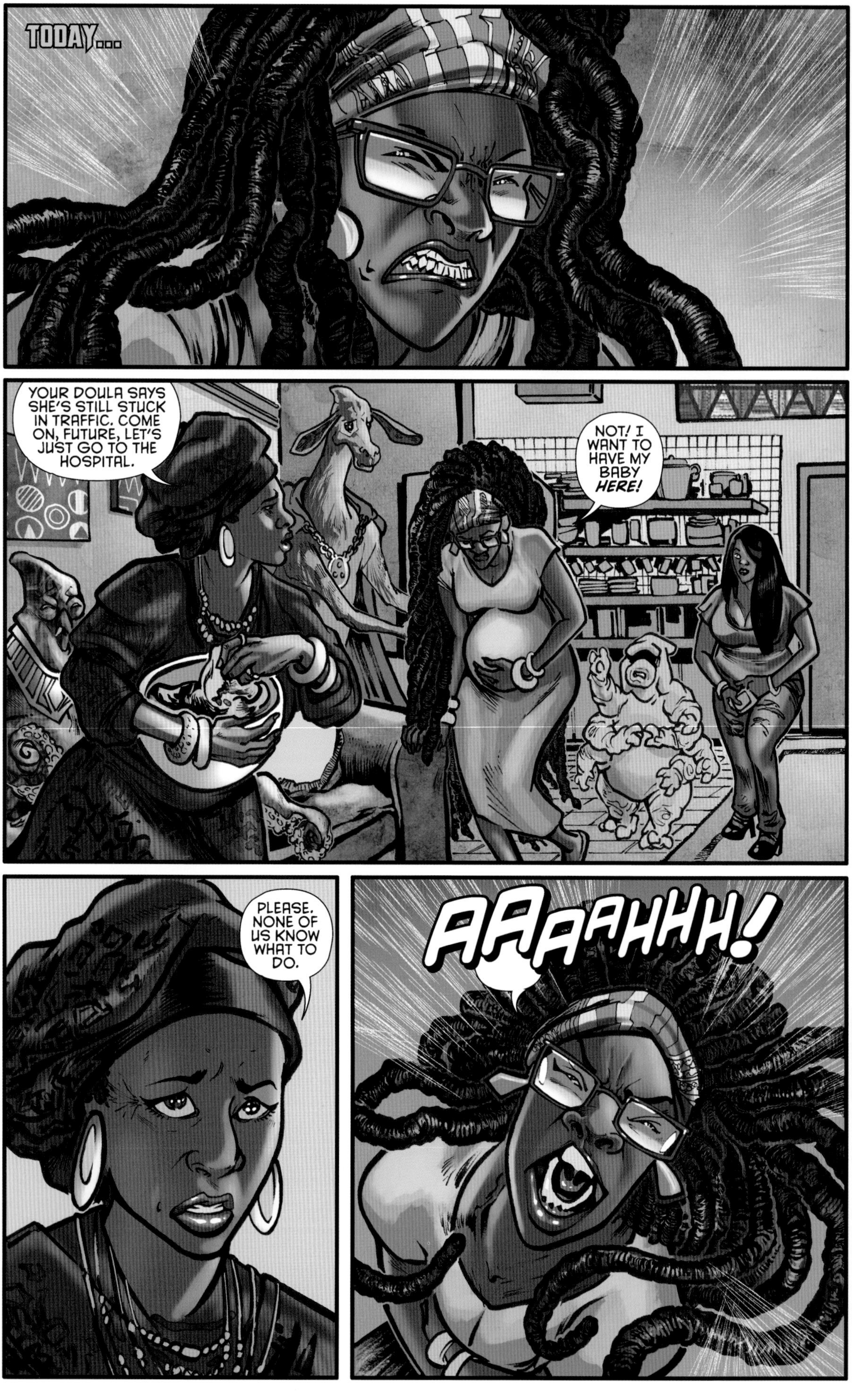
TODAY...
YOUR DOULA SAYS SHE'S STILL STUCK IN TRAFFIC. COME ON, FUTURE, LET'S JUST GO TO THE HOSPITAL.
NOT! I WANT TO HAVE MY BABY *HERE!*
PLEASE. NONE OF US KNOW WHAT TO DO.
AAAAHHH!

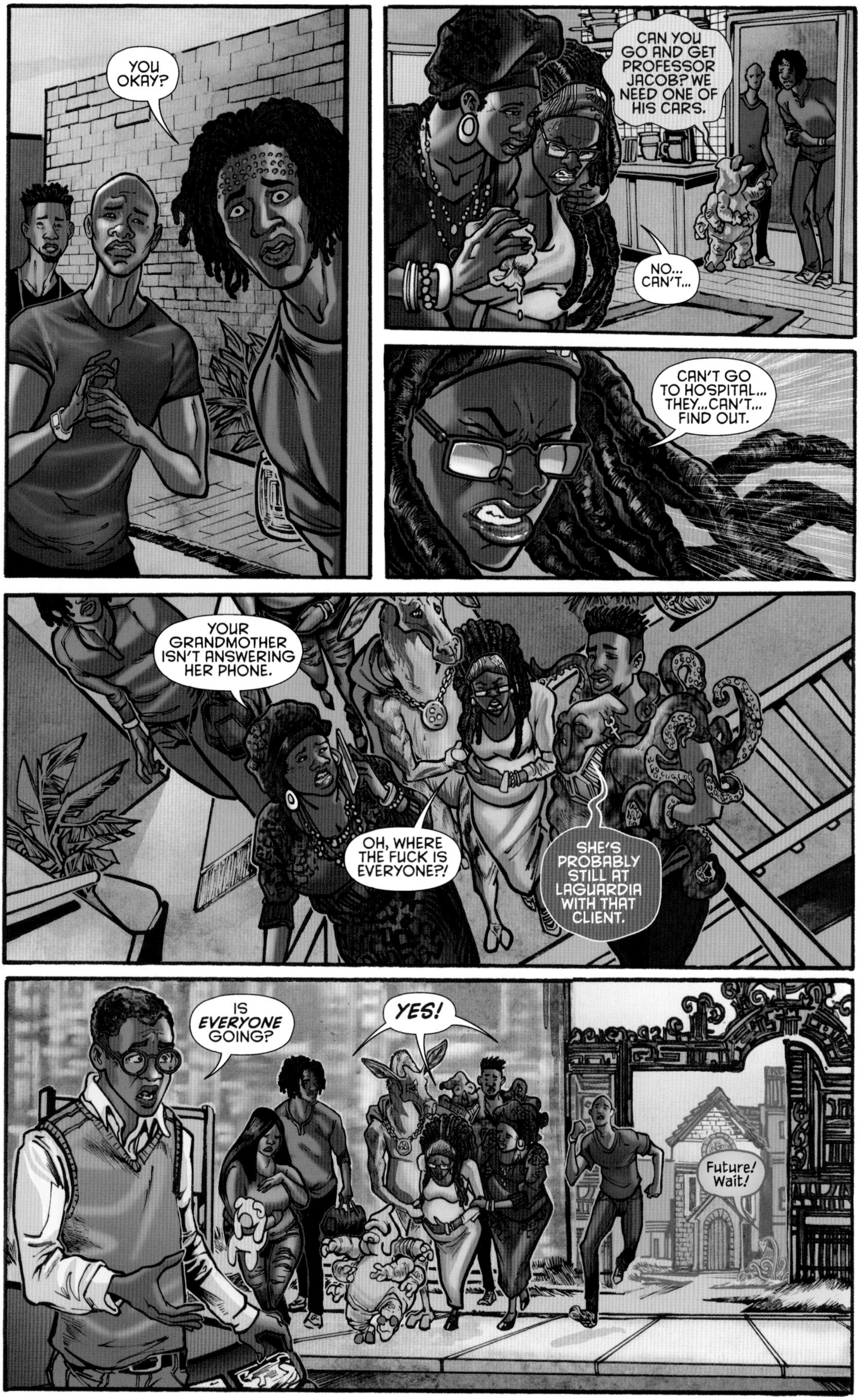
YOU OKAY?
CAN YOU GO AND GET PROFESSOR JACOB? WE NEED ONE OF HIS CARS.
NO... CAN'T...
CAN'T GO TO HOSPITAL... THEY...CAN'T... FIND OUT.
YOUR GRANDMOTHER ISN'T ANSWERING HER PHONE.
OH, WHERE THE FUCK IS EVERYONE?!
SHE'S PROBABLY STILL AT LAGUARDIA WITH THAT CLIENT.
IS EVERYONE GOING?
YES!
Future! Wait!

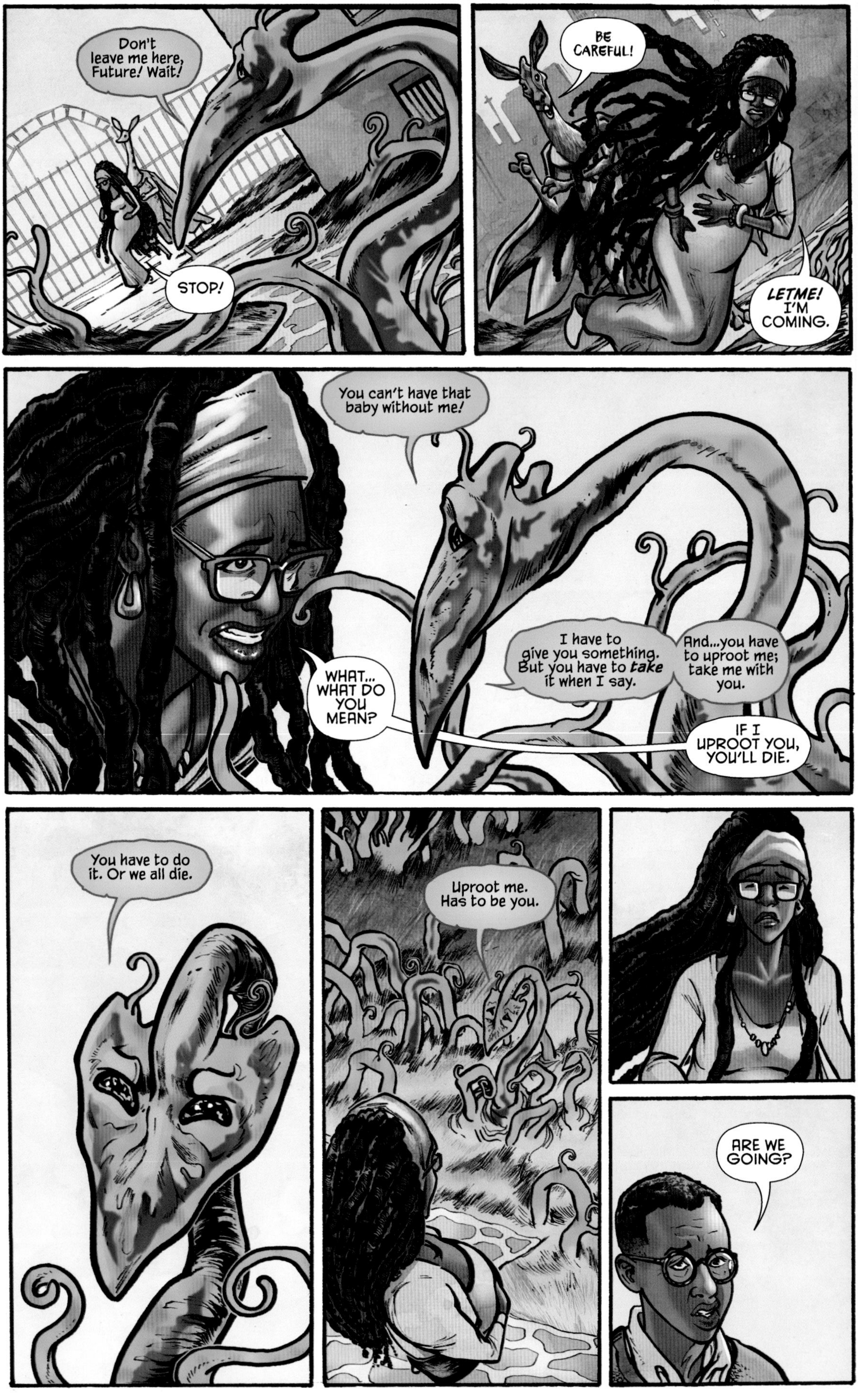
Don't leave me here, Future! Wait!
STOP!
BE CAREFUL!
LETME! I'M COMING.
You can't have that baby without me!
WHAT... WHAT DO YOU MEAN?
I have to give you something. But you have to take it when I say.
And...you have to uproot me; take me with you.
IF I UPROOT YOU, YOU'LL DIE.
You have to do it. Or we all die.
Uproot me. Has to be you.
ARE WE GOING?

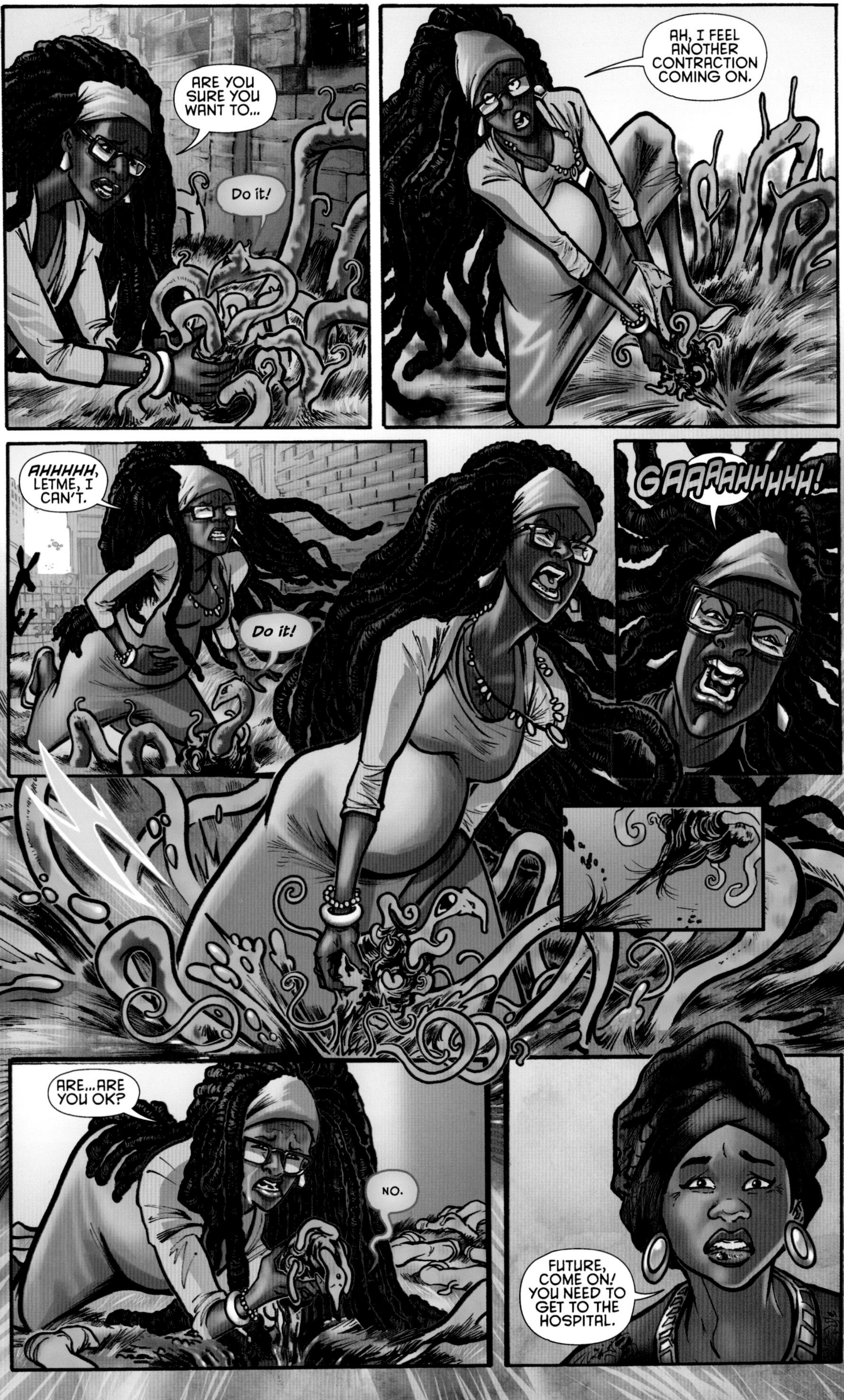
ARE YOU SURE YOU WANT TO...
Do it!
AH, I FEEL ANOTHER CONTRACTION COMING ON.
AHHHHH, LETME, I CAN'T.
Do it!
GAAAAHHHHHH!
ARE...ARE YOU OK?
NO.
FUTURE, COME ON! YOU NEED TO GET TO THE HOSPITAL.

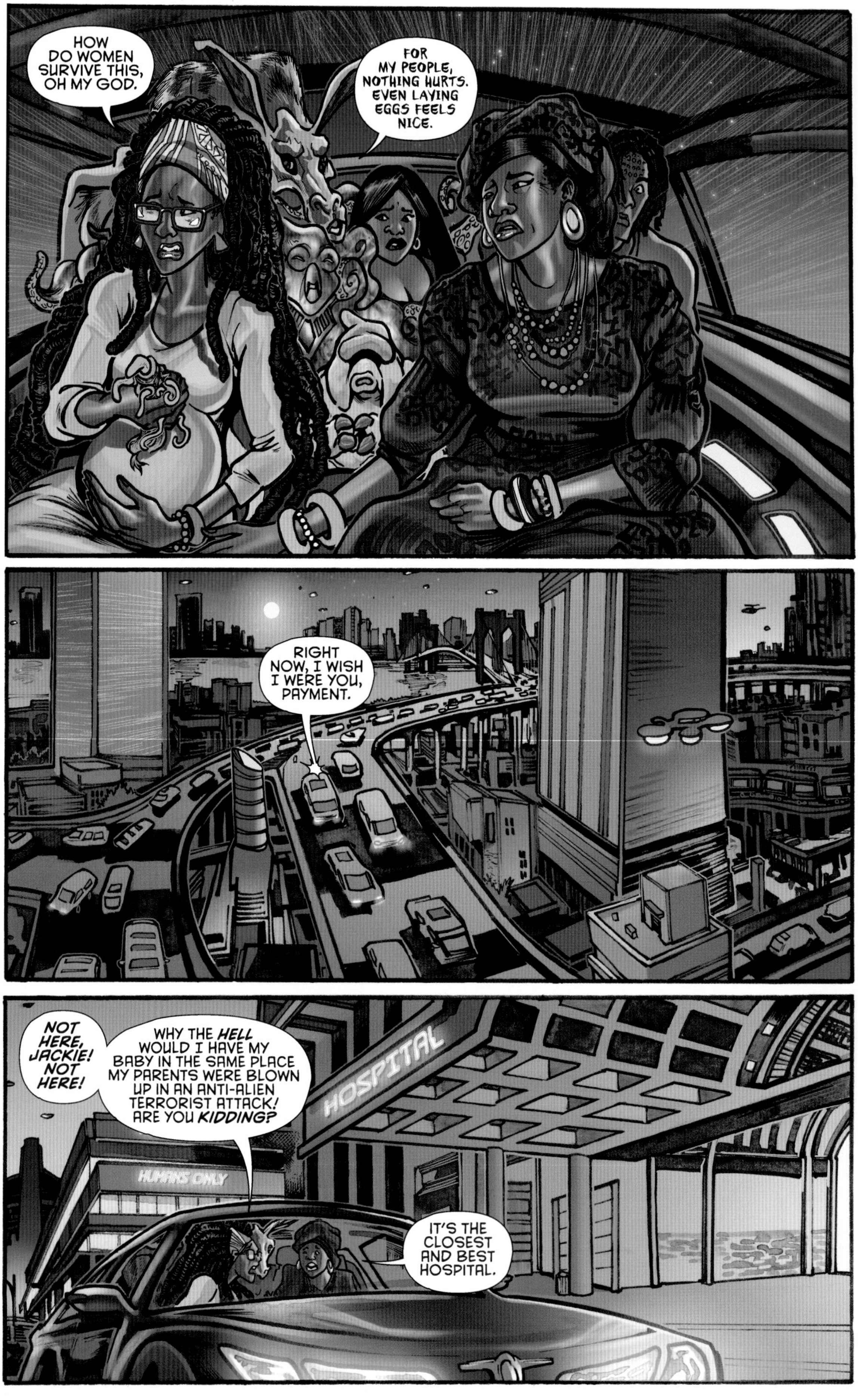
HOW DO WOMEN SURVIVE THIS, OH MY GOD.
FOR MY PEOPLE, NOTHING HURTS. EVEN LAYING EGGS FEELS NICE.
RIGHT NOW, I WISH I WERE YOU, PAYMENT.
NOT HERE, JACKIE! NOT HERE!
WHY THE HELL WOULD I HAVE MY BABY IN THE SAME PLACE MY PARENTS WERE BLOWN UP IN AN ANTI-ALIEN TERRORIST ATTACK! ARE YOU KIDDING?
HOSPITAL
HUMANS ONLY
IT'S THE CLOSEST AND BEST HOSPITAL.

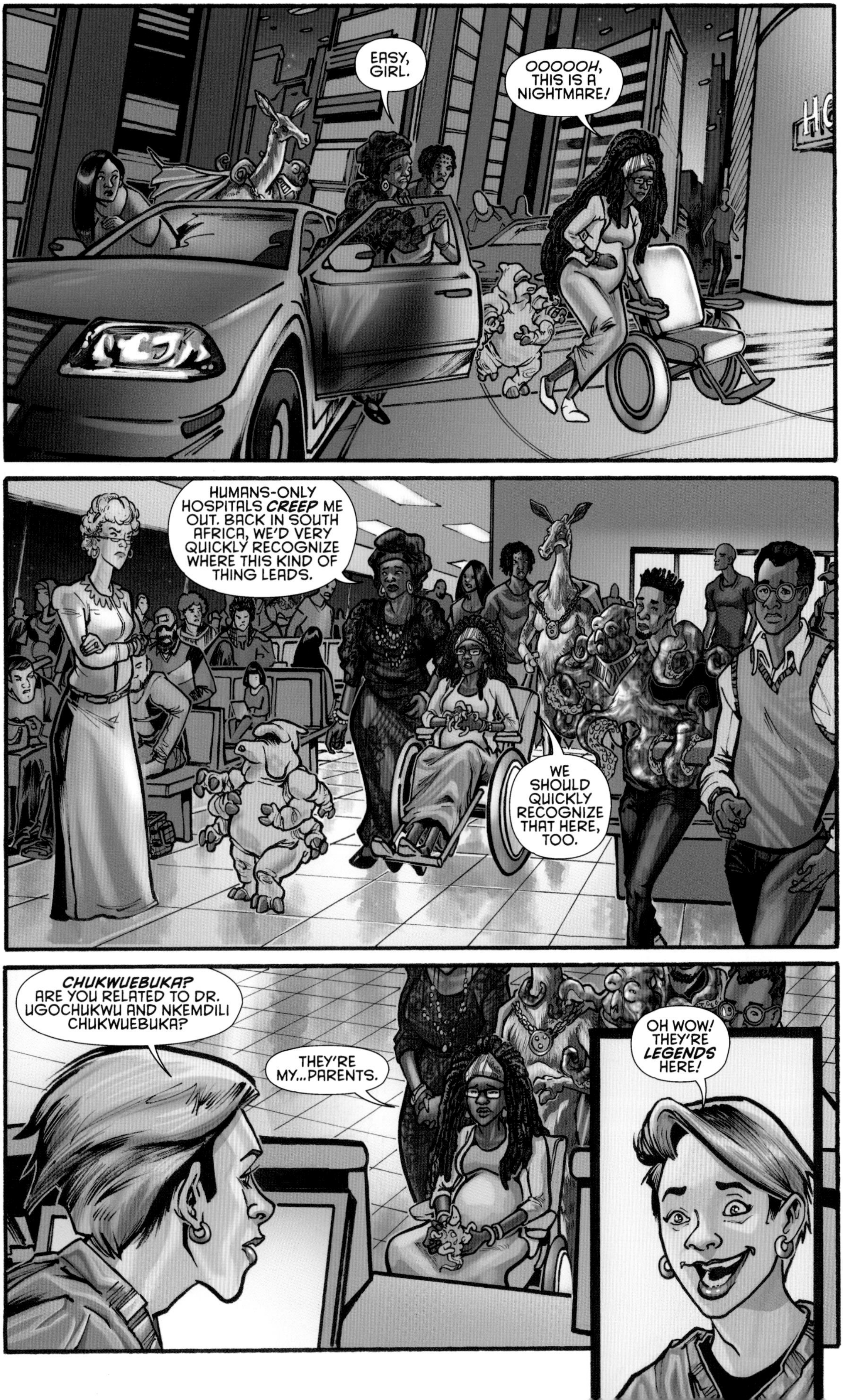
EASY, GIRL.
OOOOOH, THIS IS A NIGHTMARE!
HUMANS-ONLY HOSPITALS CREEP ME OUT. BACK IN SOUTH AFRICA, WE'D VERY QUICKLY RECOGNIZE WHERE THIS KIND OF THING LEADS.
WE SHOULD QUICKLY RECOGNIZE THAT HERE, TOO.
CHUKWUEBUKA? ARE YOU RELATED TO DR. UGOCHUKWU AND NKEMDILI CHUKWUEBUKA?
THEY'RE MY...PARENTS.
OH WOW! THEY'RE LEGENDS HERE!

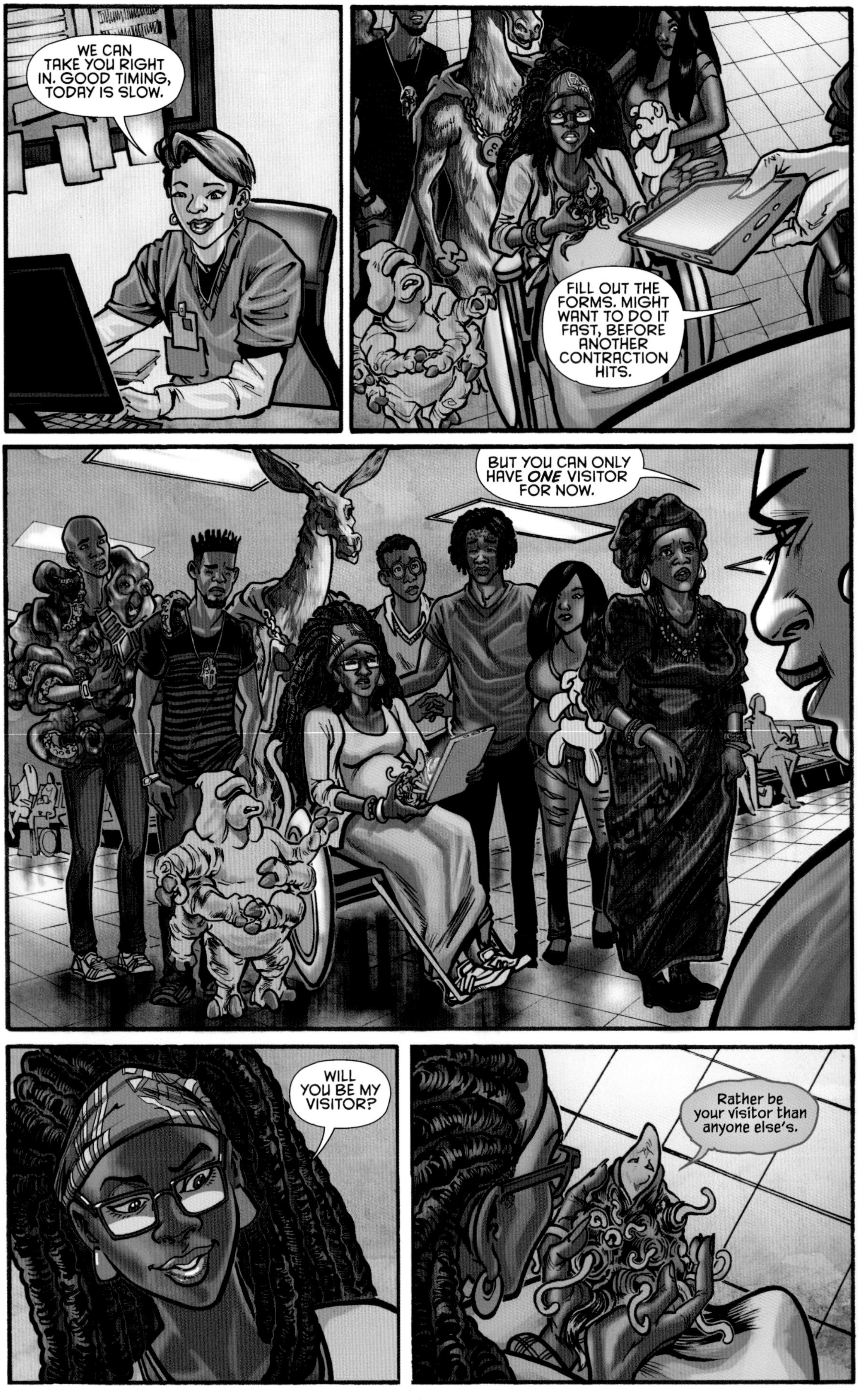
WE CAN TAKE YOU RIGHT IN. GOOD TIMING, TODAY IS SLOW.
FILL OUT THE FORMS. MIGHT WANT TO DO IT FAST, BEFORE ANOTHER CONTRACTION HITS.
BUT YOU CAN ONLY HAVE *ONE* VISITOR FOR NOW.
WILL YOU BE MY VISITOR?
Rather be your visitor than anyone else's.

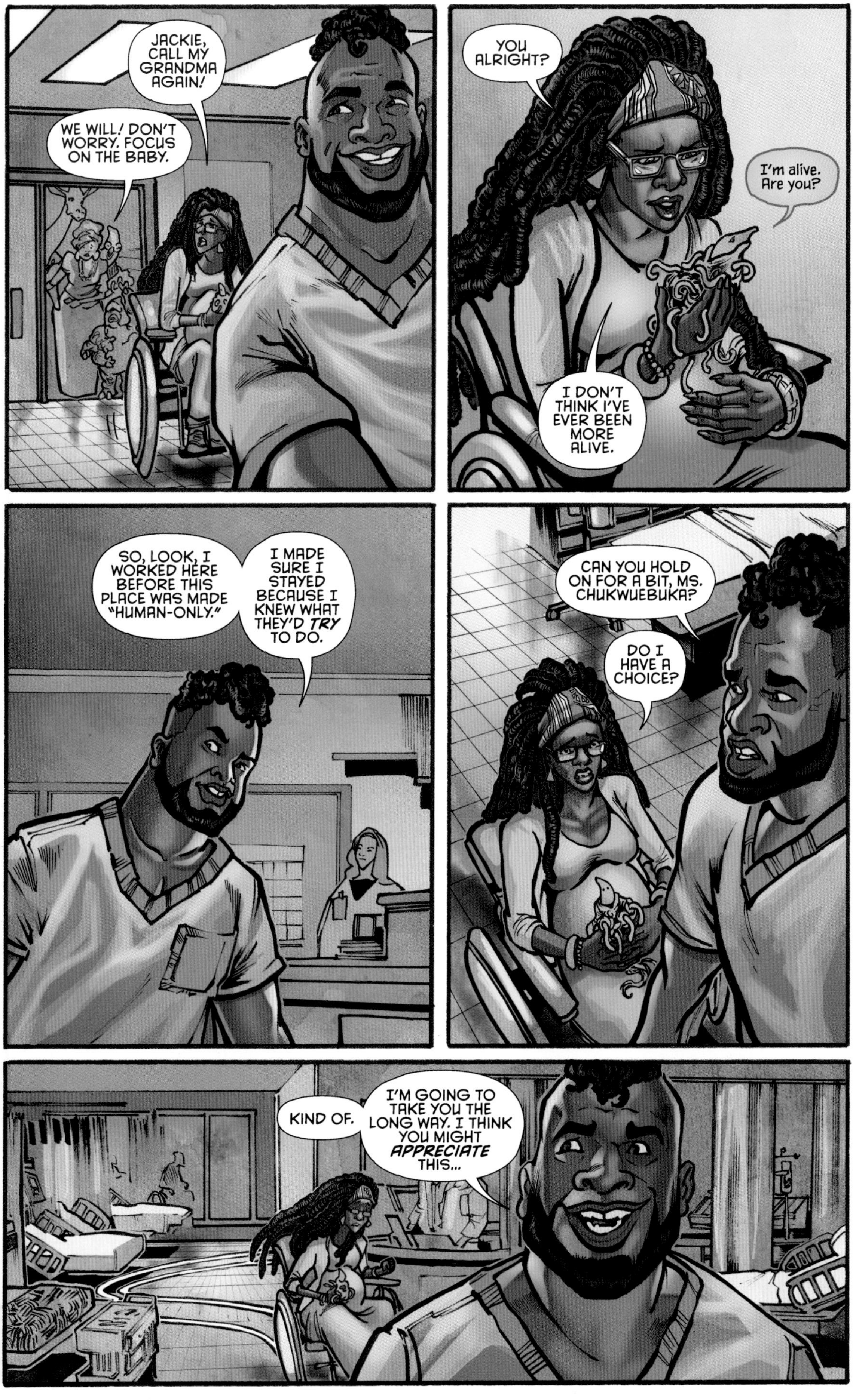
JACKIE, CALL MY GRANDMA AGAIN!
WE WILL! DON'T WORRY. FOCUS ON THE BABY.
YOU ALRIGHT?
I'm alive. Are you?
I DON'T THINK I'VE EVER BEEN MORE ALIVE.
SO, LOOK, I WORKED HERE BEFORE THIS PLACE WAS MADE "HUMAN-ONLY."
I MADE SURE I STAYED BECAUSE I KNEW WHAT THEY'D *TRY* TO DO.
CAN YOU HOLD ON FOR A BIT, MS. CHUKWUEBUKA?
DO I HAVE A CHOICE?
KIND OF.
I'M GOING TO TAKE YOU THE LONG WAY. I THINK YOU MIGHT *APPRECIATE* THIS...

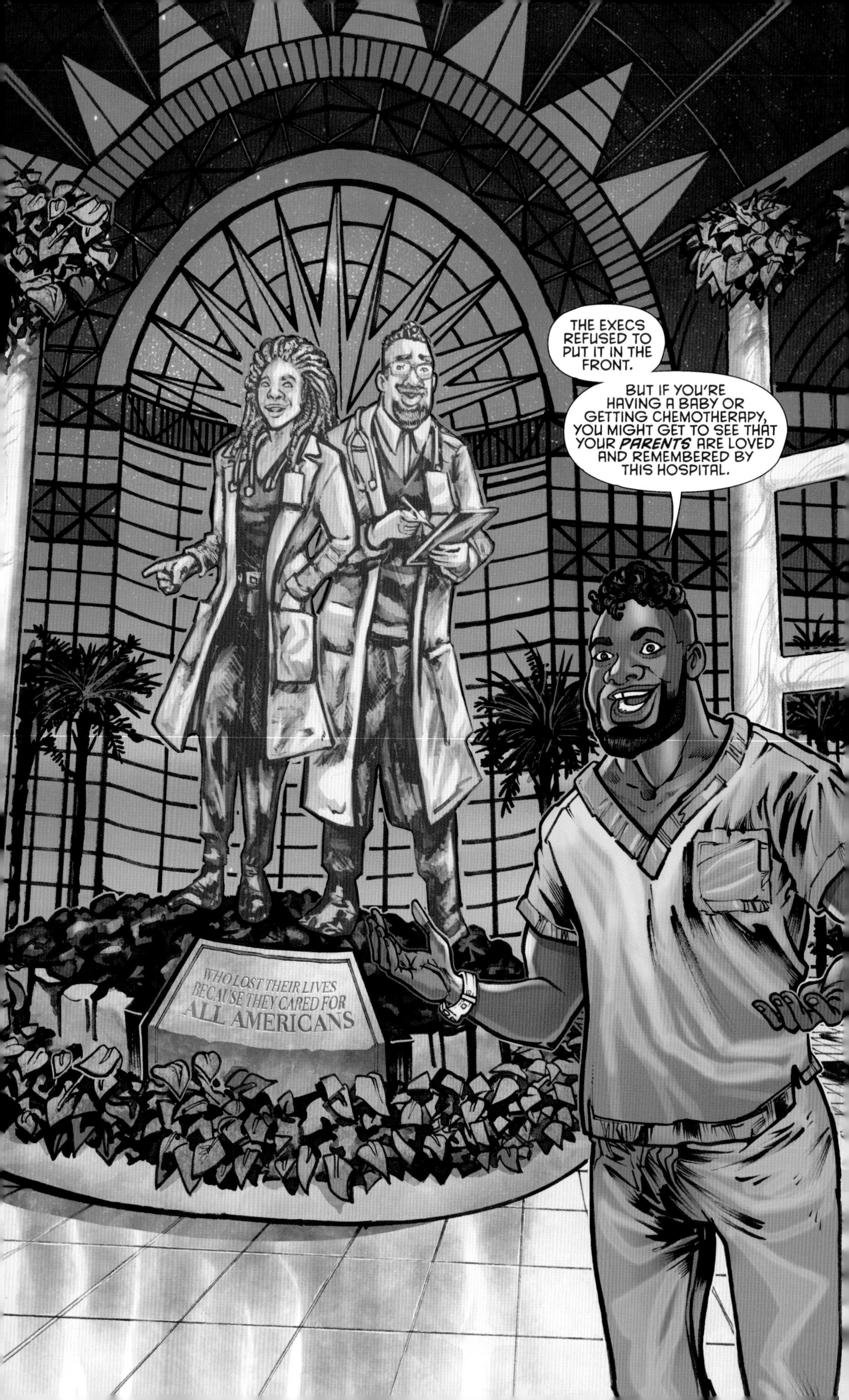
WHO LOST THEIR LIVES
BECAUSE THEY CARED FOR
ALL AMERICANS
THE EXECS REFUSED TO PUT IT IN THE FRONT.
BUT IF YOU'RE HAVING A BABY OR GETTING CHEMOTHERAPY, YOU MIGHT GET TO SEE THAT YOUR *PARENTS* ARE LOVED AND REMEMBERED BY THIS HOSPITAL.

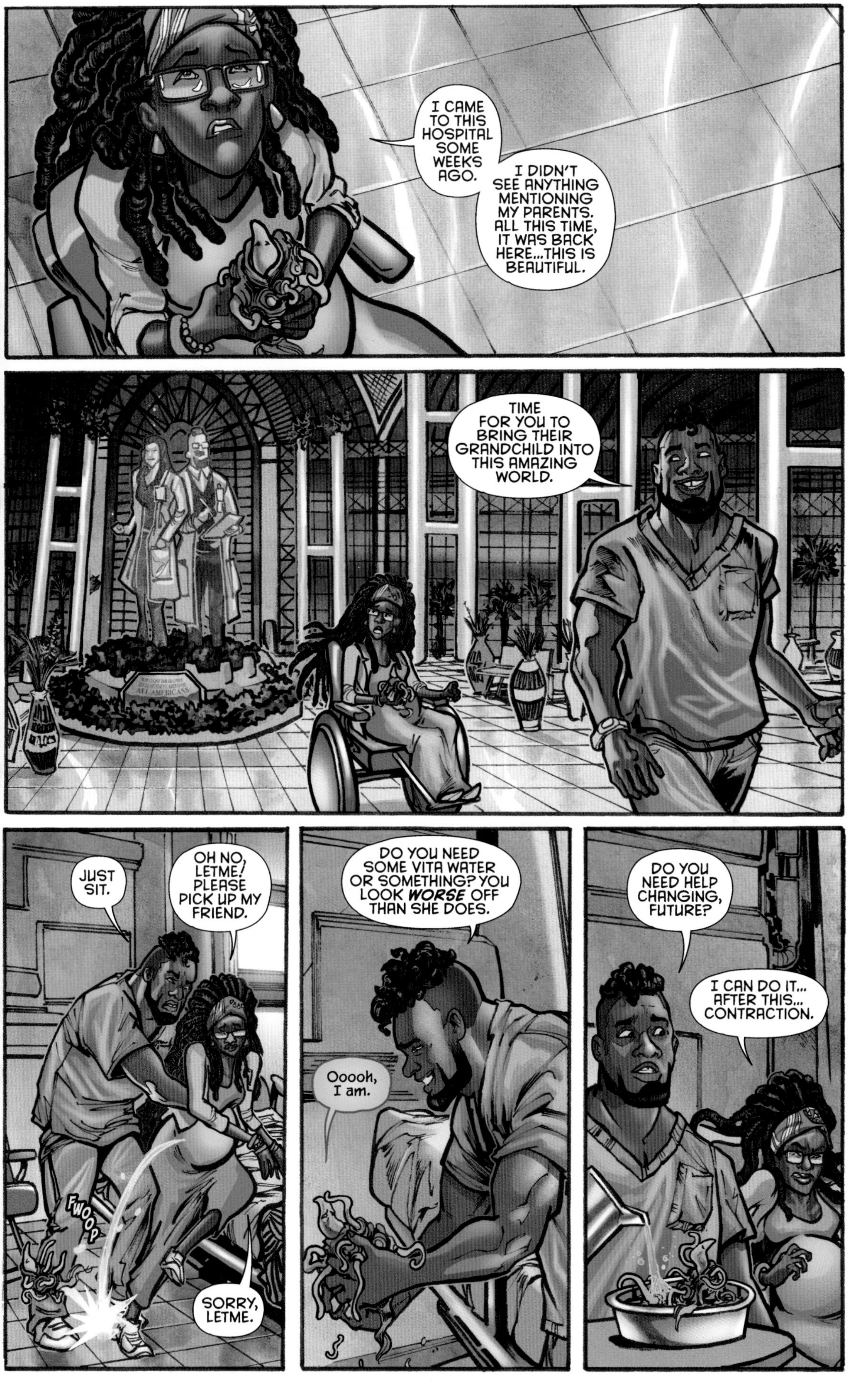
I CAME TO THIS HOSPITAL SOME WEEKS AGO.
I DIDN'T SEE ANYTHING MENTIONING MY PARENTS. ALL THIS TIME, IT WAS BACK HERE...THIS IS BEAUTIFUL.
ALL AMERICANS
TIME FOR YOU TO BRING THEIR GRANDCHILD INTO THIS AMAZING WORLD.
JUST SIT.
OH NO, LETME! PLEASE PICK UP MY FRIEND.
FWOOP
SORRY, LETME.
DO YOU NEED SOME VITA WATER OR SOMETHING? YOU LOOK *WORSE* OFF THAN SHE DOES.
Ooooh, I am.
DO YOU NEED HELP CHANGING, FUTURE?
I CAN DO IT... AFTER THIS... CONTRACTION.

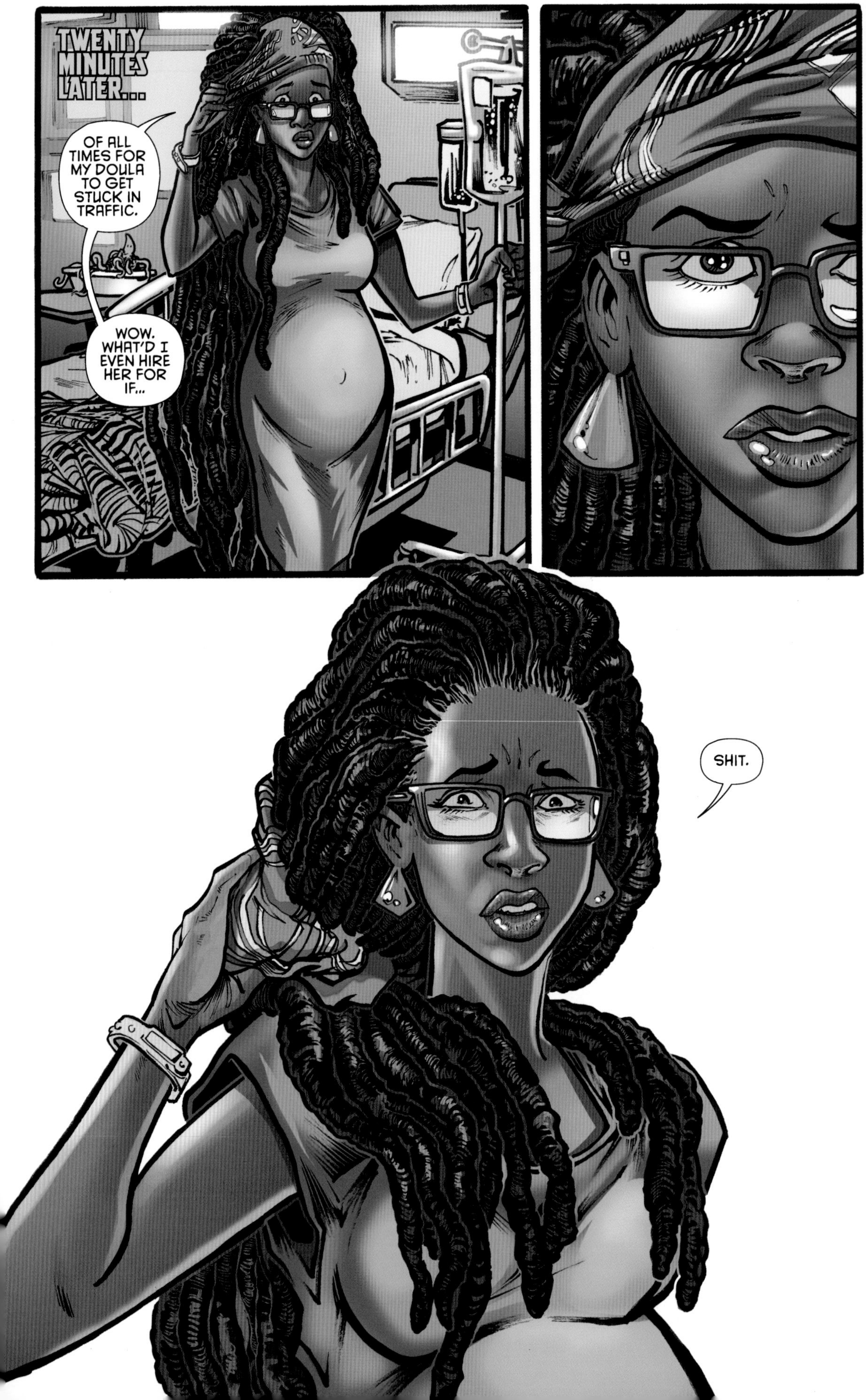
TWENTY MINUTES LATER...
OF ALL TIMES FOR MY DOULA TO GET STUCK IN TRAFFIC.
WOW. WHAT'D I EVEN HIRE HER FOR IF...
SHIT.

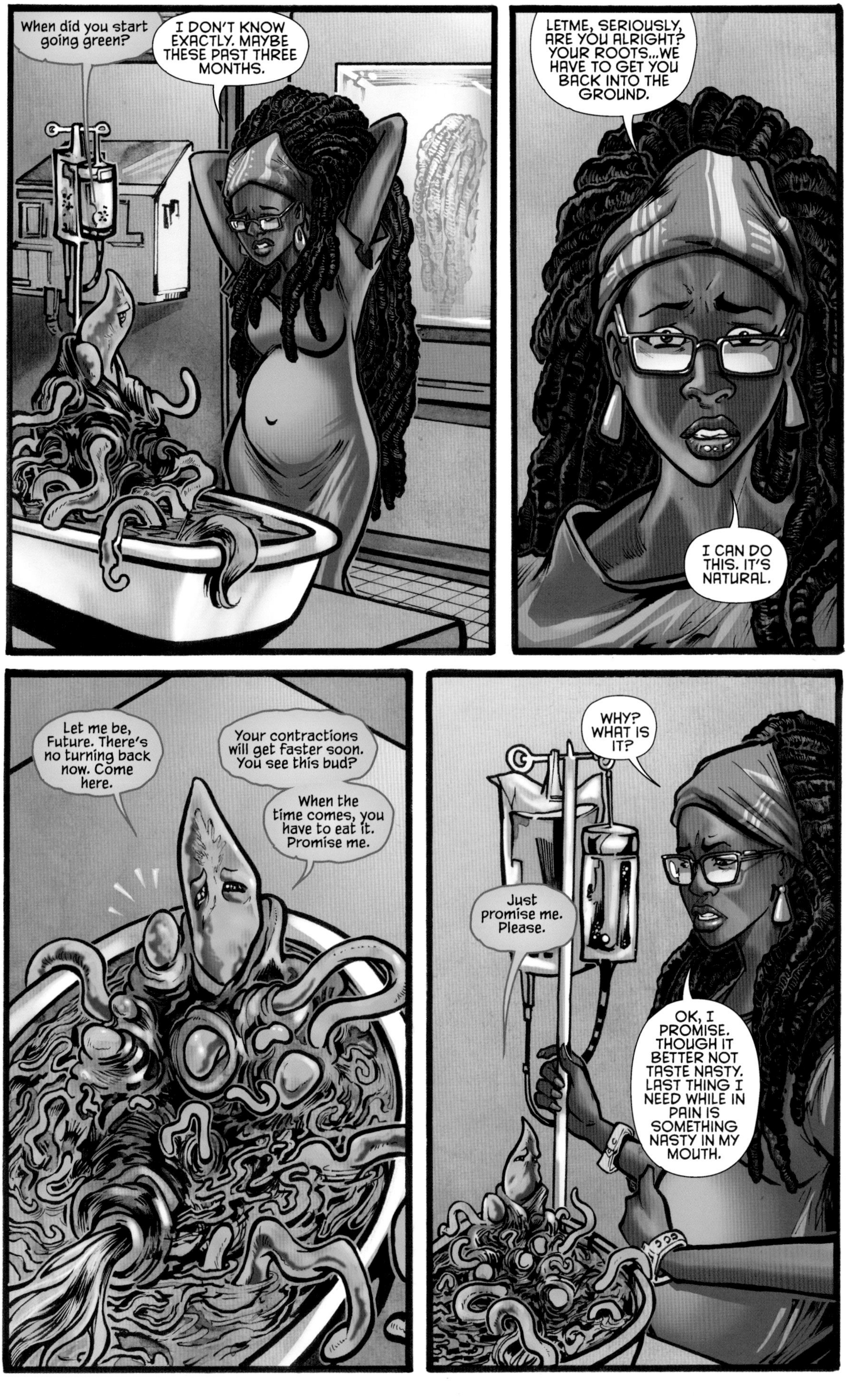
When did you start going green?
I DON'T KNOW EXACTLY. MAYBE THESE PAST THREE MONTHS.
LETME, SERIOUSLY, ARE YOU ALRIGHT? YOUR ROOTS...WE HAVE TO GET YOU BACK INTO THE GROUND.
I CAN DO THIS. IT'S NATURAL.
Let me be, Future. There's no turning back now. Come here.
Your contractions will get faster soon. You see this bud?
When the time comes, you have to eat it. Promise me.
WHY? WHAT IS IT?
Just promise me. Please.
OK, I PROMISE. THOUGH IT BETTER NOT TASTE NASTY. LAST THING I NEED WHILE IN PAIN IS SOMETHING NASTY IN MY MOUTH.

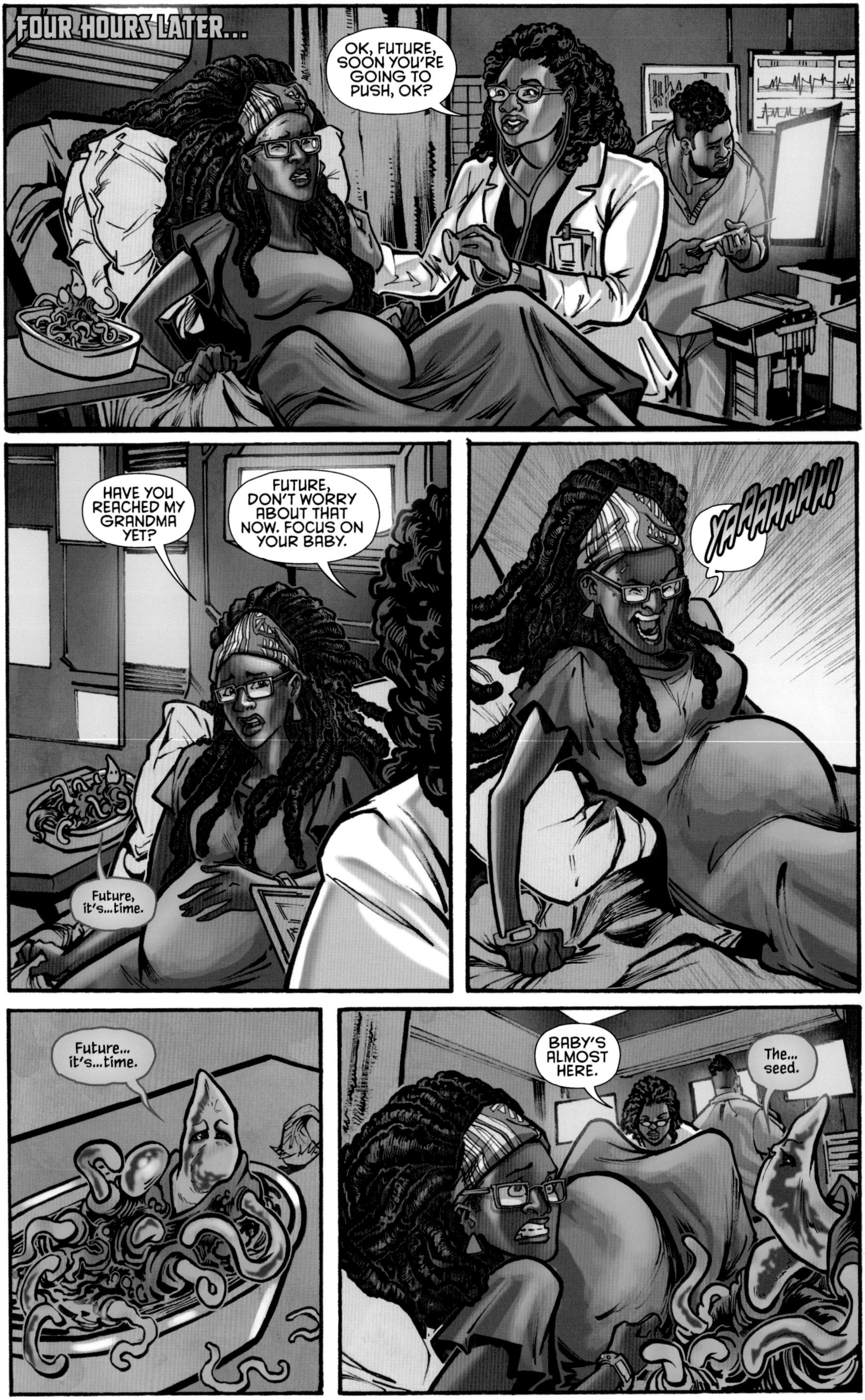
FOUR HOURS LATER...
OK, FUTURE, SOON YOU'RE GOING TO PUSH, OK?
HAVE YOU REACHED MY GRANDMA YET?
FUTURE, DON'T WORRY ABOUT THAT NOW. FOCUS ON YOUR BABY.
Future, it's...time.
YAAAHHHH!
Future... it's...time.
BABY'S ALMOST HERE.
The... seed.

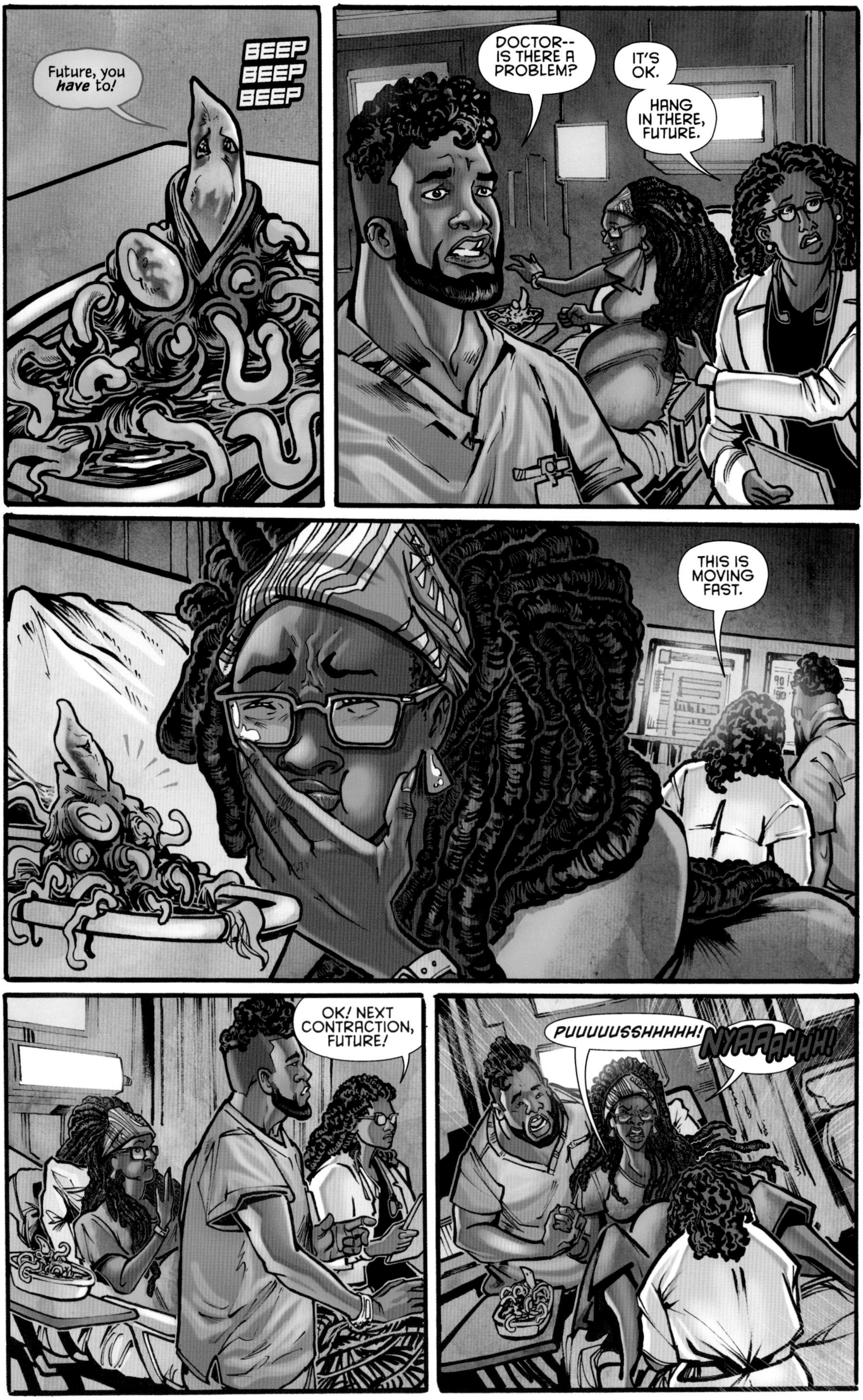
Future, you *have* to!
BEEP BEEP BEEP
DOCTOR-- IS THERE A PROBLEM?
IT'S OK.
HANG IN THERE, FUTURE.
THIS IS MOVING FAST.
OK! NEXT CONTRACTION, FUTURE!
PUUUUUSSHHHHH!
NYAAAHHH!

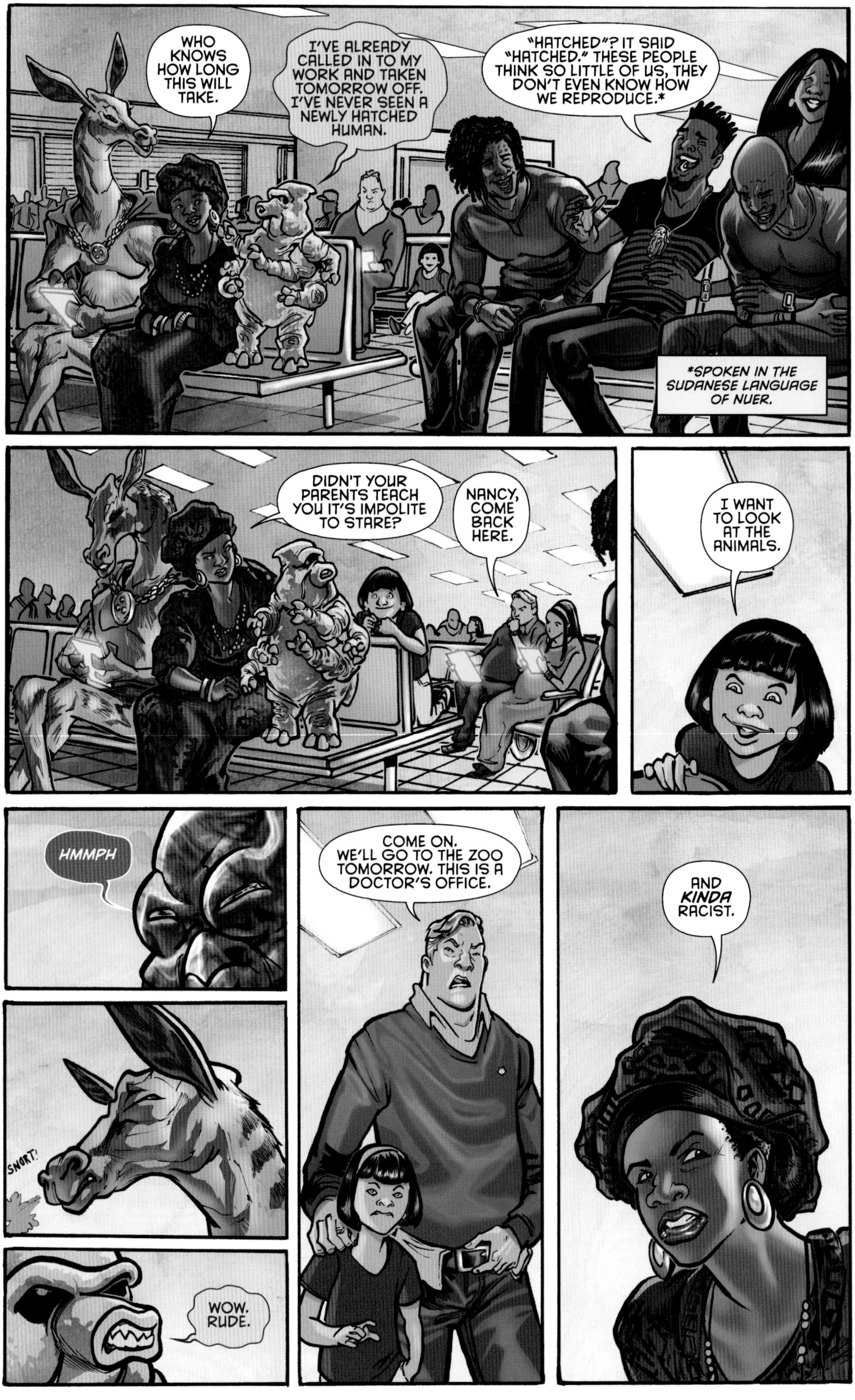
WHO KNOWS HOW LONG THIS WILL TAKE.
I'VE ALREADY CALLED IN TO MY WORK AND TAKEN TOMORROW OFF. I'VE NEVER SEEN A NEWLY HATCHED HUMAN.
"HATCHED"? IT SAID "HATCHED." THESE PEOPLE THINK SO LITTLE OF US, THEY DON'T EVEN KNOW HOW WE REPRODUCE.*
*SPOKEN IN THE SUDANESE LANGUAGE OF NUER.
DIDN'T YOUR PARENTS TEACH YOU IT'S IMPOLITE TO STARE?
NANCY, COME BACK HERE.
I WANT TO LOOK AT THE ANIMALS.
HMMPH
SNORT!
WOW. RUDE.
COME ON. WE'LL GO TO THE ZOO TOMORROW. THIS IS A DOCTOR'S OFFICE.
AND KINDA RACIST.

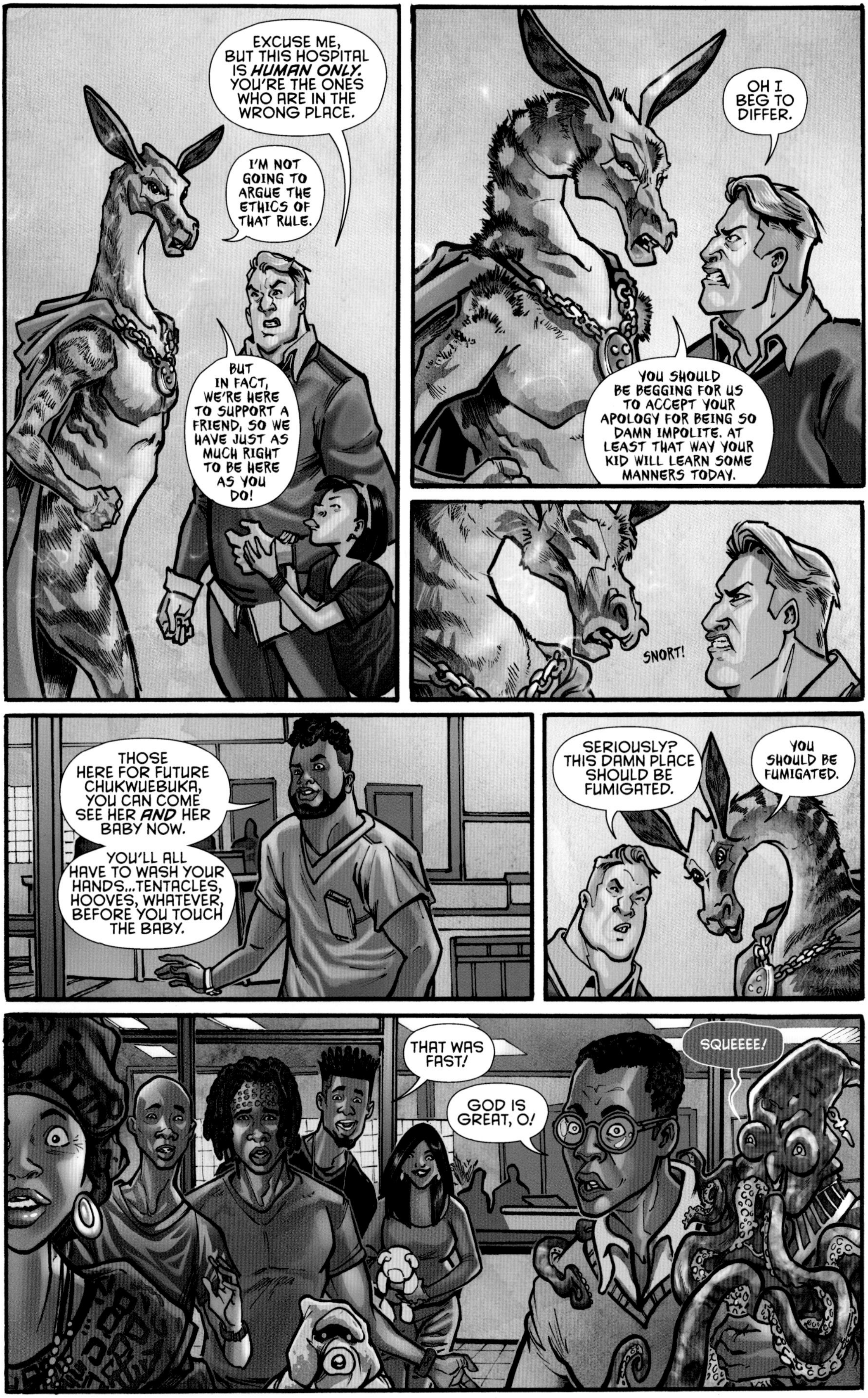
EXCUSE ME, BUT THIS HOSPITAL IS *HUMAN ONLY.* YOU'RE THE ONES WHO ARE IN THE WRONG PLACE.
I'M NOT GOING TO ARGUE THE ETHICS OF THAT RULE.
BUT IN FACT, WE'RE HERE TO SUPPORT A FRIEND, SO WE HAVE JUST AS MUCH RIGHT TO BE HERE AS YOU DO!
OH I BEG TO DIFFER.
YOU SHOULD BE BEGGING FOR US TO ACCEPT YOUR APOLOGY FOR BEING SO DAMN IMPOLITE. AT LEAST THAT WAY YOUR KID WILL LEARN SOME MANNERS TODAY.
SNORT!
THOSE HERE FOR FUTURE CHUKWUEBUKA, YOU CAN COME SEE HER *AND* HER BABY NOW.
YOU'LL ALL HAVE TO WASH YOUR HANDS...TENTACLES, HOOVES, WHATEVER, BEFORE YOU TOUCH THE BABY.
SERIOUSLY? THIS DAMN PLACE SHOULD BE FUMIGATED.
YOU SHOULD BE FUMIGATED.
THAT WAS FAST!
GOD IS GREAT, O!
SQUEEEE!

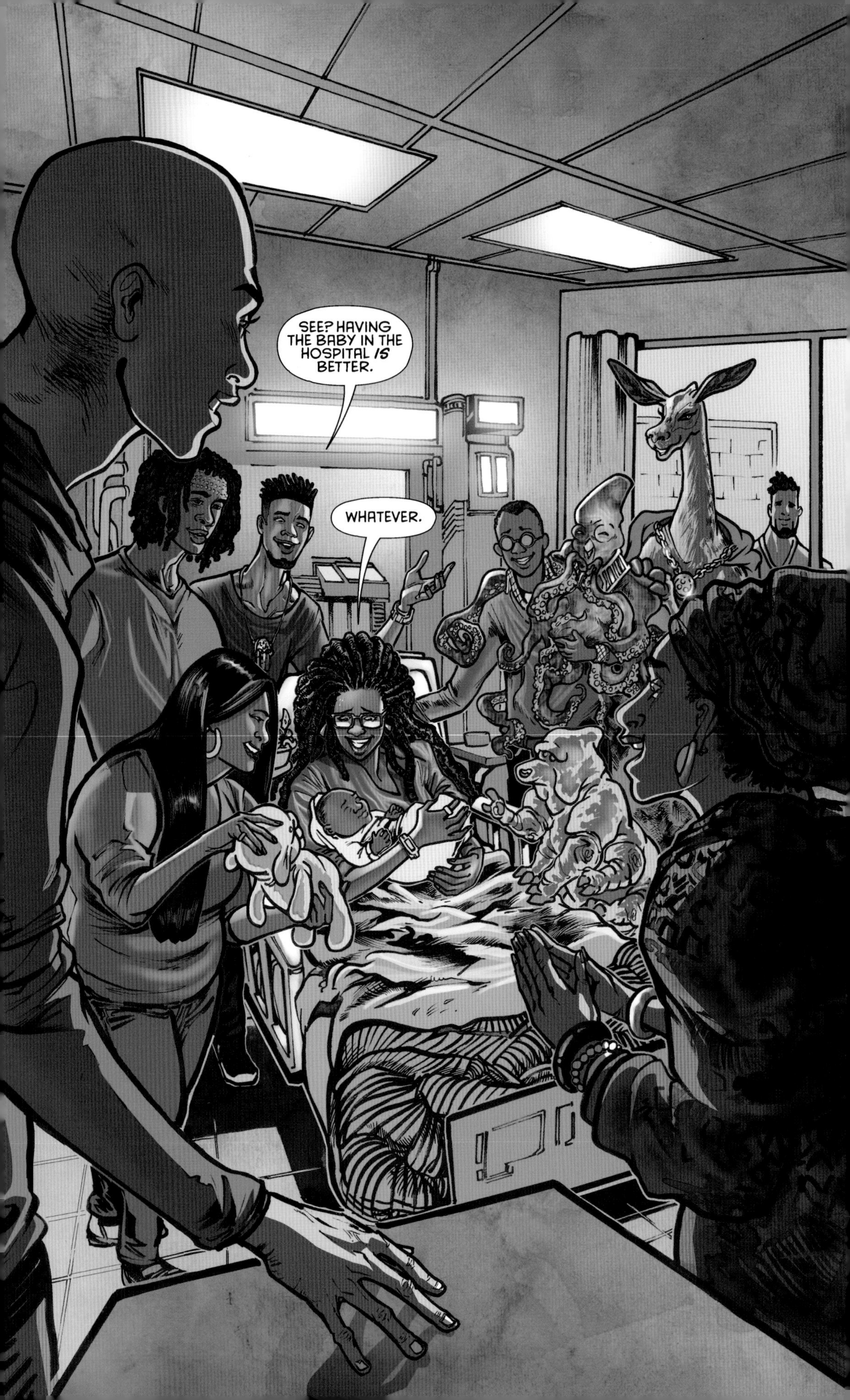
SEE? HAVING THE BABY IN THE HOSPITAL *IS* BETTER.
WHATEVER.

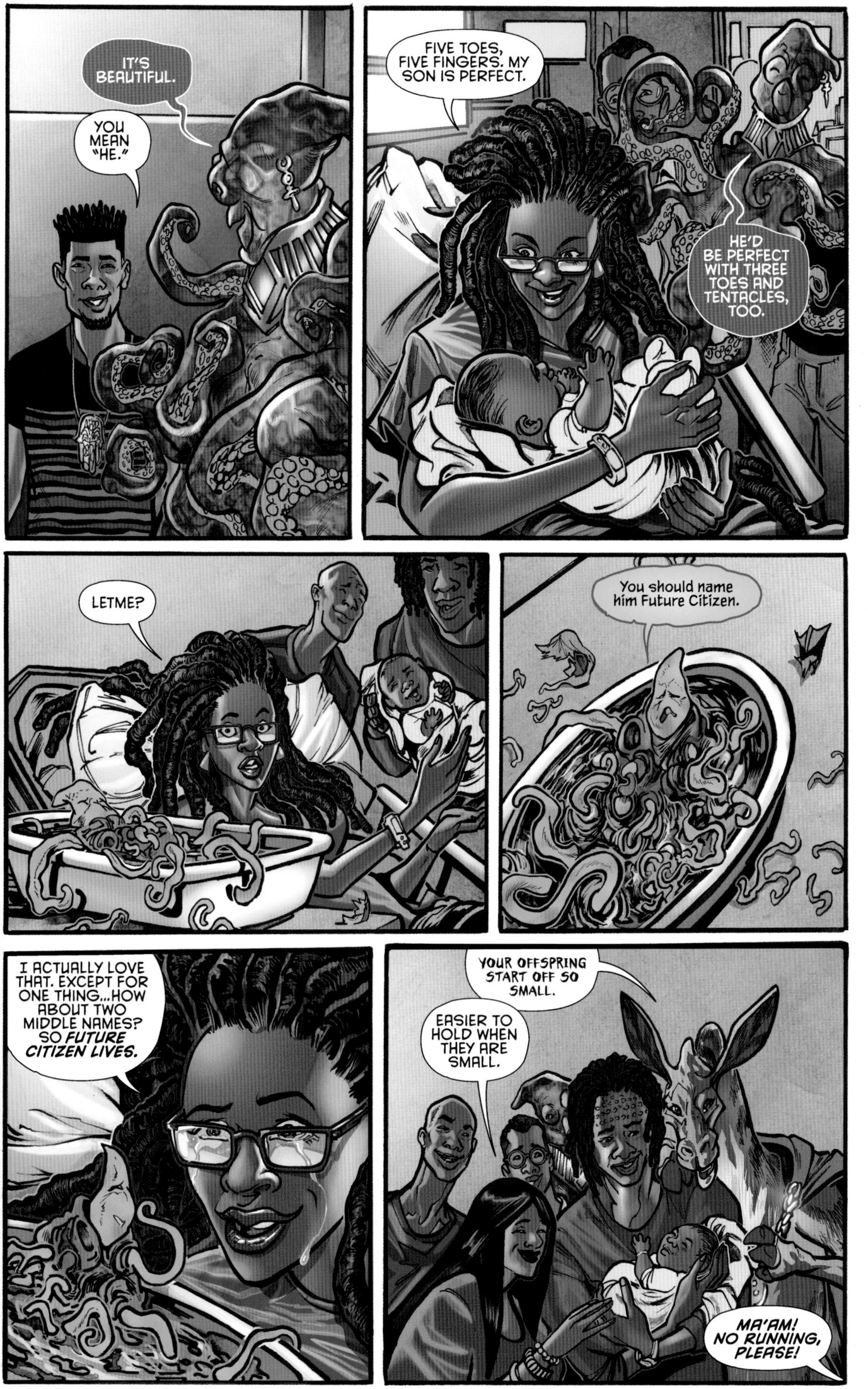
IT'S BEAUTIFUL.
YOU MEAN "HE."
FIVE TOES, FIVE FINGERS. MY SON IS PERFECT.
HE'D BE PERFECT WITH THREE TOES AND TENTACLES, TOO.
LETME?
You should name him Future Citizen.
I ACTUALLY LOVE THAT. EXCEPT FOR ONE THING...HOW ABOUT TWO MIDDLE NAMES? SO FUTURE CITIZEN LIVES.
YOUR OFFSPRING START OFF SO SMALL.
EASIER TO HOLD WHEN THEY ARE SMALL.
MA'AM! NO RUNNING, PLEASE!

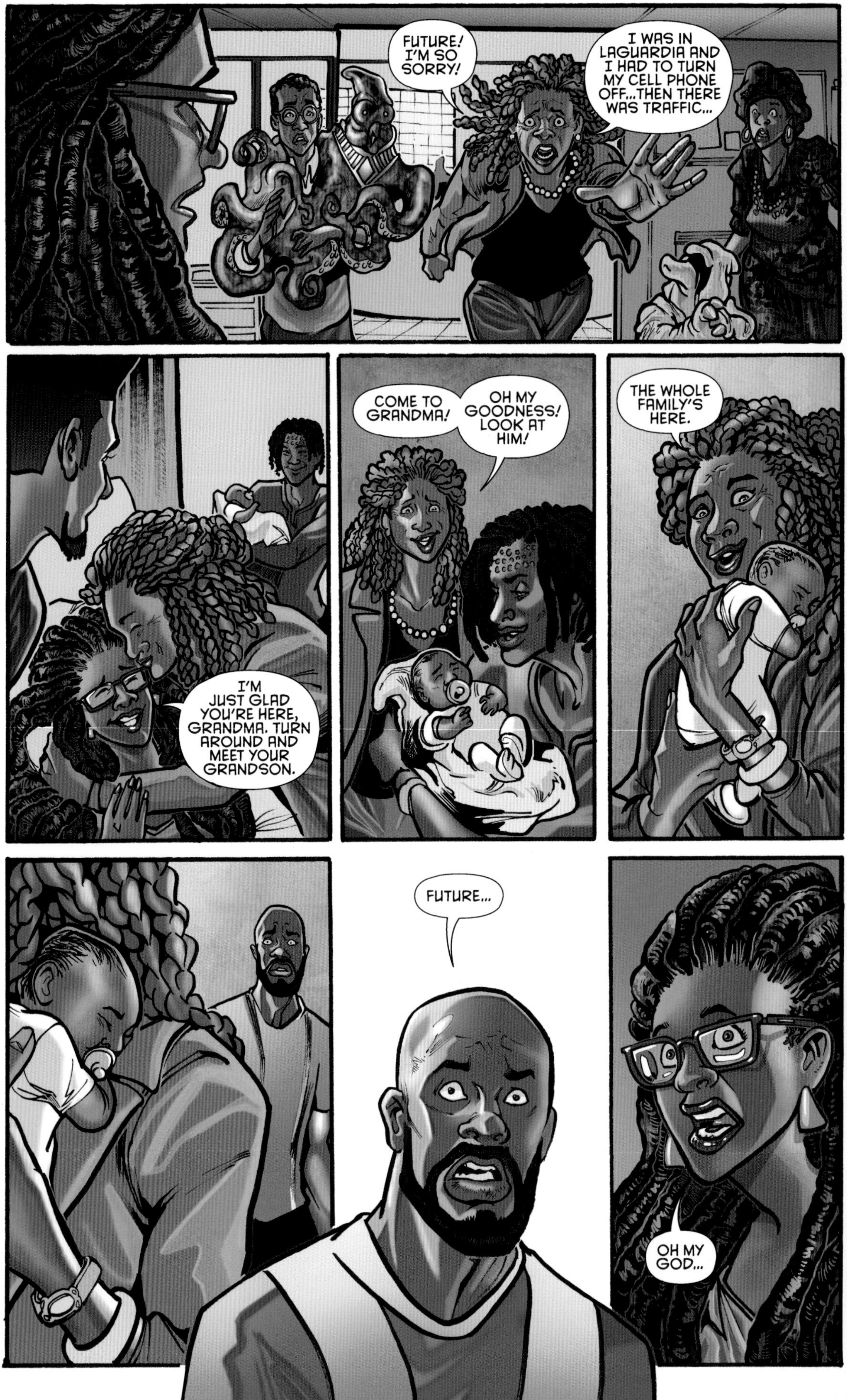
FUTURE! I'M SO SORRY!
I WAS IN LAGUARDIA AND I HAD TO TURN MY CELL PHONE OFF...THEN THERE WAS TRAFFIC...
I'M JUST GLAD YOU'RE HERE, GRANDMA. TURN AROUND AND MEET YOUR GRANDSON.
COME TO GRANDMA!
OH MY GOODNESS! LOOK AT HIM!
THE WHOLE FAMILY'S HERE.
FUTURE...
OH MY GOD...

CHAPTER 4

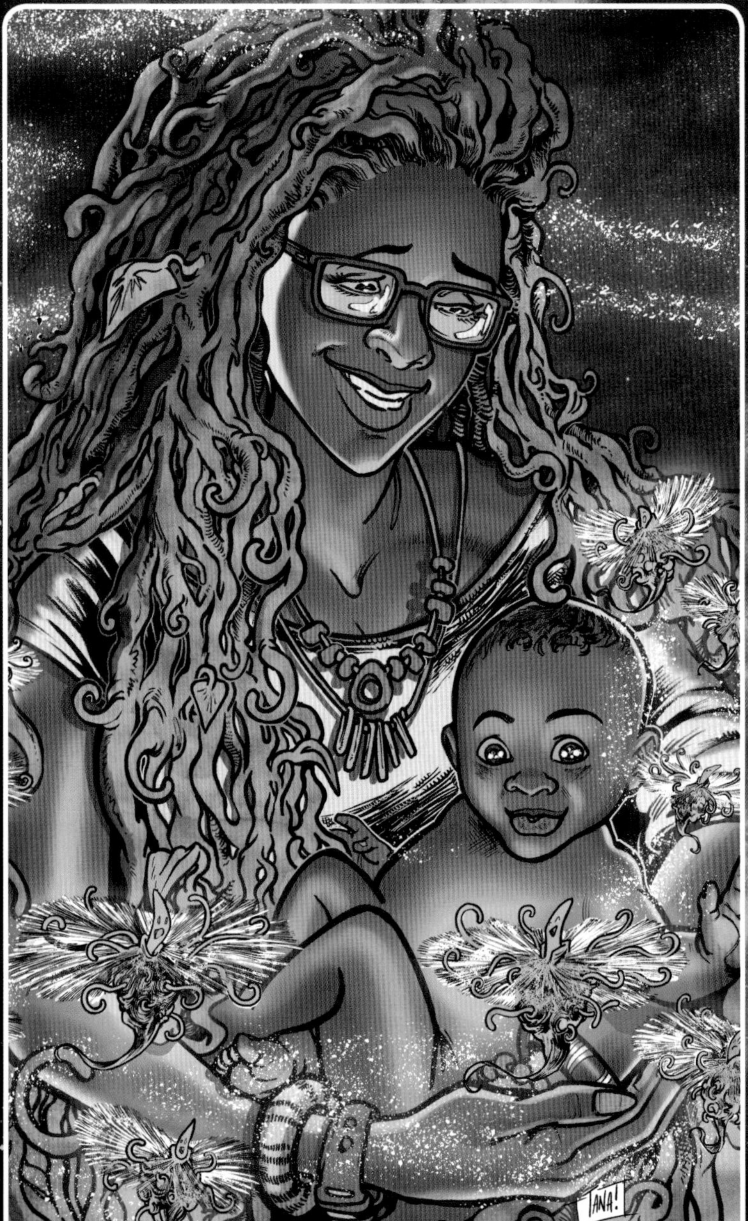
ANA!

FUTURE CITIZEN

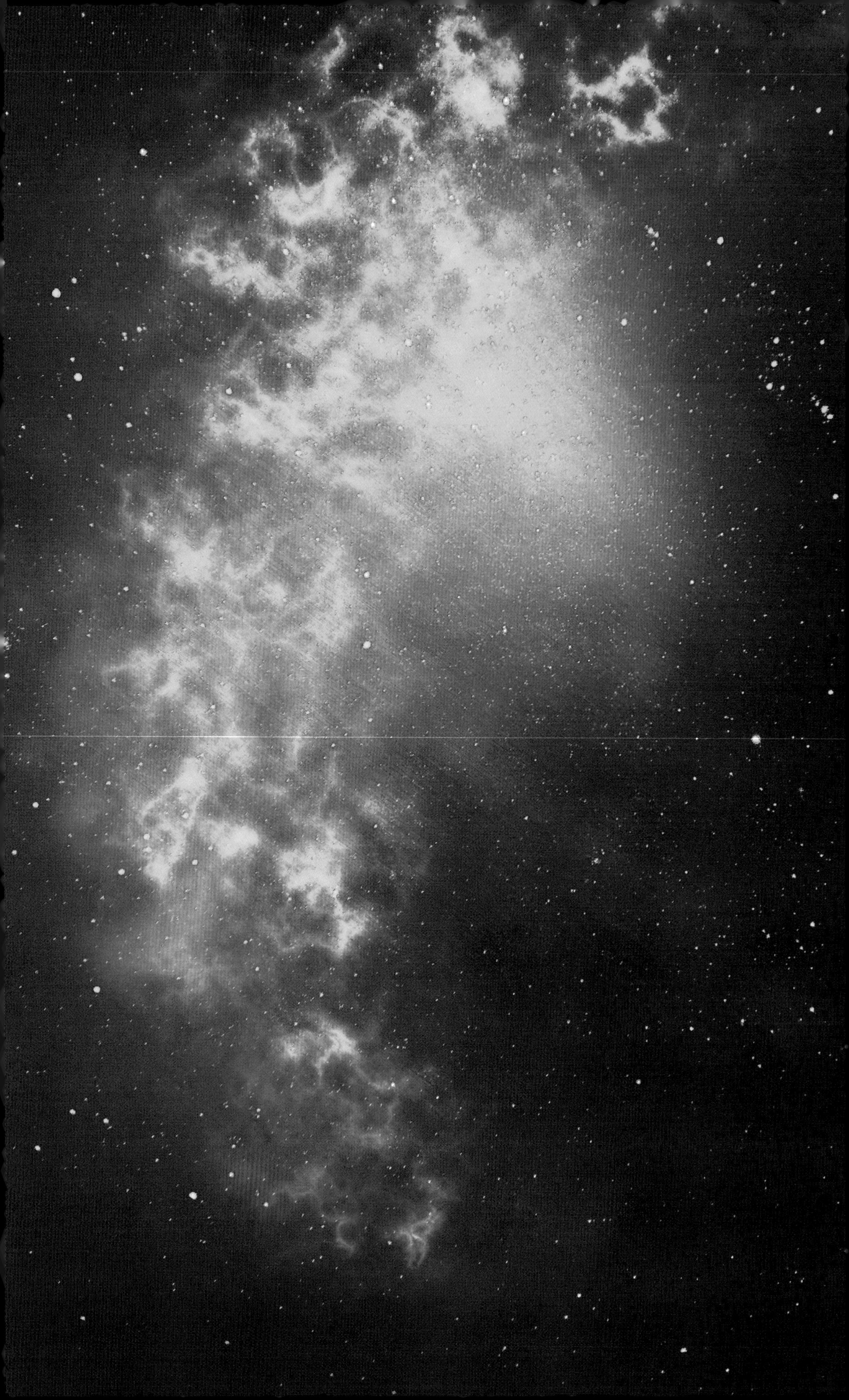

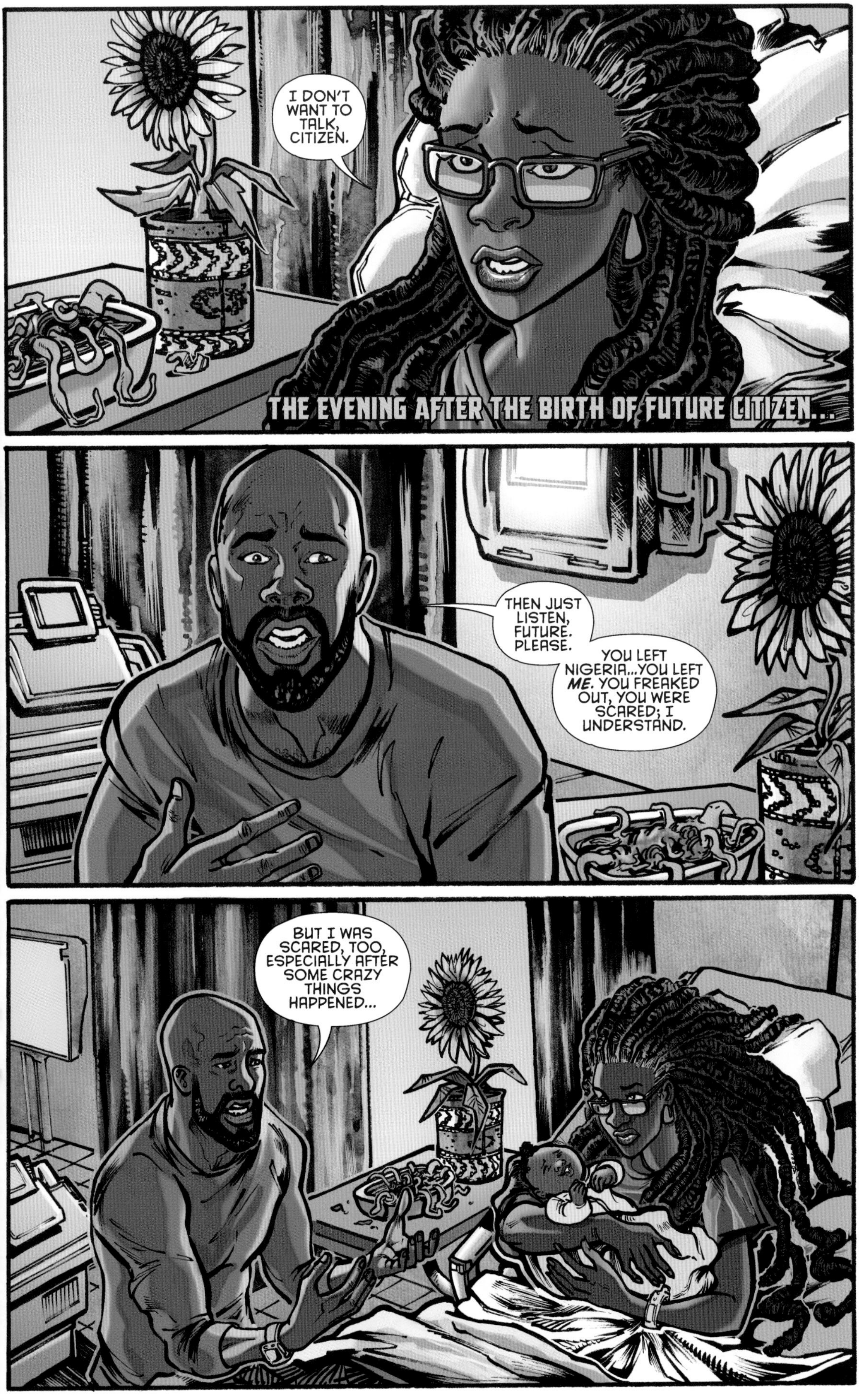
I DON'T WANT TO TALK, CITIZEN.
THE EVENING AFTER THE BIRTH OF FUTURE CITIZEN...
THEN JUST LISTEN, FUTURE. PLEASE.
YOU LEFT NIGERIA...YOU LEFT *ME*. YOU FREAKED OUT, YOU WERE SCARED; I UNDERSTAND.
BUT I WAS SCARED, TOO, ESPECIALLY AFTER SOME CRAZY THINGS HAPPENED...

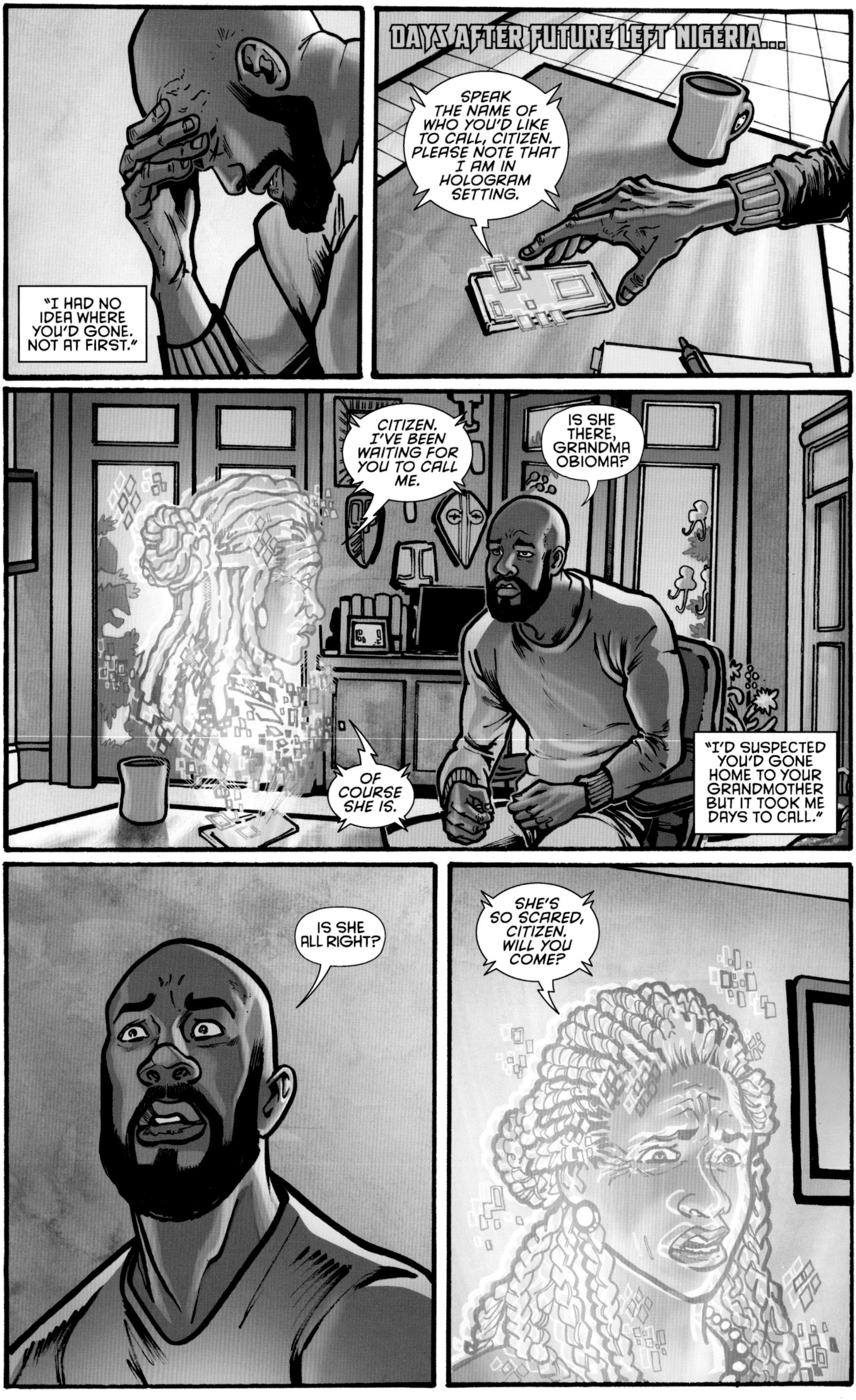
"I HAD NO IDEA WHERE YOU'D GONE. NOT AT FIRST."
DAYS AFTER FUTURE LEFT NIGERIA...
SPEAK THE NAME OF WHO YOU'D LIKE TO CALL, CITIZEN. PLEASE NOTE THAT I AM IN HOLOGRAM SETTING.
CITIZEN. I'VE BEEN WAITING FOR YOU TO CALL ME.
IS SHE THERE, GRANDMA OBIOMA?
OF COURSE SHE IS.
"I'D SUSPECTED YOU'D GONE HOME TO YOUR GRANDMOTHER BUT IT TOOK ME DAYS TO CALL."
IS SHE ALL RIGHT?
SHE'S SO SCARED, CITIZEN. WILL YOU COME?

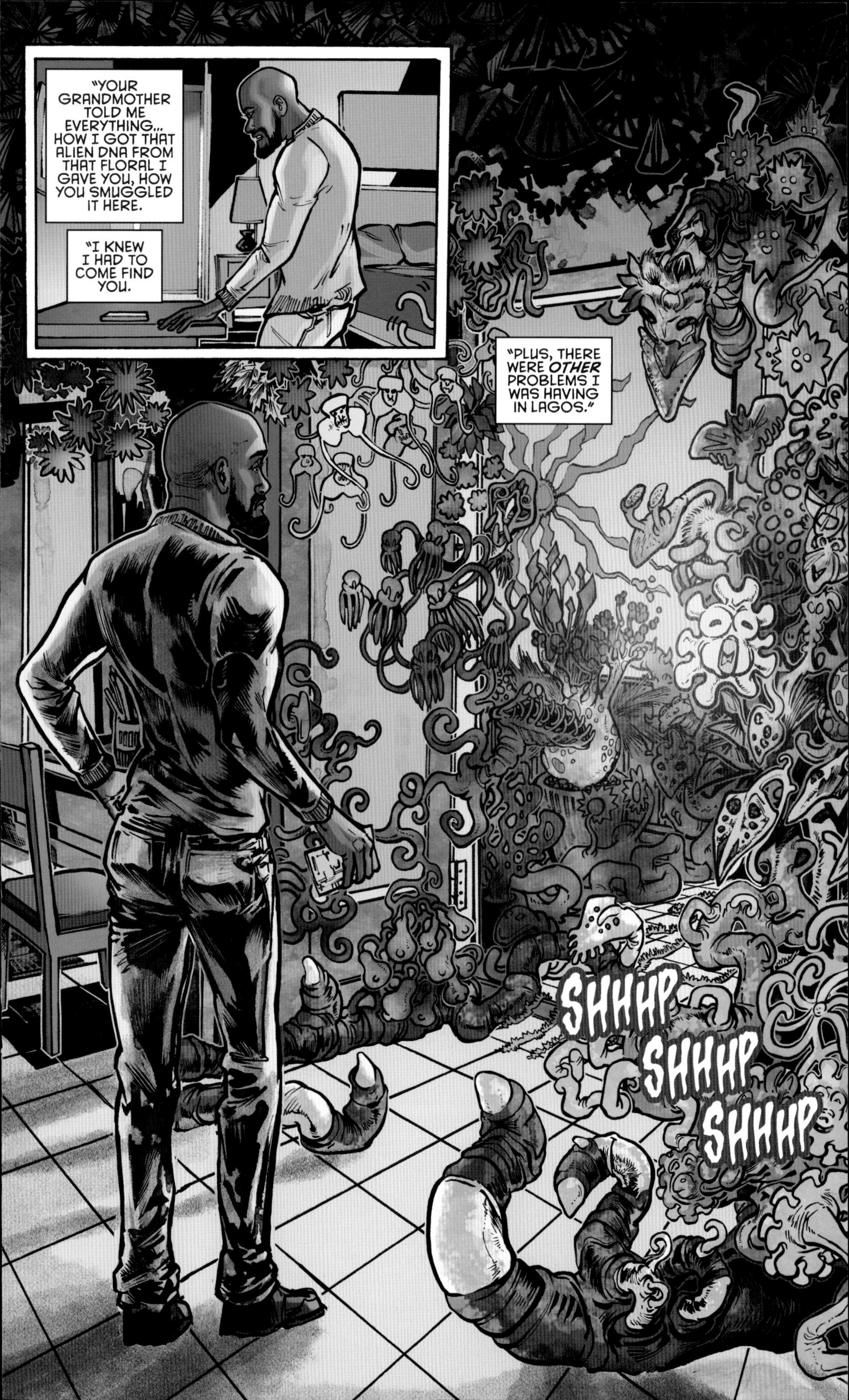
"YOUR GRANDMOTHER TOLD ME EVERYTHING... HOW I GOT THAT ALIEN DNA FROM THAT FLORAL I GAVE YOU, HOW YOU SMUGGLED IT HERE.
"I KNEW I HAD TO COME FIND YOU.
"PLUS, THERE WERE *OTHER* PROBLEMS I WAS HAVING IN LAGOS."
SHHHP
SHHHP
SHHHP

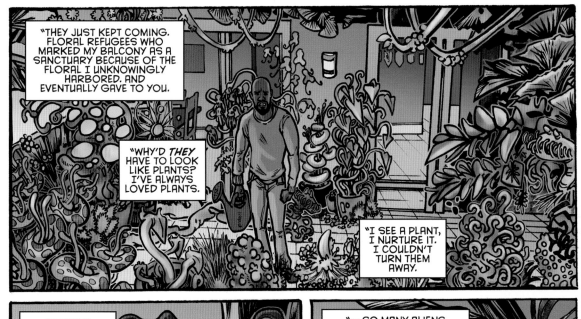

"THEY JUST KEPT COMING. FLORAL REFUGEES WHO MARKED MY BALCONY AS A SANCTUARY BECAUSE OF THE FLORAL I UNKNOWINGLY HARBORED. AND EVENTUALLY GAVE TO YOU.

"WHY'D *THEY* HAVE TO LOOK LIKE PLANTS? I'VE ALWAYS LOVED PLANTS.

"I SEE A PLANT, I NURTURE IT. I COULDN'T TURN THEM AWAY.

"I WAS A *NEO-BIAFRAN.* I WAS ALL ABOUT THE STRONG INDUSTRIOUS *PURE* NATION IN THE SOUTHEAST.

"FLORALS, SHAPE CHANGERS, SPACE OGBANJES--

"-- SO MANY ALIENS ARRIVED AND *ALL* LOOKED TO THE FUTURE, HOW TO MAKE *NIGERIA* GREATER.

"NONE CARED TO KNOW *OUR* HISTORY AND WHY IGBOS LIKE ME *STILL* WANTED THE SOUTHEAST TO SECEDE FROM NIGERIA AND HAVE OUR OWN COUNTRY OF BIAFRA.

"I DIDN'T EVEN KNOW FLORAL WARS WERE HAPPENING IN NIGERIA. YET MY BALCONY MADE ME LOOK LIKE I WAS SOME DOUBLE AGENT.

"AND I KEPT GETTING THOSE DAMN *GREEN* HAIRS IN MY BEARD.

"WHAT HAPPENED NEXT... WAS INEVITABLE."

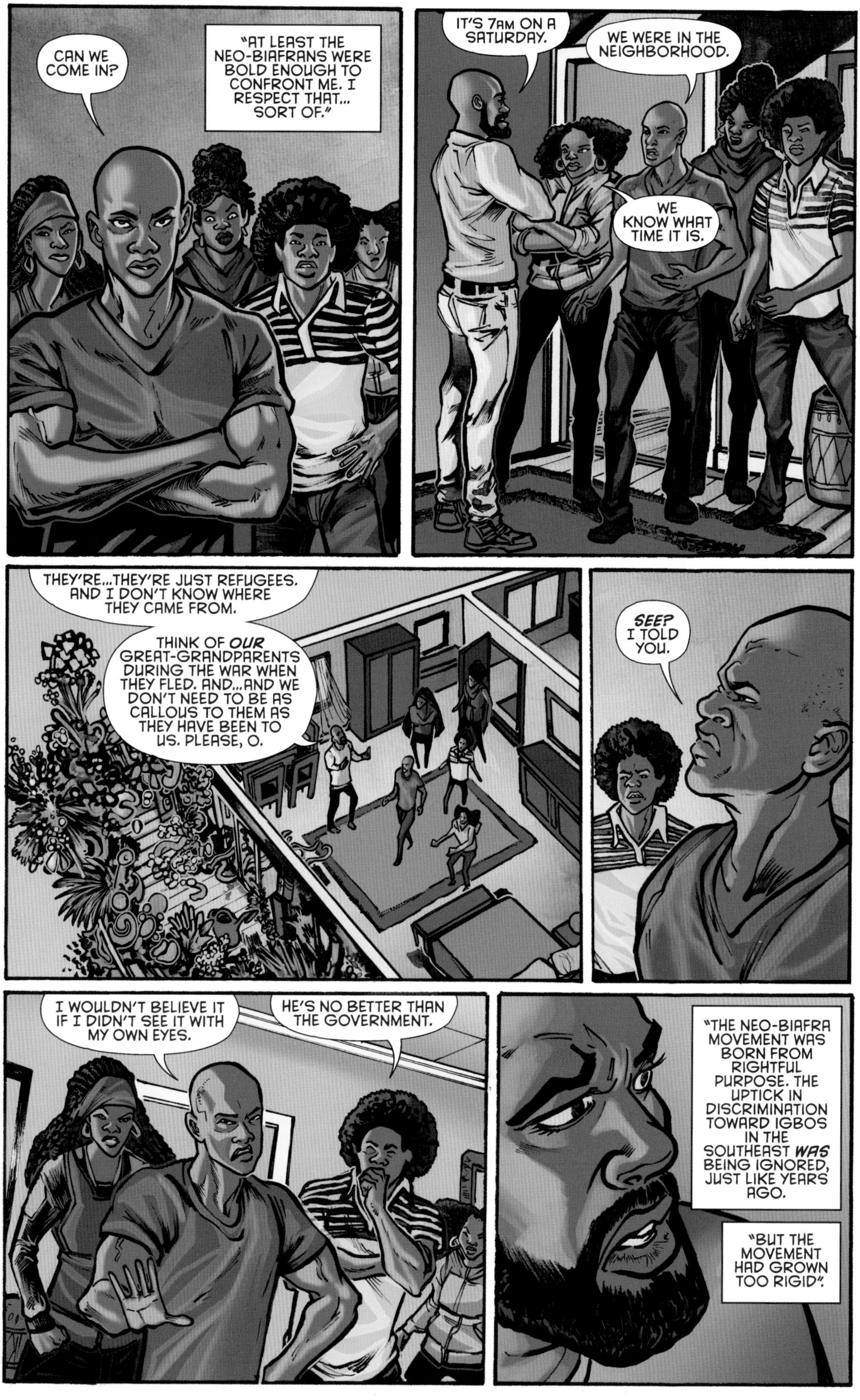
CAN WE COME IN?
"AT LEAST THE NEO-BIAFRANS WERE BOLD ENOUGH TO CONFRONT ME. I RESPECT THAT... SORT OF."
IT'S 7AM ON A SATURDAY.
WE WERE IN THE NEIGHBORHOOD.
WE KNOW WHAT TIME IT IS.
THEY'RE...THEY'RE JUST REFUGEES. AND I DON'T KNOW WHERE THEY CAME FROM.
THINK OF *OUR* GREAT-GRANDPARENTS DURING THE WAR WHEN THEY FLED. AND...AND WE DON'T NEED TO BE AS CALLOUS TO THEM AS THEY HAVE BEEN TO US. PLEASE, O.
SEE? I TOLD YOU.
I WOULDN'T BELIEVE IT IF I DIDN'T SEE IT WITH MY OWN EYES.
HE'S NO BETTER THAN THE GOVERNMENT.
"THE NEO-BIAFRA MOVEMENT WAS BORN FROM RIGHTFUL PURPOSE. THE UPTICK IN DISCRIMINATION TOWARD IGBOS IN THE SOUTHEAST *WAS* BEING IGNORED, JUST LIKE YEARS AGO.
"BUT THE MOVEMENT HAD GROWN TOO RIGID".

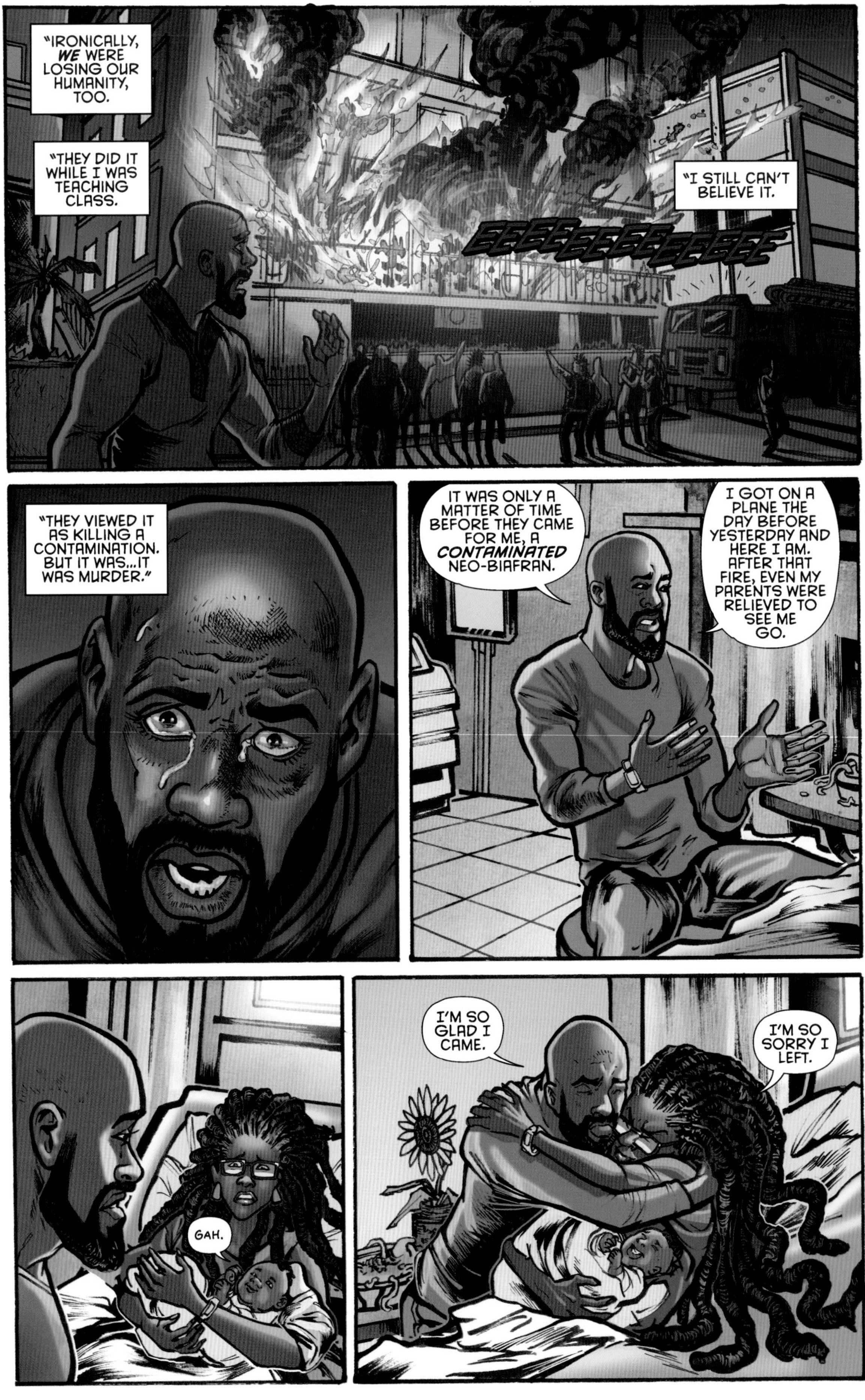
"IRONICALLY, WE WERE LOSING OUR HUMANITY, TOO.
"THEY DID IT WHILE I WAS TEACHING CLASS.
"I STILL CAN'T BELIEVE IT.
EEEEEEEEEEEEEEE
"THEY VIEWED IT AS KILLING A CONTAMINATION. BUT IT WAS...IT WAS MURDER."
IT WAS ONLY A MATTER OF TIME BEFORE THEY CAME FOR ME, A CONTAMINATED NEO-BIAFRAN.
I GOT ON A PLANE THE DAY BEFORE YESTERDAY AND HERE I AM. AFTER THAT FIRE, EVEN MY PARENTS WERE RELIEVED TO SEE ME GO.
GAH.
I'M SO GLAD I CAME.
I'M SO SORRY I LEFT.

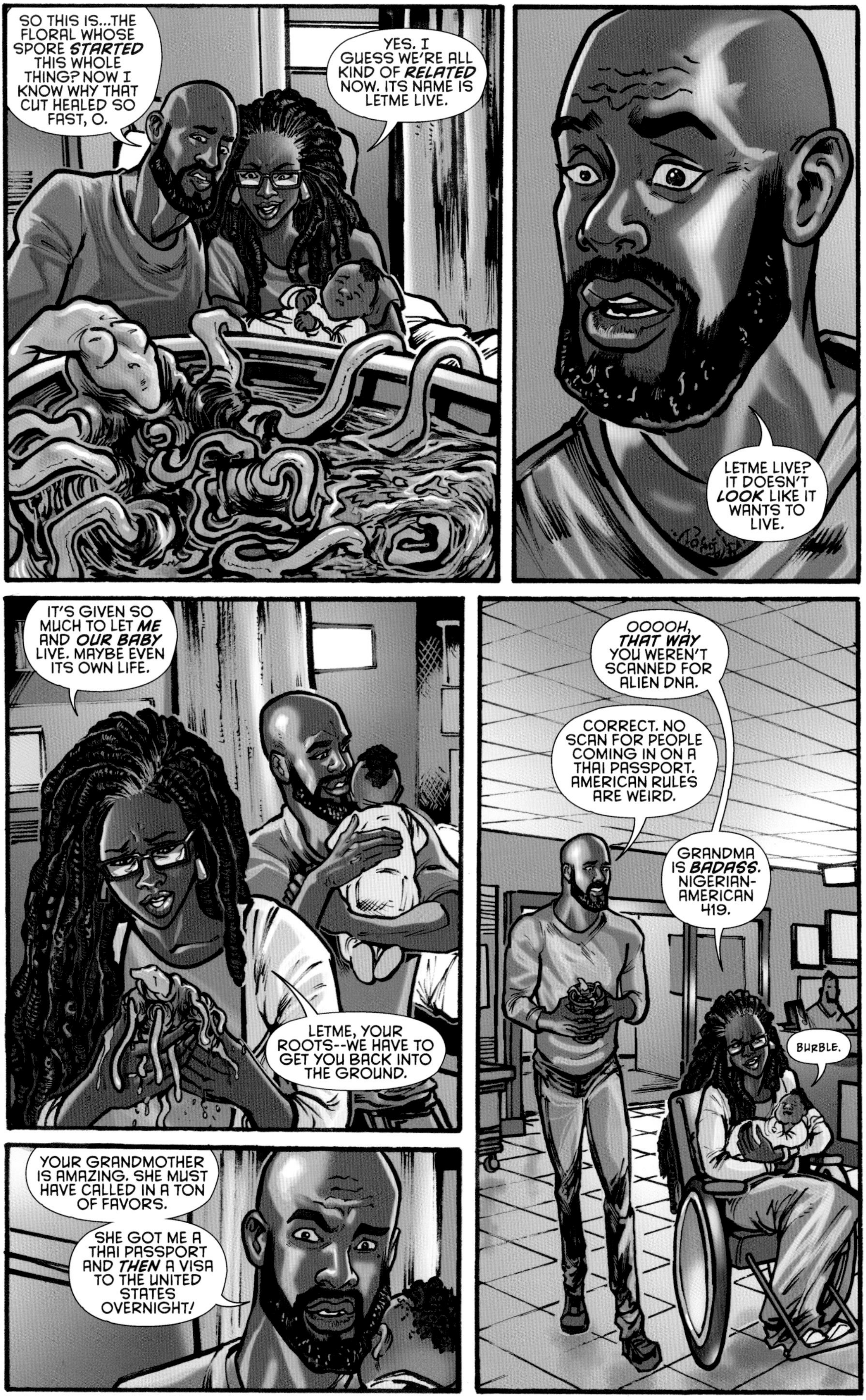
SO THIS IS...THE FLORAL WHOSE SPORE STARTED THIS WHOLE THING? NOW I KNOW WHY THAT CUT HEALED SO FAST, O.
YES. I GUESS WE'RE ALL KIND OF RELATED NOW. ITS NAME IS LETME LIVE.
LETME LIVE? IT DOESN'T LOOK LIKE IT WANTS TO LIVE.
IT'S GIVEN SO MUCH TO LET ME AND OUR BABY LIVE. MAYBE EVEN ITS OWN LIFE.
LETME, YOUR ROOTS--WE HAVE TO GET YOU BACK INTO THE GROUND.
YOUR GRANDMOTHER IS AMAZING. SHE MUST HAVE CALLED IN A TON OF FAVORS.
SHE GOT ME A THAI PASSPORT AND THEN A VISA TO THE UNITED STATES OVERNIGHT!
OOOOH, THAT WAY YOU WEREN'T SCANNED FOR ALIEN DNA.
CORRECT. NO SCAN FOR PEOPLE COMING IN ON A THAI PASSPORT. AMERICAN RULES ARE WEIRD.
GRANDMA IS BADASS. NIGERIAN-AMERICAN 419.
BURBLE.

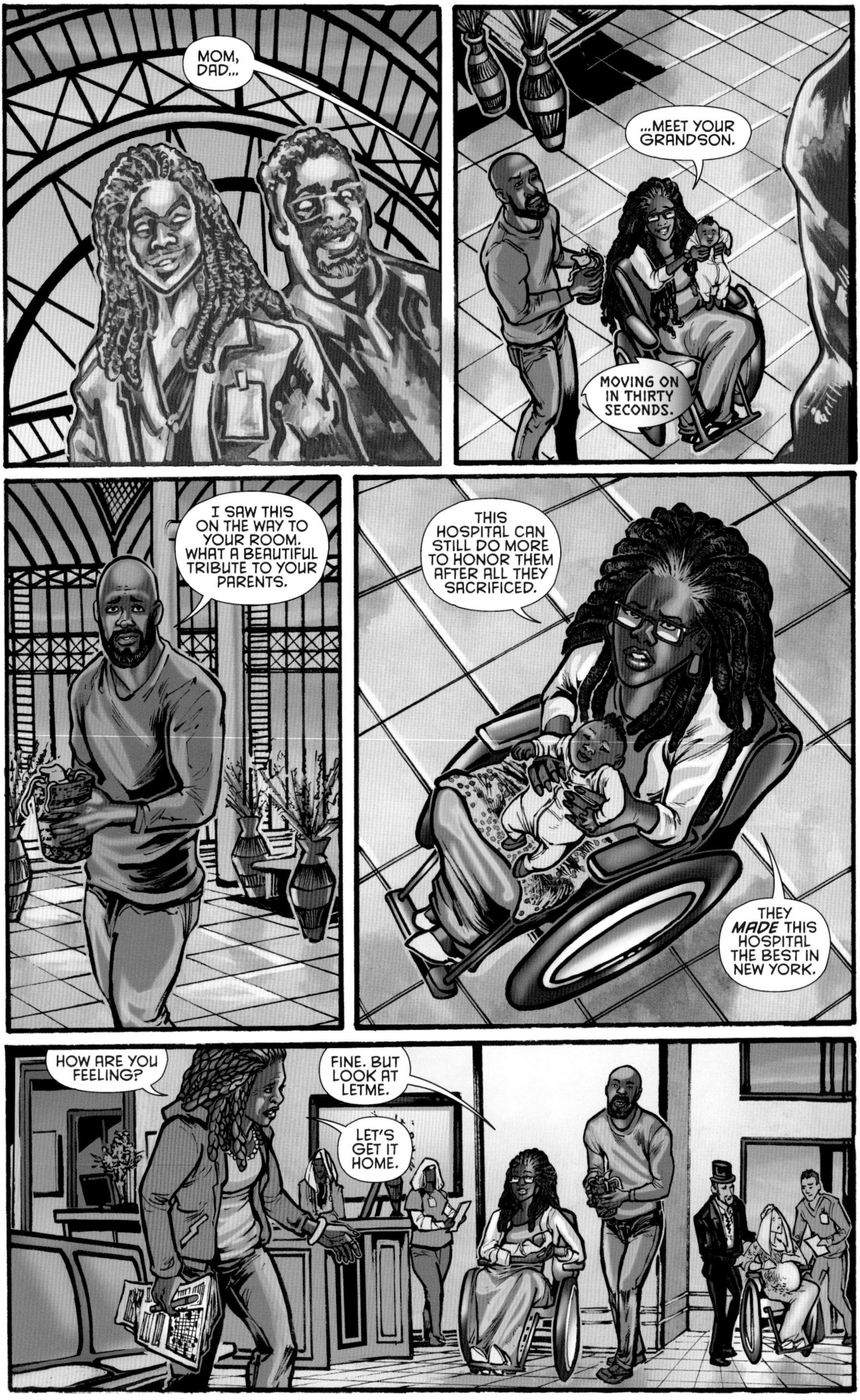
MOM, DAD...
...MEET YOUR GRANDSON.
MOVING ON IN THIRTY SECONDS.
I SAW THIS ON THE WAY TO YOUR ROOM. WHAT A BEAUTIFUL TRIBUTE TO YOUR PARENTS.
THIS HOSPITAL CAN STILL DO MORE TO HONOR THEM AFTER ALL THEY SACRIFICED.
THEY *MADE* THIS HOSPITAL THE BEST IN NEW YORK.
HOW ARE YOU FEELING?
FINE. BUT LOOK AT LETME.
LET'S GET IT HOME.

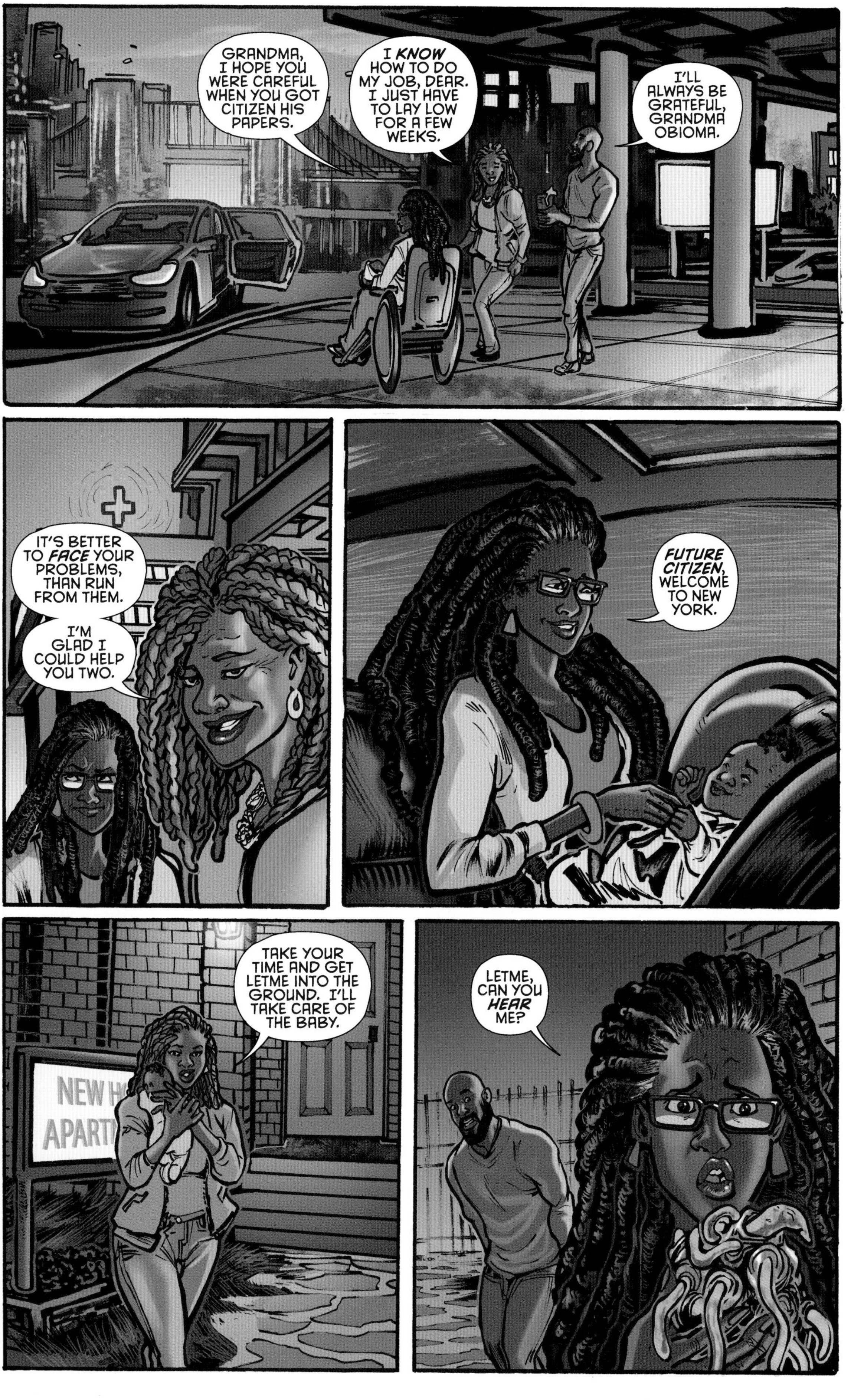
GRANDMA, I HOPE YOU WERE CAREFUL WHEN YOU GOT CITIZEN HIS PAPERS.
I KNOW HOW TO DO MY JOB, DEAR. I JUST HAVE TO LAY LOW FOR A FEW WEEKS.
I'LL ALWAYS BE GRATEFUL, GRANDMA OBIOMA.
IT'S BETTER TO FACE YOUR PROBLEMS, THAN RUN FROM THEM.
I'M GLAD I COULD HELP YOU TWO.
FUTURE CITIZEN, WELCOME TO NEW YORK.
TAKE YOUR TIME AND GET LETME INTO THE GROUND. I'LL TAKE CARE OF THE BABY.
NEW H
APART
LETME, CAN YOU HEAR ME?

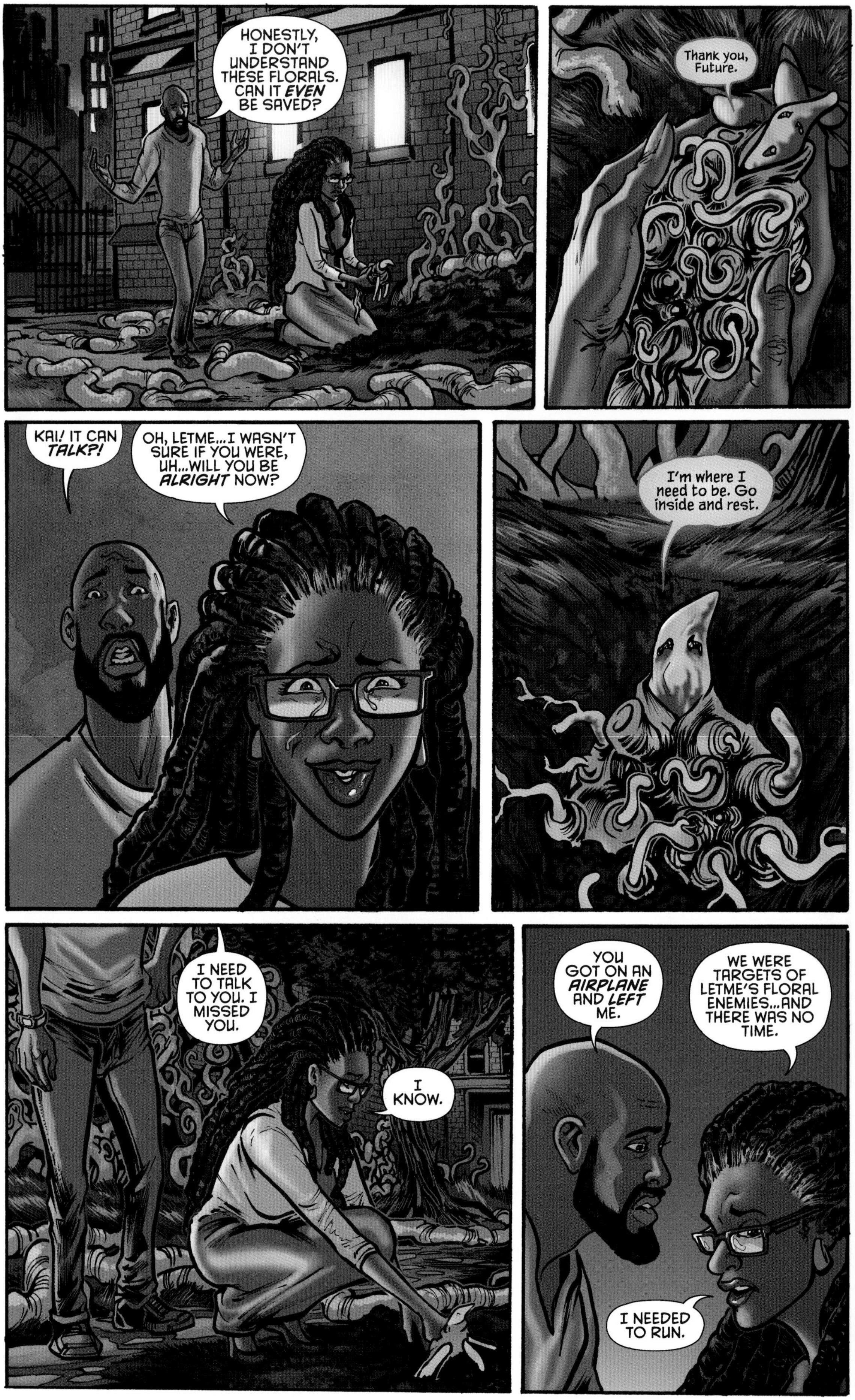
HONESTLY, I DON'T UNDERSTAND THESE FLORALS. CAN IT EVEN BE SAVED?
Thank you, Future.
KAI! IT CAN TALK?!
OH, LETME... I WASN'T SURE IF YOU WERE, UH... WILL YOU BE ALRIGHT NOW?
I'm where I need to be. Go inside and rest.
I NEED TO TALK TO YOU. I MISSED YOU.
I KNOW.
YOU GOT ON AN AIRPLANE AND LEFT ME.
WE WERE TARGETS OF LETME'S FLORAL ENEMIES... AND THERE WAS NO TIME.
I NEEDED TO RUN.

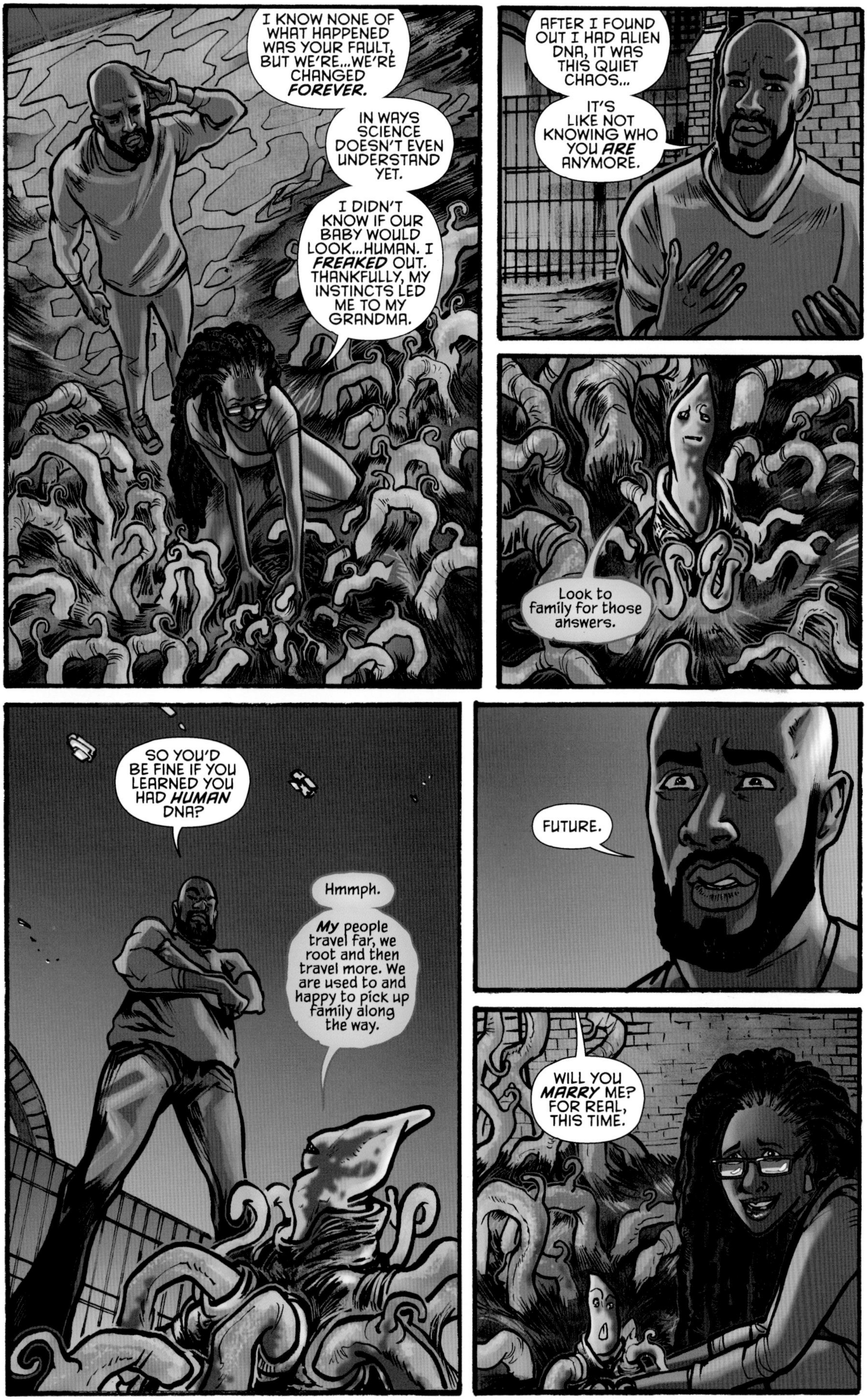
I KNOW NONE OF WHAT HAPPENED WAS YOUR FAULT, BUT WE'RE...WE'RE CHANGED FOREVER.
IN WAYS SCIENCE DOESN'T EVEN UNDERSTAND YET.
I DIDN'T KNOW IF OUR BABY WOULD LOOK...HUMAN. I FREAKED OUT. THANKFULLY, MY INSTINCTS LED ME TO MY GRANDMA.
AFTER I FOUND OUT I HAD ALIEN DNA, IT WAS THIS QUIET CHAOS...
IT'S LIKE NOT KNOWING WHO YOU ARE ANYMORE.
Look to family for those answers.
SO YOU'D BE FINE IF YOU LEARNED YOU HAD HUMAN DNA?
Hmmph.
My people travel far, we root and then travel more. We are used to and happy to pick up family along the way.
FUTURE.
WILL YOU MARRY ME? FOR REAL, THIS TIME.

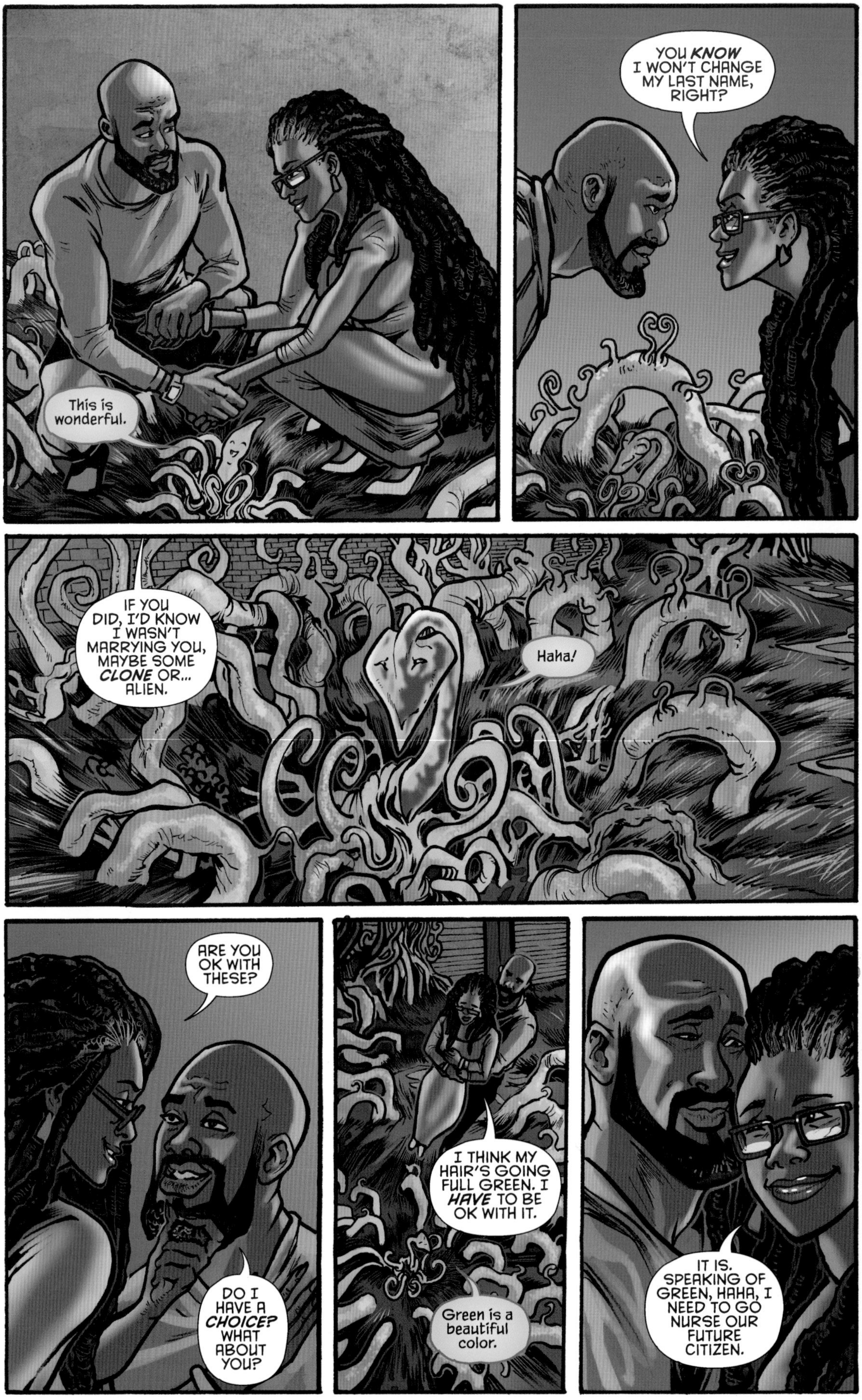
This is wonderful.
YOU KNOW I WON'T CHANGE MY LAST NAME, RIGHT?
IF YOU DID, I'D KNOW I WASN'T MARRYING YOU, MAYBE SOME CLONE OR... ALIEN.
Haha!
ARE YOU OK WITH THESE?
DO I HAVE A CHOICE? WHAT ABOUT YOU?
I THINK MY HAIR'S GOING FULL GREEN. I HAVE TO BE OK WITH IT.
Green is a beautiful color.
IT IS. SPEAKING OF GREEN, HAHA, I NEED TO GO NURSE OUR FUTURE CITIZEN.

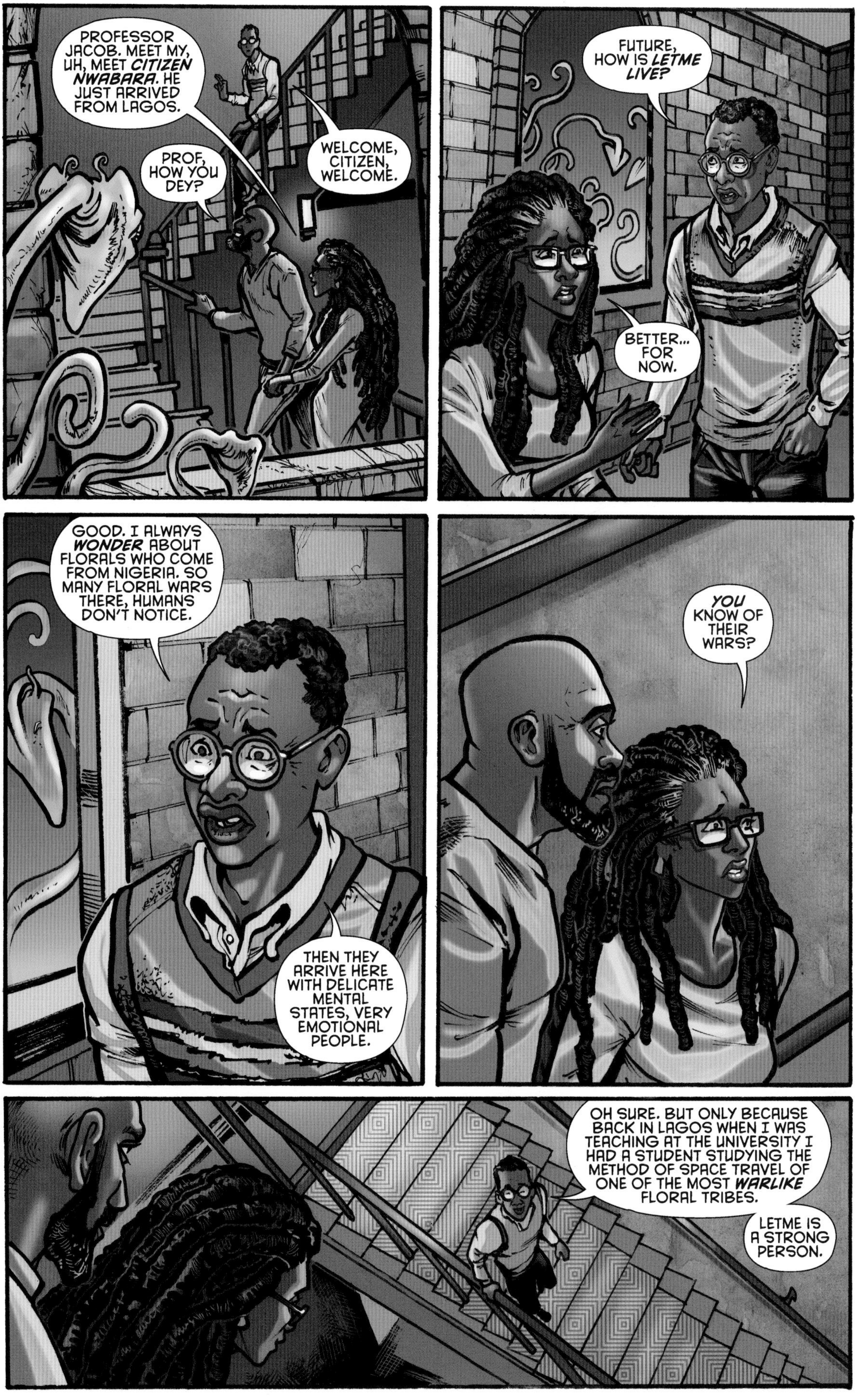
PROFESSOR JACOB. MEET MY, UH, MEET CITIZEN NWABARA. HE JUST ARRIVED FROM LAGOS.
PROF, HOW YOU DEY?
WELCOME, CITIZEN, WELCOME.
FUTURE, HOW IS LETME LIVE?
BETTER... FOR NOW.
GOOD. I ALWAYS WONDER ABOUT FLORALS WHO COME FROM NIGERIA. SO MANY FLORAL WARS THERE, HUMANS DON'T NOTICE.
THEN THEY ARRIVE HERE WITH DELICATE MENTAL STATES, VERY EMOTIONAL PEOPLE.
YOU KNOW OF THEIR WARS?
OH SURE. BUT ONLY BECAUSE BACK IN LAGOS WHEN I WAS TEACHING AT THE UNIVERSITY I HAD A STUDENT STUDYING THE METHOD OF SPACE TRAVEL OF ONE OF THE MOST WARLIKE FLORAL TRIBES.
LETME IS A STRONG PERSON.

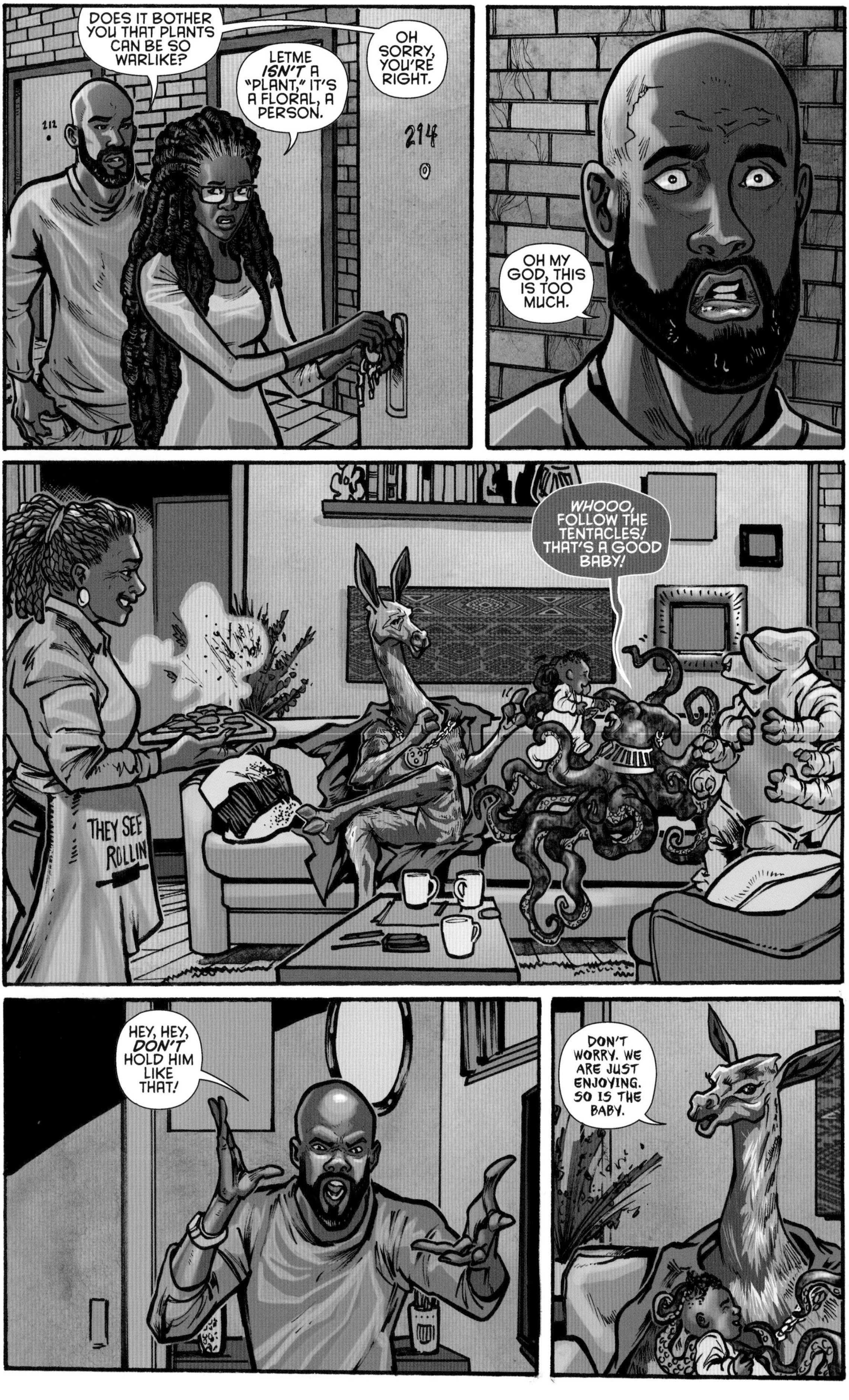
DOES IT BOTHER YOU THAT PLANTS CAN BE SO WARLIKE?
LETME ISN'T A "PLANT," IT'S A FLORAL, A PERSON.
OH SORRY, YOU'RE RIGHT.
212
214
OH MY GOD, THIS IS TOO MUCH.
WHOOO, FOLLOW THE TENTACLES! THAT'S A GOOD BABY!
THEY SEE ROLLIN
HEY, HEY, DON'T HOLD HIM LIKE THAT!
DON'T WORRY. WE ARE JUST ENJOYING. SO IS THE BABY.

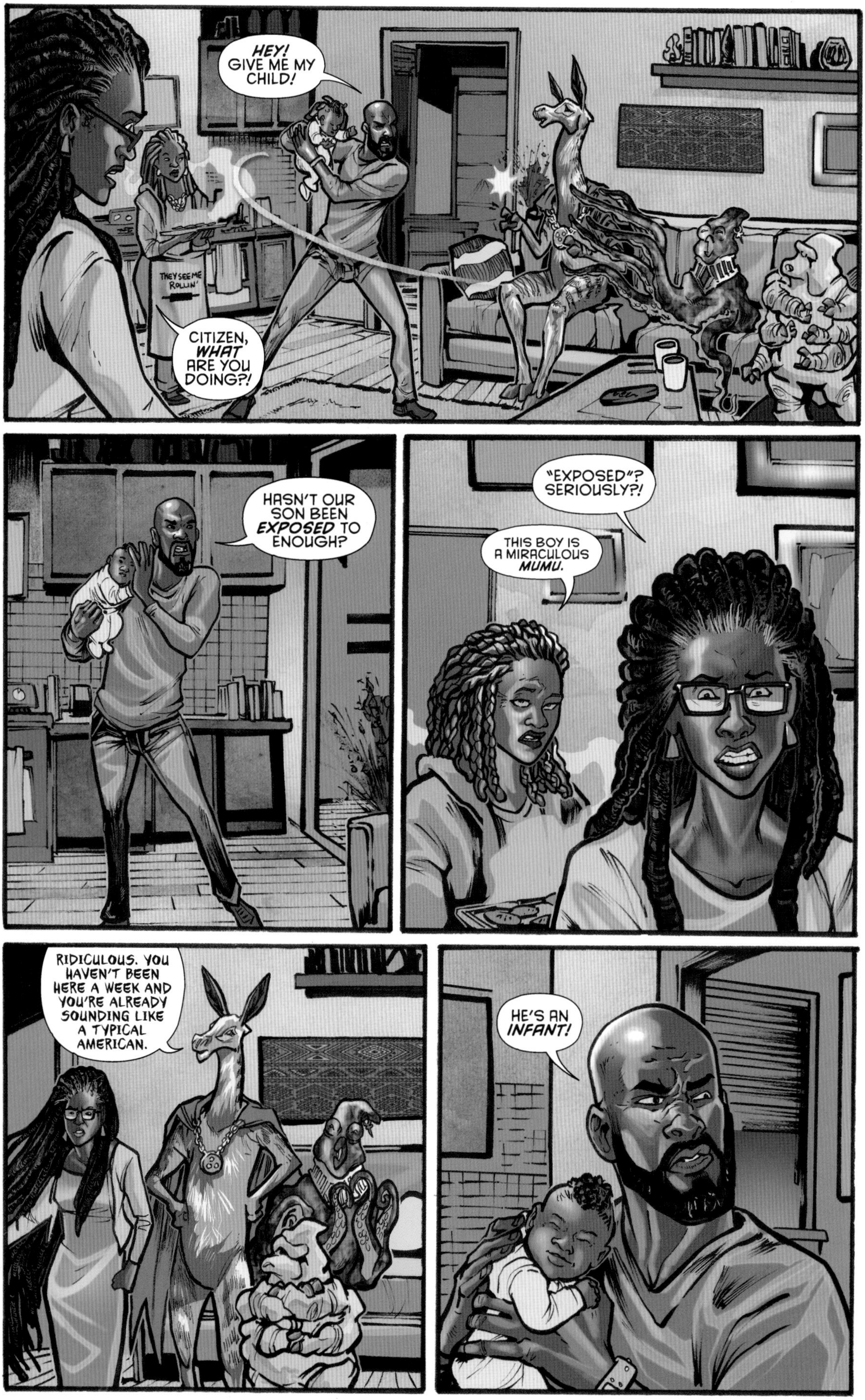
HEY! GIVE ME MY CHILD!
THEY SEE ME ROLLIN'
CITIZEN, WHAT ARE YOU DOING?!
HASN'T OUR SON BEEN EXPOSED TO ENOUGH?
"EXPOSED"? SERIOUSLY?!
THIS BOY IS A MIRACULOUS MUMU.
RIDICULOUS. YOU HAVEN'T BEEN HERE A WEEK AND YOU'RE ALREADY SOUNDING LIKE A TYPICAL AMERICAN.
HE'S AN INFANT!

I KNOW YOUR BIAFRA MOVEMENT. YOU NEO-BIAFRANS DON'T GET IT, IT'S NOT JUST YOU IGBO HUMANS WHO ARE DEALING WITH HARDSHIP.

WHAT DO YOU KNOW OF BIAFRA? YOU *BARELY* KNOW EARTH!

SNORT!

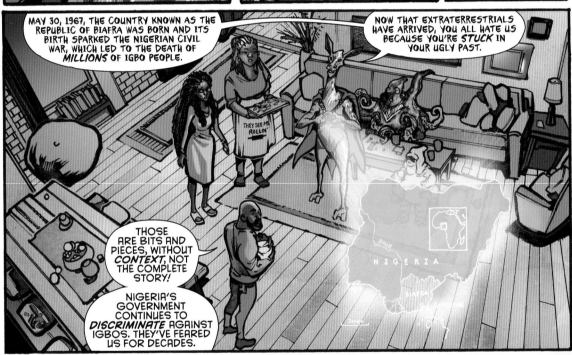

MAY 30, 1967, THE COUNTRY KNOWN AS THE REPUBLIC OF BIAFRA WAS BORN AND ITS BIRTH SPARKED THE NIGERIAN CIVIL WAR, WHICH LED TO THE DEATH OF *MILLIONS* OF IGBO PEOPLE.

NOW THAT EXTRATERRESTRIALS HAVE ARRIVED, YOU ALL HATE US BECAUSE YOU'RE *STUCK* IN YOUR UGLY PAST.

THOSE ARE BITS AND PIECES, WITHOUT *CONTEXT*, NOT THE COMPLETE STORY!

NIGERIA'S GOVERNMENT CONTINUES TO *DISCRIMINATE* AGAINST IGBOS. THEY'VE FEARED US FOR DECADES.

THEY SEE ME ROLLIN'

NIGERIA

BIAFRA

YOU ARRIVED AND THINK THAT'S THE *BEGINNING* OF EARTH'S STORY. NOT AT ALL.

REGARDLESS, CITIZEN, THESE ARE MY FRIENDS. I'M HAPPY TO HAVE *WHATEVER* IS IN THEM...IN OUR CHILD... IN ME.

I'M HAPPY WITH WHAT I AM NOW. AREN'T YOU?

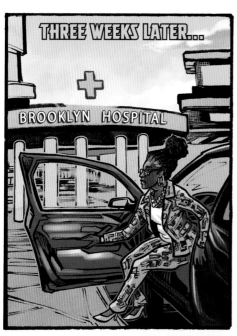

THREE WEEKS LATER...

BROOKLYN HOSPITAL

I'M HERE TO SEE, DR. MICHAEL SHELLEY.

HE'LL BE WITH YOU, SHORTLY. PLEASE HAVE A SEAT.

PLEASE HAVE PROOF OF
AND/OR YOUR MEDICARE FOR ALL CARD
ACCESIBLE AT THE TIME OF SERVICE

HUMANS PREFERRED

ASE HAVE PROOF OF INSURANCE
OR YOUR MEDICARE FOR ALL CARD
ESIBLE AT THE TIME OF SERVICE

GO RIGHT IN, DR. CHUCK... CHOOK... *CHUKWUEBUKA.* THANKS.

HUMANS PREFERRED

THANKS SO MUCH FOR COMING, FUTURE. I...I KNOW THIS MUST BE *STRANGE* FOR YOU.

YES. I NEARLY IGNORED YOUR CALL. I JUST HAD A BABY.

I'M GLAD YOU DIDN'T, I GUESS. SO MANY OF MY EMPLOYEES HAVE *ASKED* ABOUT YOU SINCE YOU WERE HERE...AND ABOUT YOUR PARENTS.

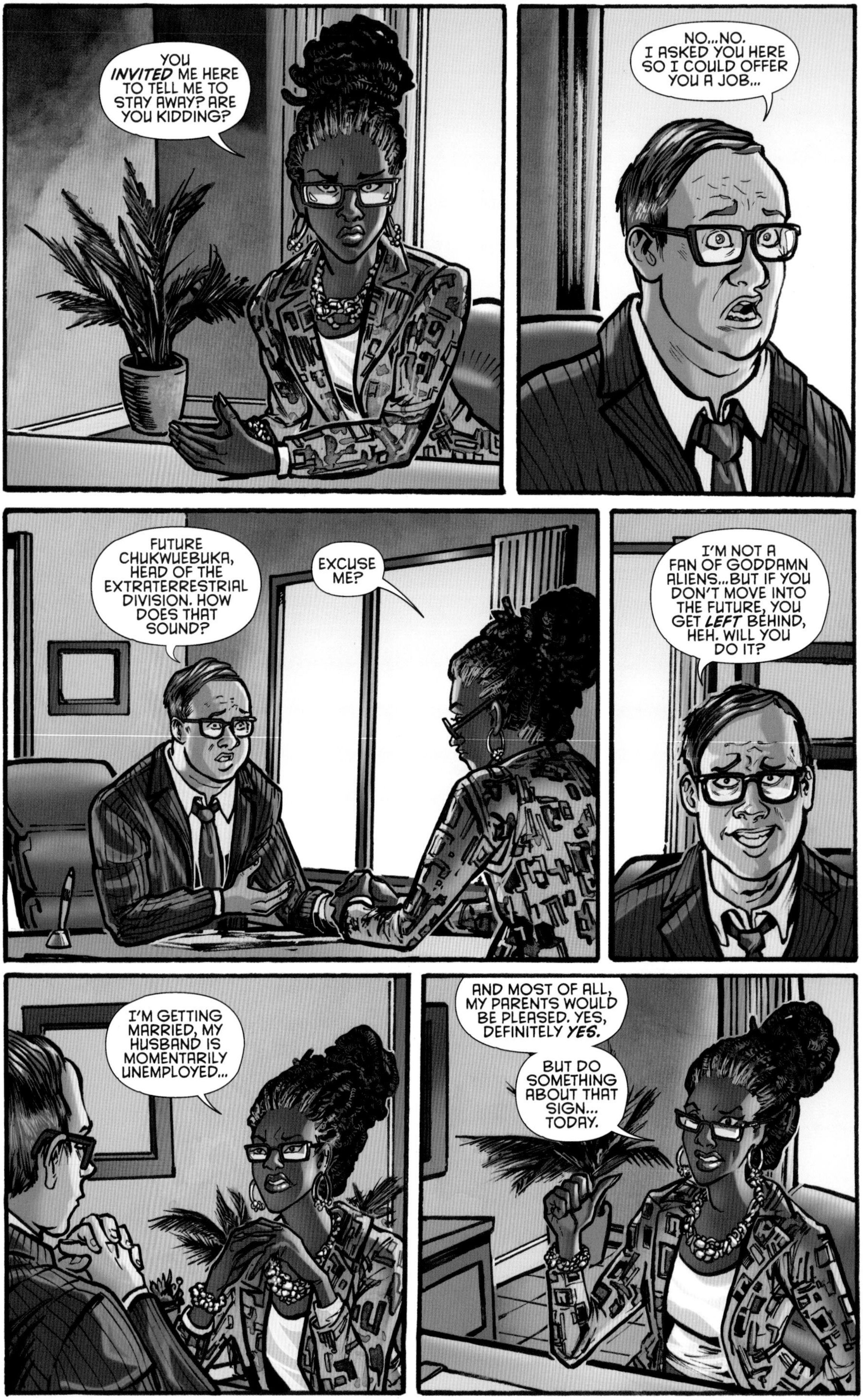
YOU *INVITED* ME HERE TO TELL ME TO STAY AWAY? ARE YOU KIDDING?
NO...NO. I ASKED YOU HERE SO I COULD OFFER YOU A JOB...
FUTURE CHUKWUEBUKA, HEAD OF THE EXTRATERRESTRIAL DIVISION. HOW DOES THAT SOUND?
EXCUSE ME?
I'M NOT A FAN OF GODDAMN ALIENS...BUT IF YOU DON'T MOVE INTO THE FUTURE, YOU GET *LEFT* BEHIND, HEH. WILL YOU DO IT?
I'M GETTING MARRIED, MY HUSBAND IS MOMENTARILY UNEMPLOYED...
AND MOST OF ALL, MY PARENTS WOULD BE PLEASED. YES, DEFINITELY *YES.*
BUT DO SOMETHING ABOUT THAT SIGN... TODAY.

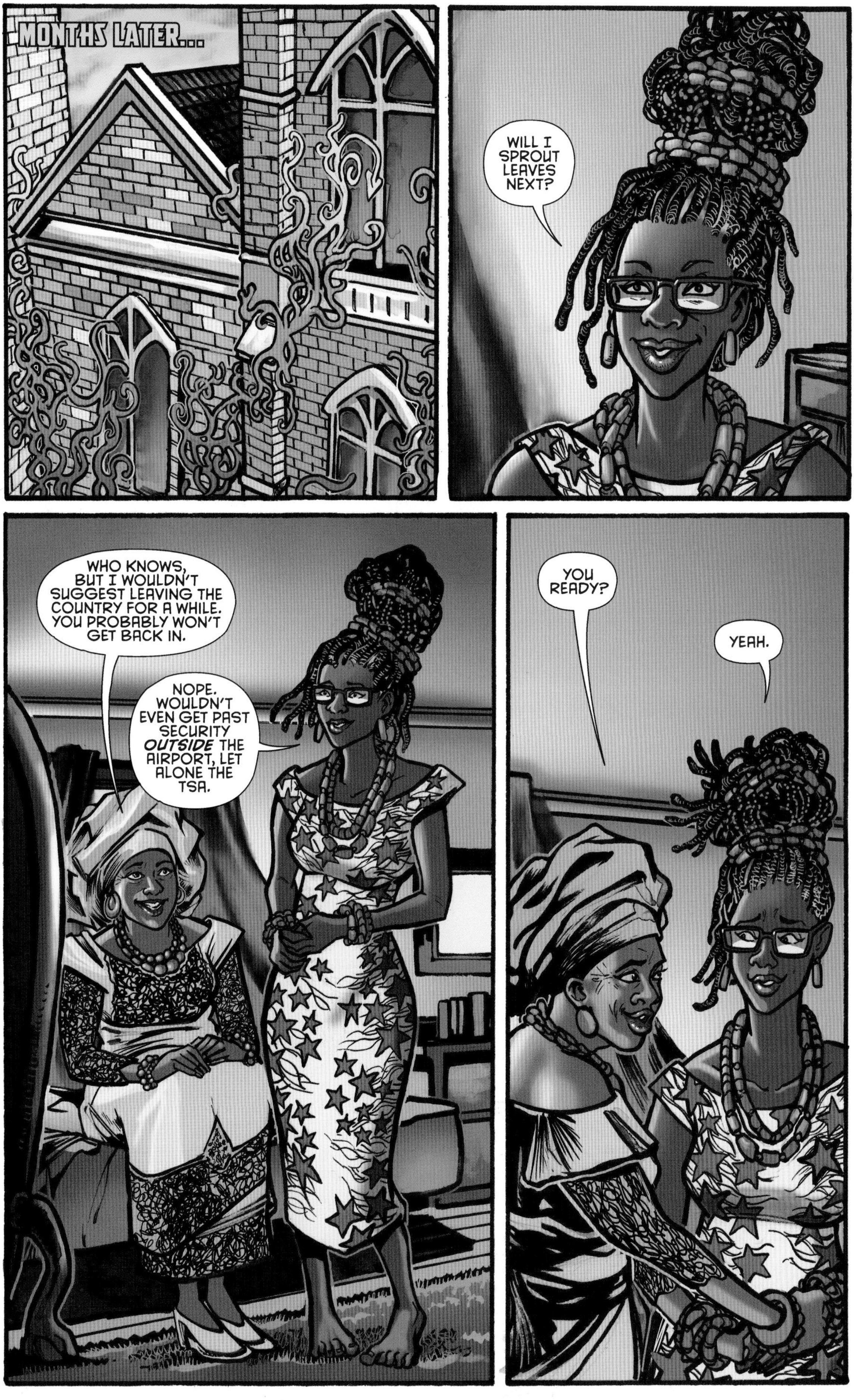
MONTHS LATER...
WILL I SPROUT LEAVES NEXT?
WHO KNOWS, BUT I WOULDN'T SUGGEST LEAVING THE COUNTRY FOR A WHILE. YOU PROBABLY WON'T GET BACK IN.
NOPE. WOULDN'T EVEN GET PAST SECURITY OUTSIDE THE AIRPORT, LET ALONE THE TSA.
YOU READY?
YEAH.

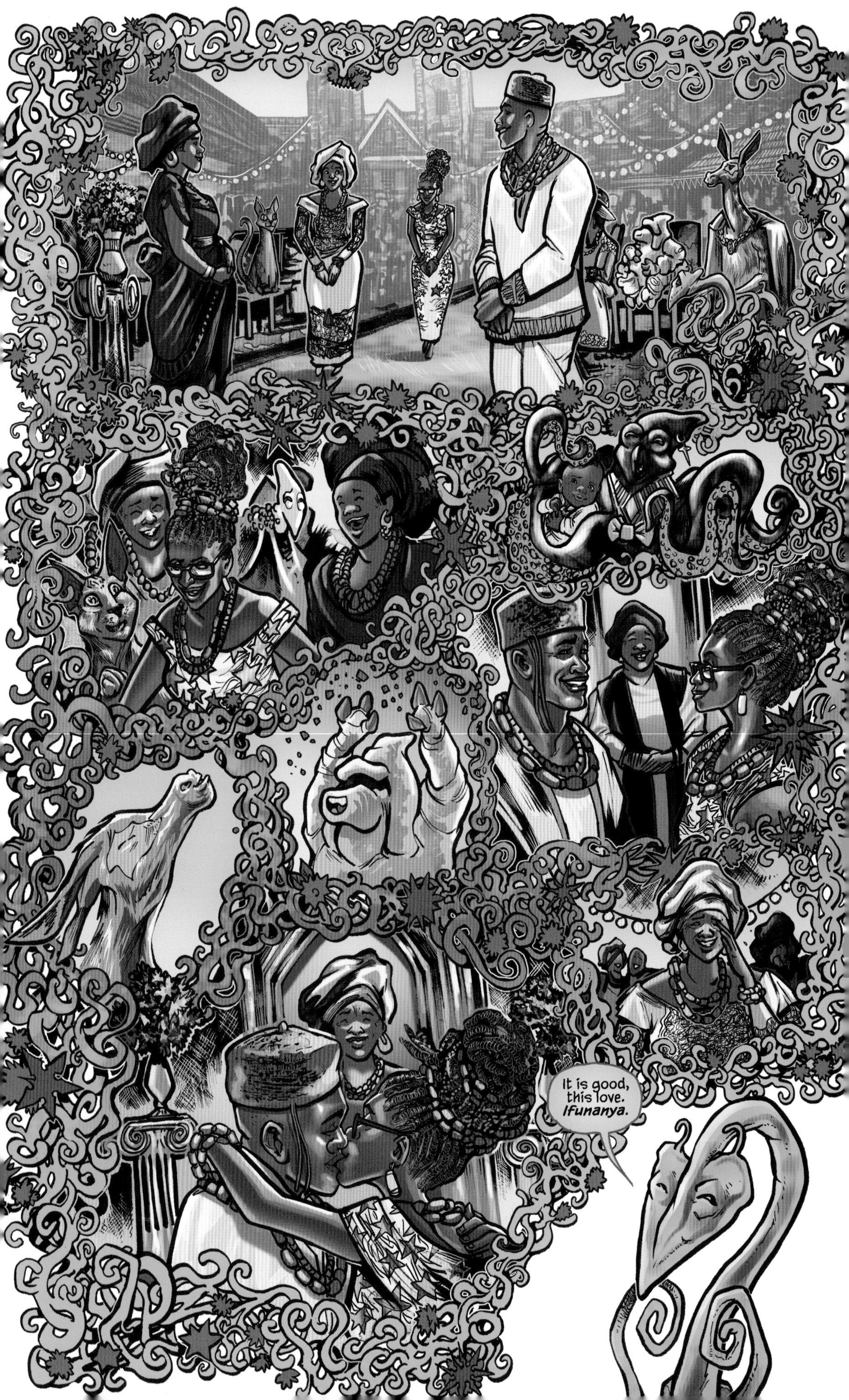
It is good, this love. *Ifunanya.*

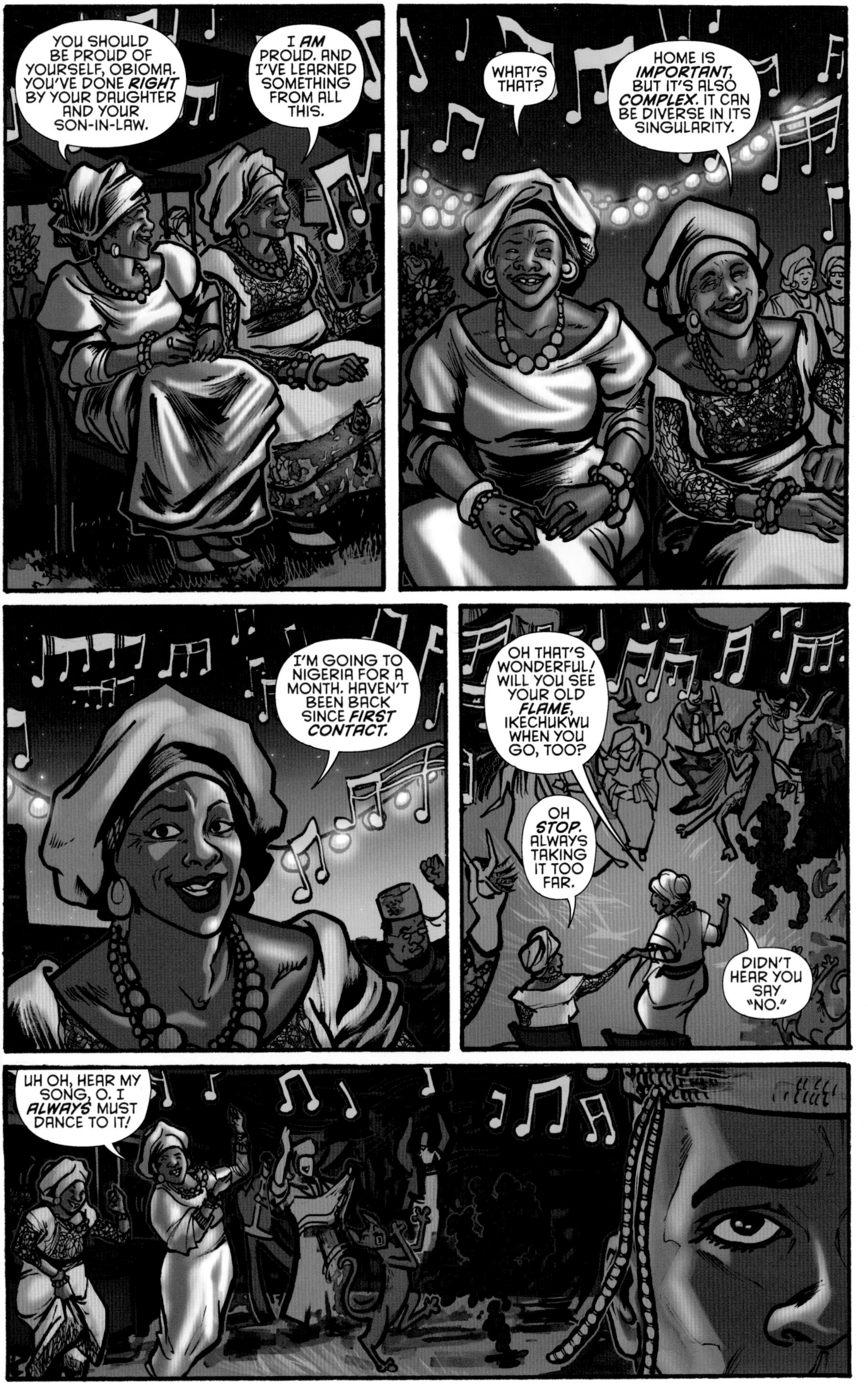
YOU SHOULD BE PROUD OF YOURSELF, OBIOMA. YOU'VE DONE RIGHT BY YOUR DAUGHTER AND YOUR SON-IN-LAW.
I AM PROUD. AND I'VE LEARNED SOMETHING FROM ALL THIS.
WHAT'S THAT?
HOME IS IMPORTANT, BUT IT'S ALSO COMPLEX. IT CAN BE DIVERSE IN ITS SINGULARITY.
I'M GOING TO NIGERIA FOR A MONTH. HAVEN'T BEEN BACK SINCE FIRST CONTACT.
OH THAT'S WONDERFUL! WILL YOU SEE YOUR OLD FLAME, IKECHUKWU WHEN YOU GO, TOO?
OH STOP. ALWAYS TAKING IT TOO FAR.
DIDN'T HEAR YOU SAY "NO."
UH OH, HEAR MY SONG, O. I ALWAYS MUST DANCE TO IT!

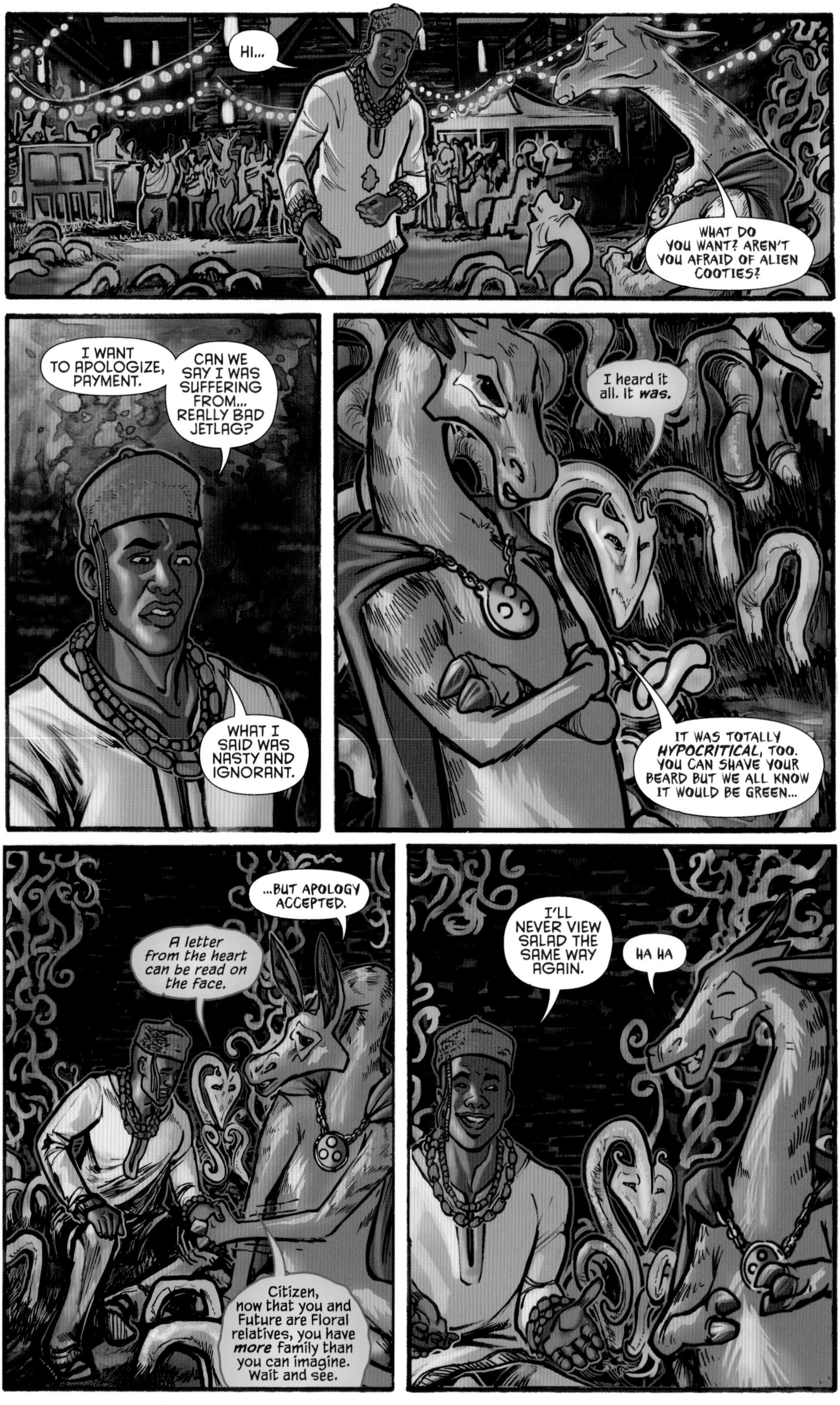
HI...
WHAT DO YOU WANT? AREN'T YOU AFRAID OF ALIEN COOTIES?
I WANT TO APOLOGIZE, PAYMENT.
CAN WE SAY I WAS SUFFERING FROM... REALLY BAD JETLAG?
WHAT I SAID WAS NASTY AND IGNORANT.
I heard it all. It *was.*
IT WAS TOTALLY *HYPOCRITICAL*, TOO. YOU CAN SHAVE YOUR BEARD BUT WE ALL KNOW IT WOULD BE GREEN...
...BUT APOLOGY ACCEPTED.
A letter from the heart can be read on the face.
Citizen, now that you and Future are Floral relatives, you have *more* family than you can imagine. Wait and see.
I'LL NEVER VIEW SALAD THE SAME WAY AGAIN.
HA HA

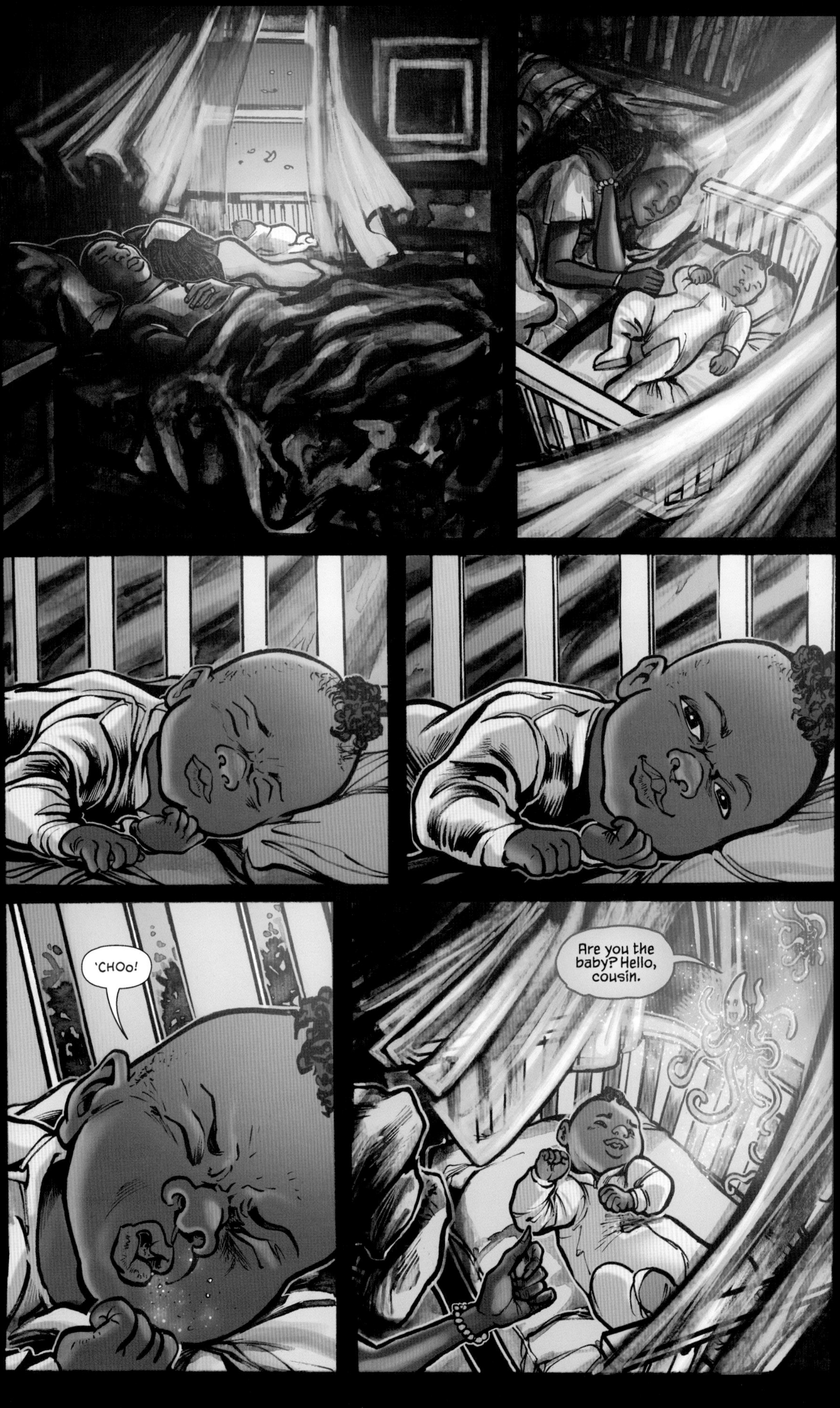
'CHOo!
Are you the baby? Hello, cousin.

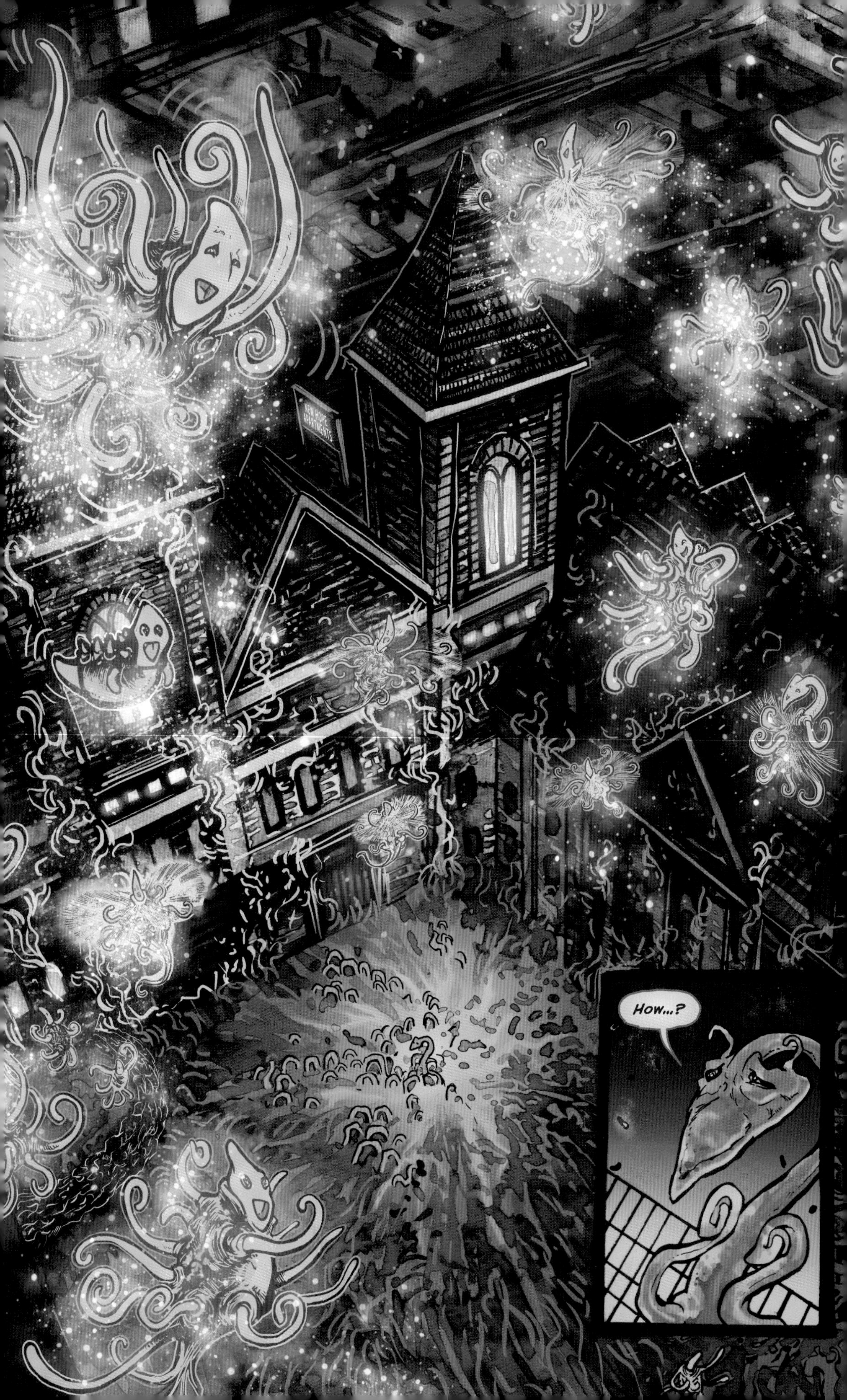
NEW HOPE APARTMENTS
HOW...?

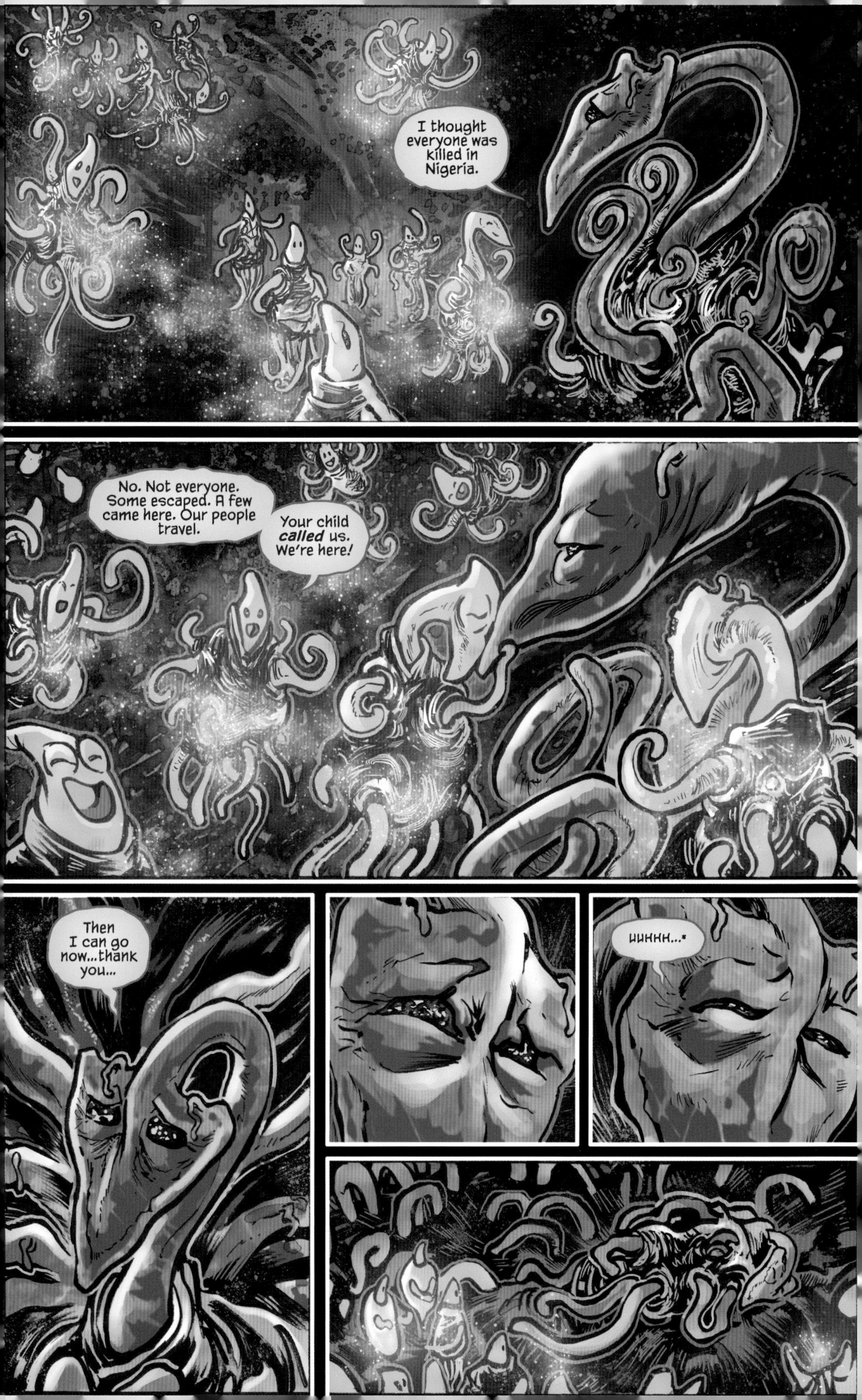
I thought everyone was killed in Nigeria.
No. Not everyone. Some escaped. A few came here. Our people travel.
Your child *called* us. We're here!
Then I can go now...thank you...
UHHHH...*

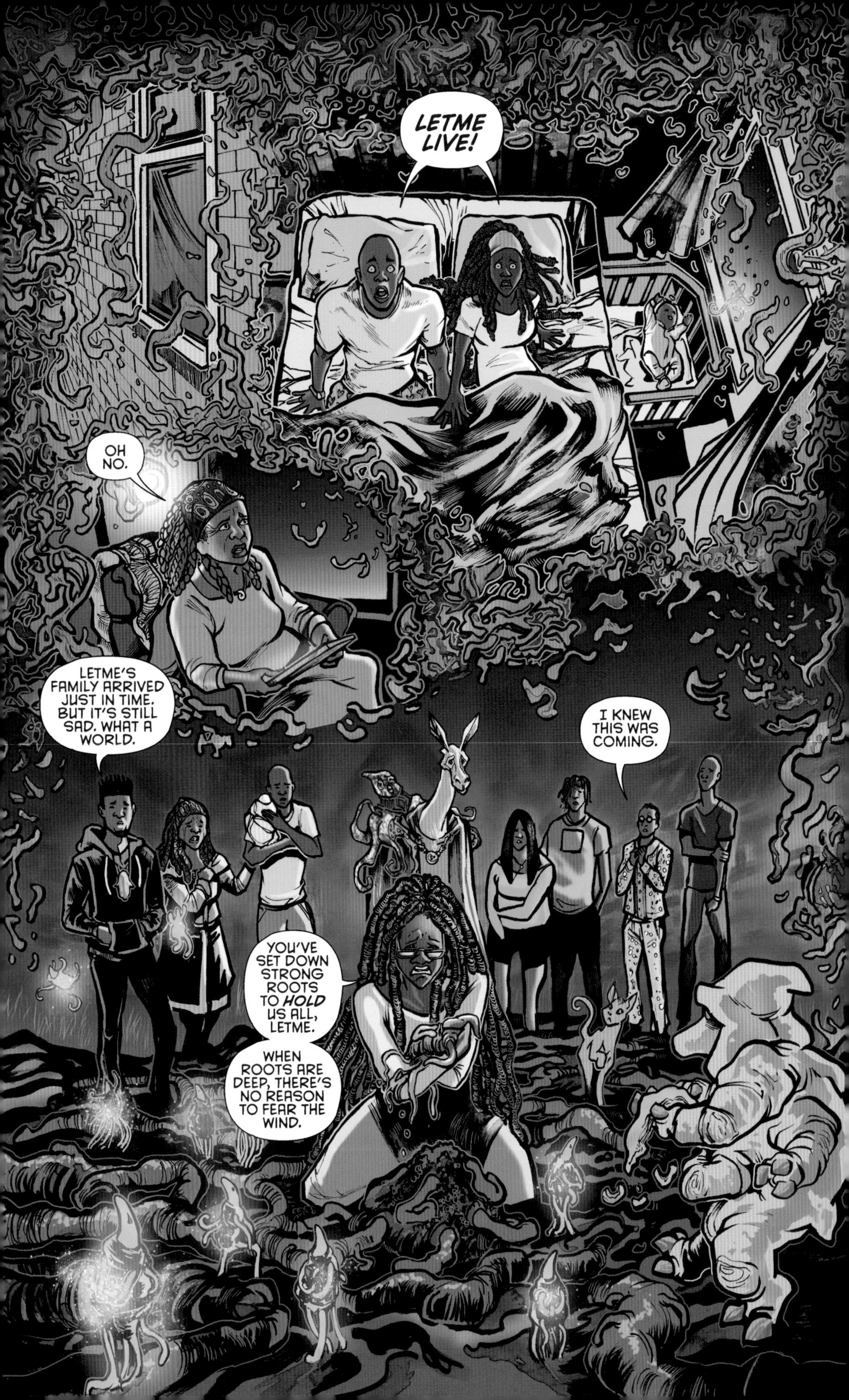
LETME LIVE!
OH NO.
LETME'S FAMILY ARRIVED JUST IN TIME. BUT IT'S STILL SAD. WHAT A WORLD.
I KNEW THIS WAS COMING.
YOU'VE SET DOWN STRONG ROOTS TO HOLD US ALL, LETME.
WHEN ROOTS ARE DEEP, THERE'S NO REASON TO FEAR THE WIND.

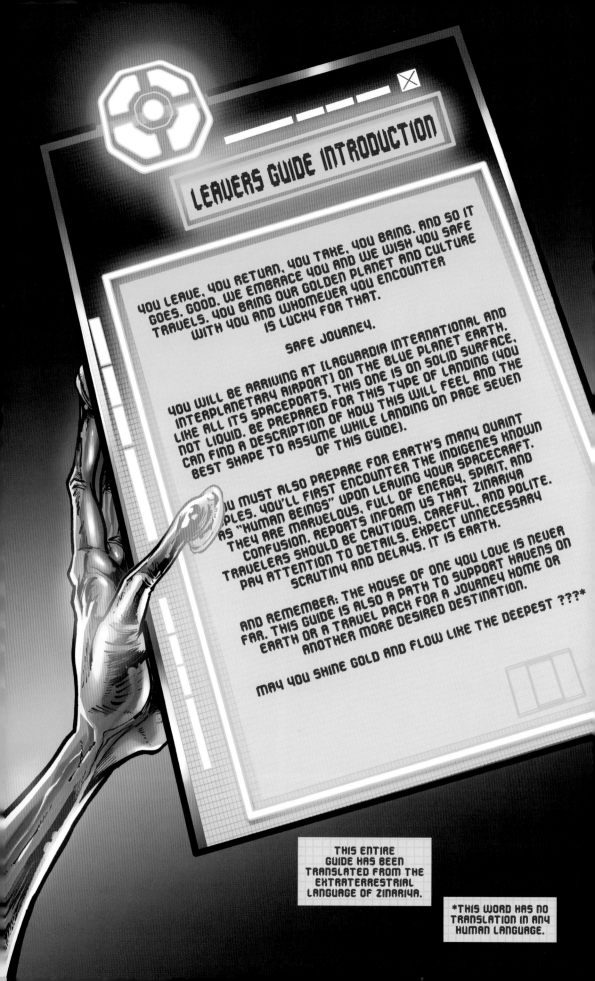

LEAVERS GUIDE INTRODUCTION

YOU LEAVE, YOU RETURN, YOU TAKE, YOU BRING. AND SO IT GOES. GOOD. WE EMBRACE YOU AND WE WISH YOU SAFE TRAVELS. YOU BRING OUR GOLDEN PLANET AND CULTURE WITH YOU AND WHOMEVER YOU ENCOUNTER IS LUCKY FOR THAT.

SAFE JOURNEY.

YOU WILL BE ARRIVING AT [LAGUARDIA INTERNATIONAL AND INTERPLANETARY AIRPORT] ON THE BLUE PLANET EARTH. LIKE ALL ITS SPACEPORTS, THIS ONE IS ON SOLID SURFACE, NOT LIQUID. BE PREPARED FOR THIS TYPE OF LANDING (YOU CAN FIND A DESCRIPTION OF HOW THIS WILL FEEL AND THE BEST SHAPE TO ASSUME WHILE LANDING ON PAGE SEVEN OF THIS GUIDE).

YOU MUST ALSO PREPARE FOR EARTH'S MANY QUAINT PEOPLES. YOU'LL FIRST ENCOUNTER THE INDIGENES KNOWN AS "HUMAN BEINGS" UPON LEAVING YOUR SPACECRAFT. THEY ARE MARVELOUS, FULL OF ENERGY, SPIRIT, AND CONFUSION. REPORTS INFORM US THAT ZINARIYA TRAVELERS SHOULD BE CAUTIOUS, CAREFUL, AND POLITE. PAY ATTENTION TO DETAILS. EXPECT UNNECESSARY SCRUTINY AND DELAYS. IT IS EARTH.

AND REMEMBER: THE HOUSE OF ONE YOU LOVE IS NEVER FAR. THIS GUIDE IS ALSO A PATH TO SUPPORT HAVENS ON EARTH OR A TRAVEL PACK FOR A JOURNEY HOME OR ANOTHER MORE DESIRED DESTINATION.

MAY YOU SHINE GOLD AND FLOW LIKE THE DEEPEST ????*

THIS ENTIRE GUIDE HAS BEEN TRANSLATED FROM THE EXTRATERRESTRIAL LANGUAGE OF ZINARIYA.

*THIS WORD HAS NO TRANSLATION IN ANY HUMAN LANGUAGE.

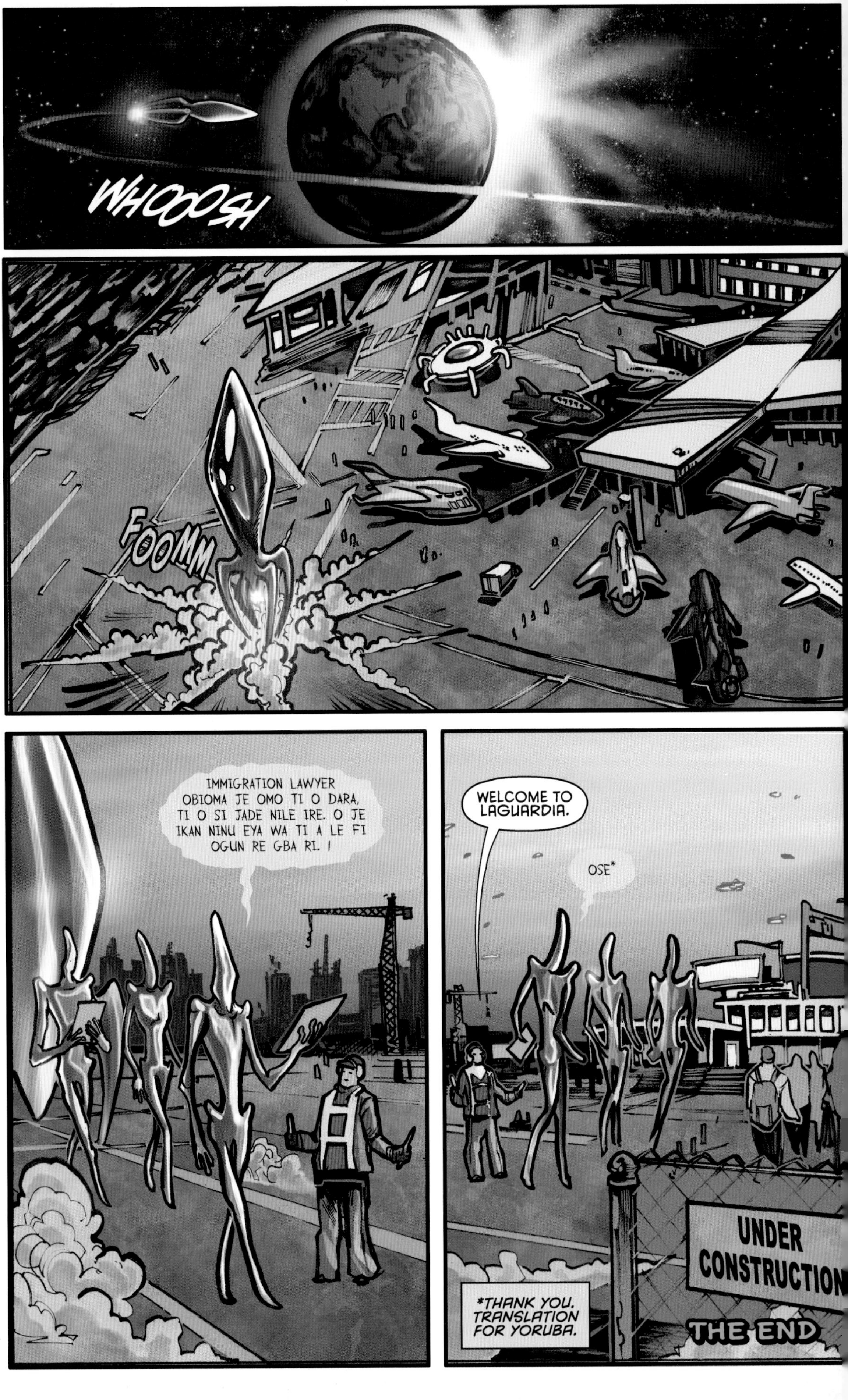
WHOOOSH
FOOMM
IMMIGRATION LAWYER OBIOMA JE OMO TI O DARA, TI O SI JADE NILE IRE. O JE IKAN NINU EYA WA TI A LE FI OGUN RE GBA RI. !
WELCOME TO LAGUARDIA.
OSE*
UNDER CONSTRUCTION
*THANK YOU. TRANSLATION FOR YORUBA.
THE END

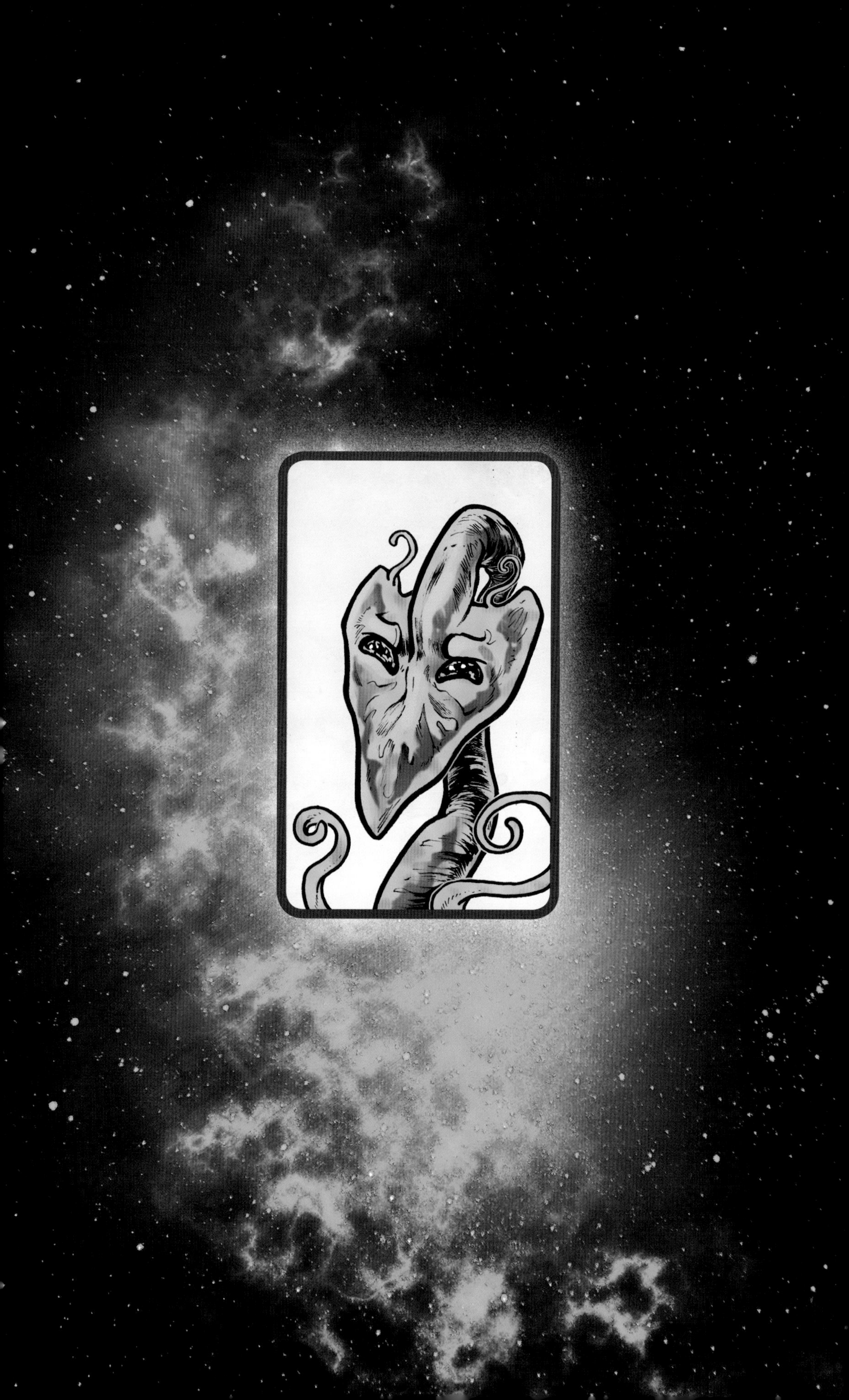

• COMING AND GOING •

I've been kicking this story around for over six years.

The first time I ever went to New York City was in 2009 for the Octavia Butler Symposium at Medgar Evers College. I arrived through LaGuardia International Airport. And I left through it, as well.

Two things: 1. What struck me most and immediately about New York was its glorious diversity. You could walk down the street and hear languages, witness customs, find restaurants, see people from all over the world in very close proximity. I prefer quiet, less urban places, away from human beings, but this aspect of New York delighted me. 2. I detested LaGuardia Airport. There was barely anywhere to sit, it was ancient in a dirty way, and the construction made getting around confusing and difficult. Over the years, I've learned that this construction is never-ending.

Nevertheless, what made the strongest impression on me was the first next-level TSA experience I had while leaving through LaGuardia that first time to fly back to Chicago. These days I have locks (less affectionately called "dreadlocks") that are over four and a half feet long. Back then, they were probably closer to two and a half. I went through the body scanner and was quickly asked to step aside. "Would you like a private room?" the female TSA officer asked. Having no idea why, I said, "Yes." My large hair bun was first "wanded." I was told to undo my bun, and then the officer proceeded to squeeze each of my thick locks from tip to root. Lastly, she massaged my scalp. It was infuriating, creepy and degrading. And it was not the last time this would happen to me when leaving LaGuardia (and at other airports, both in and outside of the United States).

I walked away from that first experience at LaGuardia furious, but also thinking about many things. About aliens. About people of African descent with our alarm-raising thick African hair. About African immigrants who'd have been kept for more in-depth questioning if they'd had my same amount and type of hair.

Hours later, I thought a lot about misdirection and how so much of airport security is just theater to make us feel safer, because when I got home and unpacked, I realized that I'd accidently left my palm-sized pink canister of pepper spray in my carry-on. So, while the LaGuardia TSA officer was busy rifling through my hair, the other officers had missed the most important item. Interesting.

I am the child of immigrants, thus my worldview has been shaped by ideas of people who move around, have multiple homes, cultures, have learned to adapt yet retain their identity and barrel-forth regardless. The Earth is big to me and humanity is diverse. Therefore, when President Trump signed the executive order to implement the infamous travel ban back in January 2017, the America and the general world climate of my story became that much clearer. I especially remember when long-distance runner Mo Farah declared "Trump has made me an alien" because the ban targeted his country of Somalia. All of this was powerful fodder for the *LAGUARDIA* series.

I believe in the existence of aliens. I fantasize about how their eventual arrival will force an amazing paradigm and identity shift in humanity and for the entire earth. I'm an irrational optimist, so I look forward to all this with excitement, anticipation and curiosity. The future portrayed in this series has its problems but it's not a dystopia.

LAGUARDIA is an exploration – it's pushback, it's playful shenanigans, it's looking forward and it's trickster tendencies all rolled up into one narrative. It's metaphor and it's literal. I hope you enjoy it.

Sincerely,
Nnedimma Nkemdili Okorafor
October 24, 2018

PS: I have since gotten TSA Pre-Check and no longer have to endure these invasive inspections. And no, I never again made the epic mistake of leaving pepper spray in my luggage while flying, haha.

TANA FORD HOW I DRAW LAGUARDIA

@tanaford

STEP 1: Digital Layout

First, I lay out all of my pages in Photoshop. This allows me to move and resize the characters, rough in the backgrounds, and get a general sense of what the final page will look like.

STEP 2: Traditional Pencils & Inks

Next, I print the digital layout lightly onto 11x17" Bristol board, and I tightly pencil and ink the page. Often, I'll use mechanical pencils with multicolor leads to draw. You can see the light blue pencils below.

STEP 3: Finishes

Finally, I scan the multocolored artwork back into Photoshop, adjust out the colored pencil marks, and clean up the black & white lines until they shine. Then, it's Jimmy Devlin's turn to work his color magic.

@tanaford

@tanaford

TOOLS of the TRADE

TANA FORD'S LAGUARDIA SKETCHBOOK

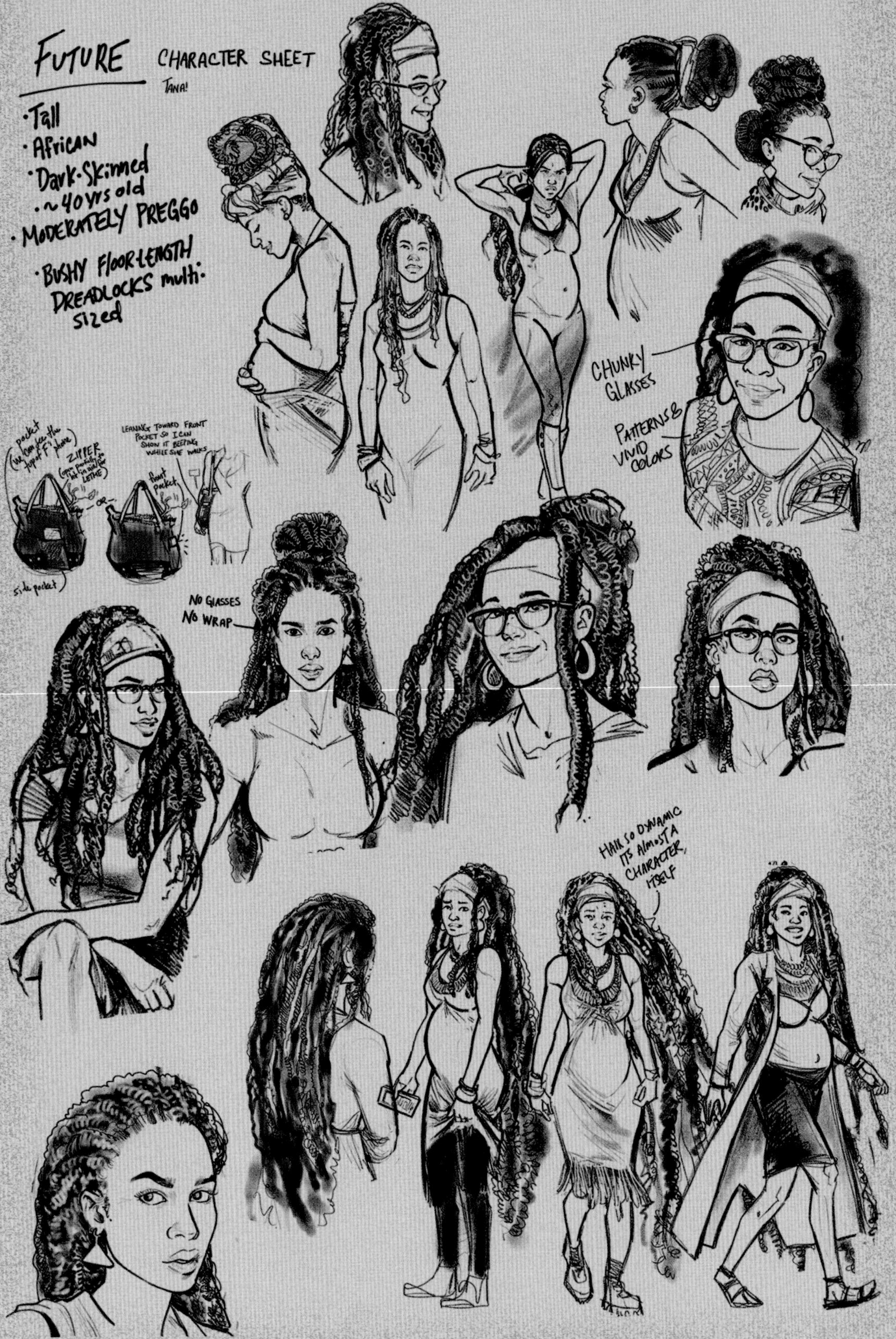

FUTURE
CHARACTER SHEET
TANA!
·Tall
·African
·Dark-Skinned
·~40 yrs old
·MODERATELY PREGGO
·BUSHY FLOOR-LENGTH DREADLOCKS multi-sized
CHUNKY GLASSES
PATTERNS & VIVID COLORS
pocket (we can see the top of F's phone)
ZIPPER
-OR-
front pocket
LEANING TOWARD FRONT POCKET SO I CAN SHOW IT BEEPING WHILE SHE WALKS
side pocket
NO GLASSES
NO WRAP
HAIR SO DYNAMIC ITS ALMOST A CHARACTER, ITSELF

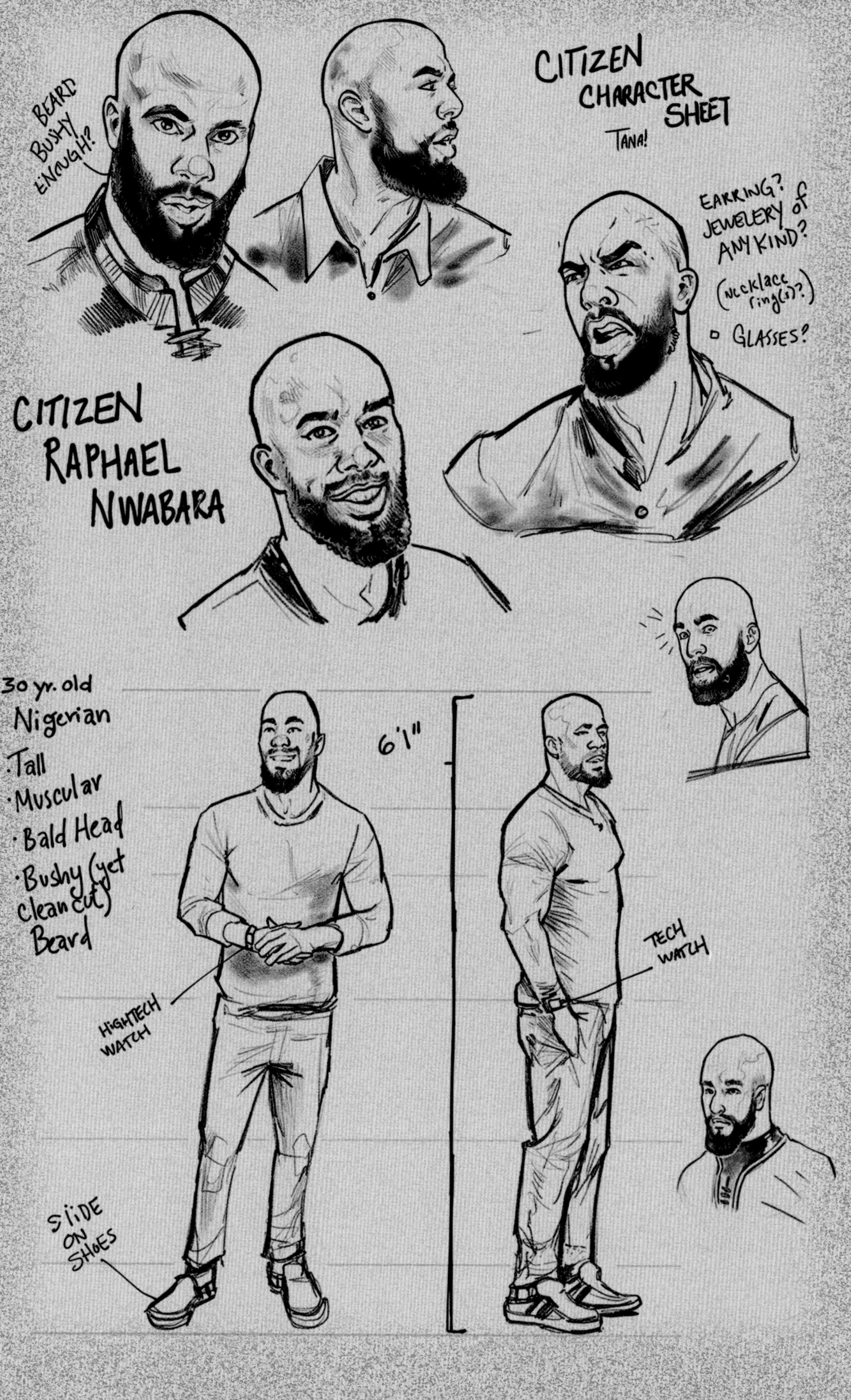

BEARD BUSHY ENOUGH?
CITIZEN CHARACTER SHEET
TANA!
EARRING? JEWELERY of ANY KIND?
(necklace ring(s)?)
GLASSES?
CITIZEN RAPHAEL NWABARA
30 yr. old
Nigerian
·Tall
·Muscular
·Bald Head
·Bushy (yet clean cut) Beard
6'1"
TECH WATCH
HIGHTECH WATCH
SLIDE ON SHOES

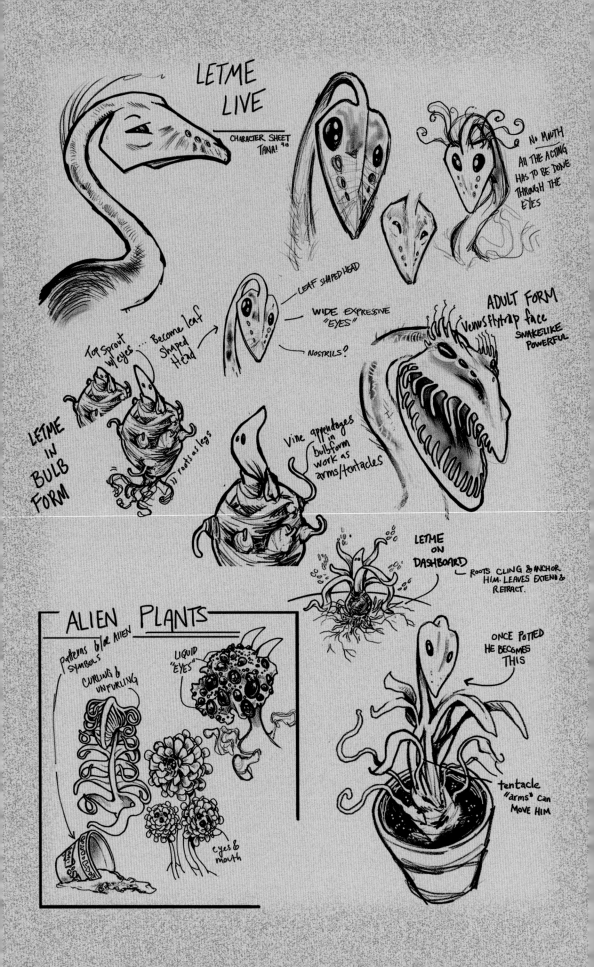

LETME LIVE

CHARACTER SHEET
TANA! 4/8

NO MOUTH
ALL THE ACTING
HAS TO BE DONE
THROUGH THE
EYES

LEAF SHAPED HEAD

WIDE EXPRESSIVE "EYES"

NOSTRILS?

Tor Sprout w/ eyes ... Become leaf shaped head →

LETME
IN
BULB
FORM

roots as legs

Vine appendages in bulbform work as arms/tentacles

ADULT FORM
Venusflytrap face
SNAKELIKE
POWERFUL

LETME ON
DASHBOARD
ROOTS CLING & ANCHOR
HIM. LEAVES EXTEND &
RETRACT.

ONCE POTTED
HE BECOMES
THIS

tentacle "arms" can MOVE HIM

ALIEN PLANTS

Patterns b/or Alien symbols

CURLING & UNFURLING

LIQUID "EYES"

eyes & mouth

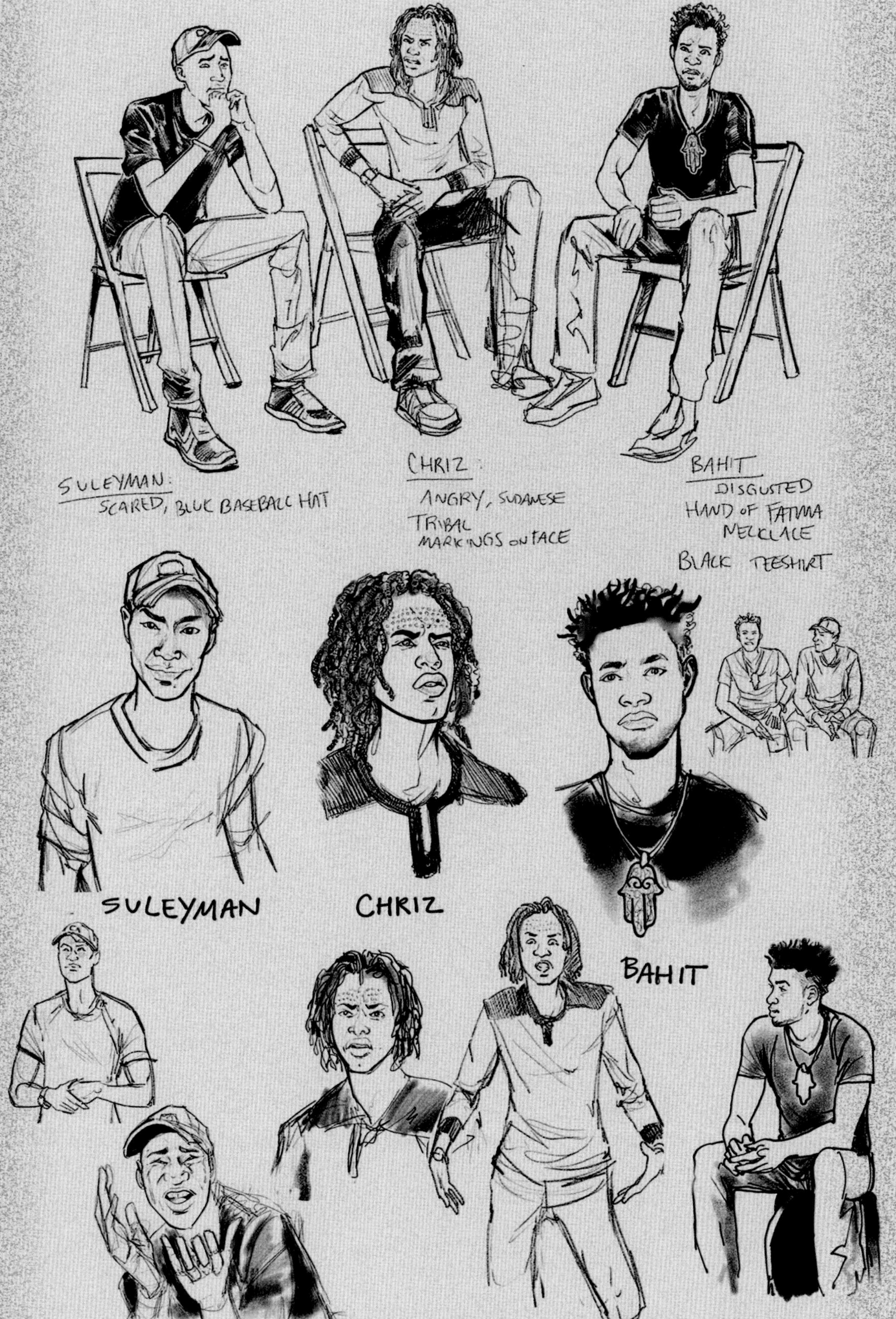
SULEYMAN:
SCARED, BLUE BASEBALL HAT
CHRIZ:
ANGRY, SUDANESE
TRIBAL
MARKINGS ON FACE
BAHIT
DISGUSTED
HAND OF FATIMA
NECKLACE
BLACK TEESHIRT
SULEYMAN
CHRIZ
BAHIT

NEW HOPE APTS.

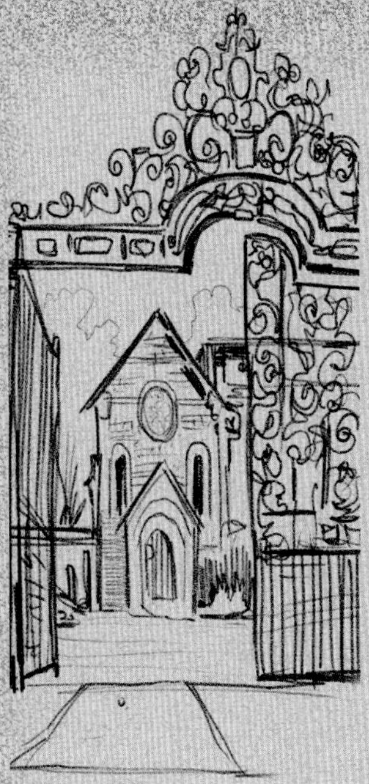

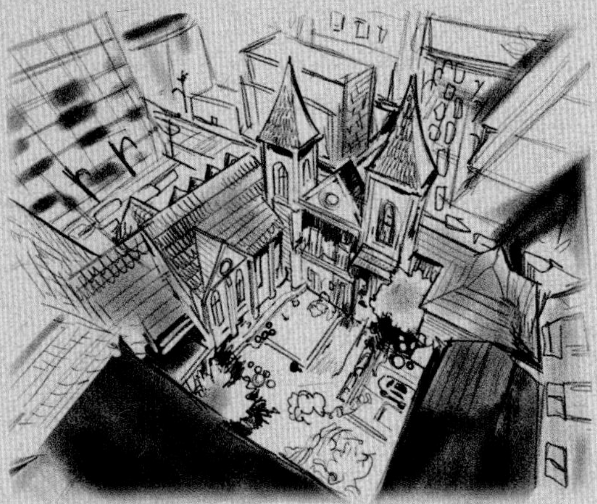

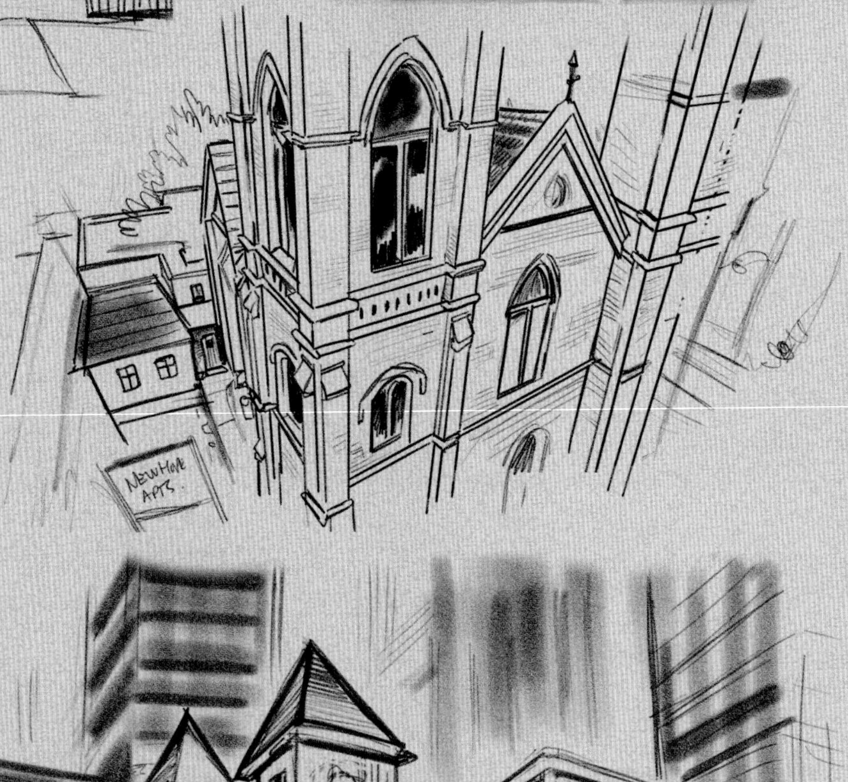
NEW HOPE
APTS.

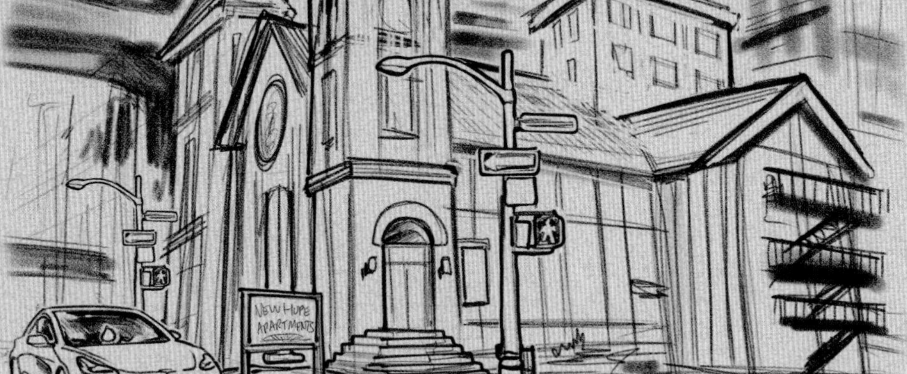
NEW HOPE
APARTMENTS

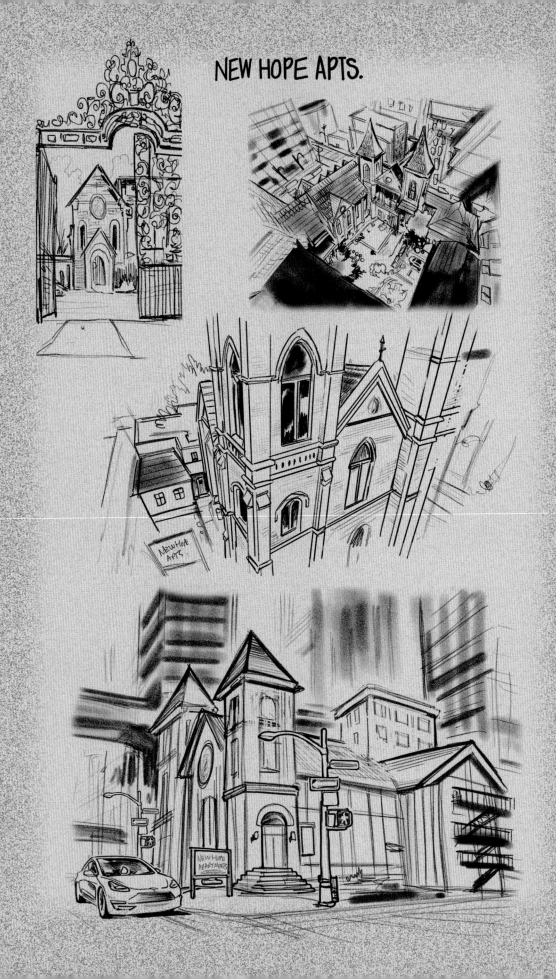

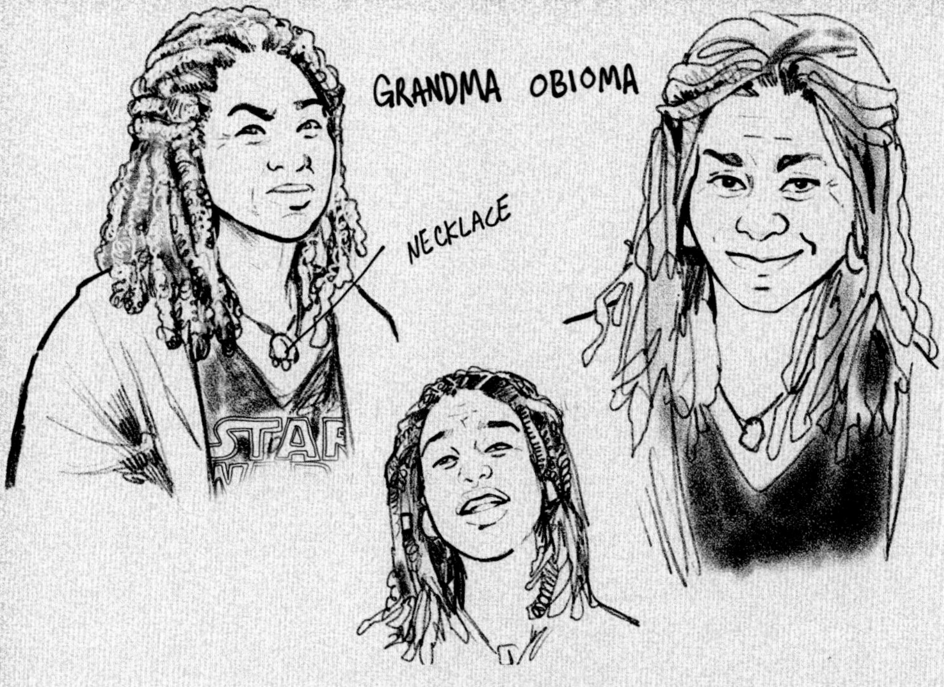
GRANDMA OBIOMA
NECKLACE

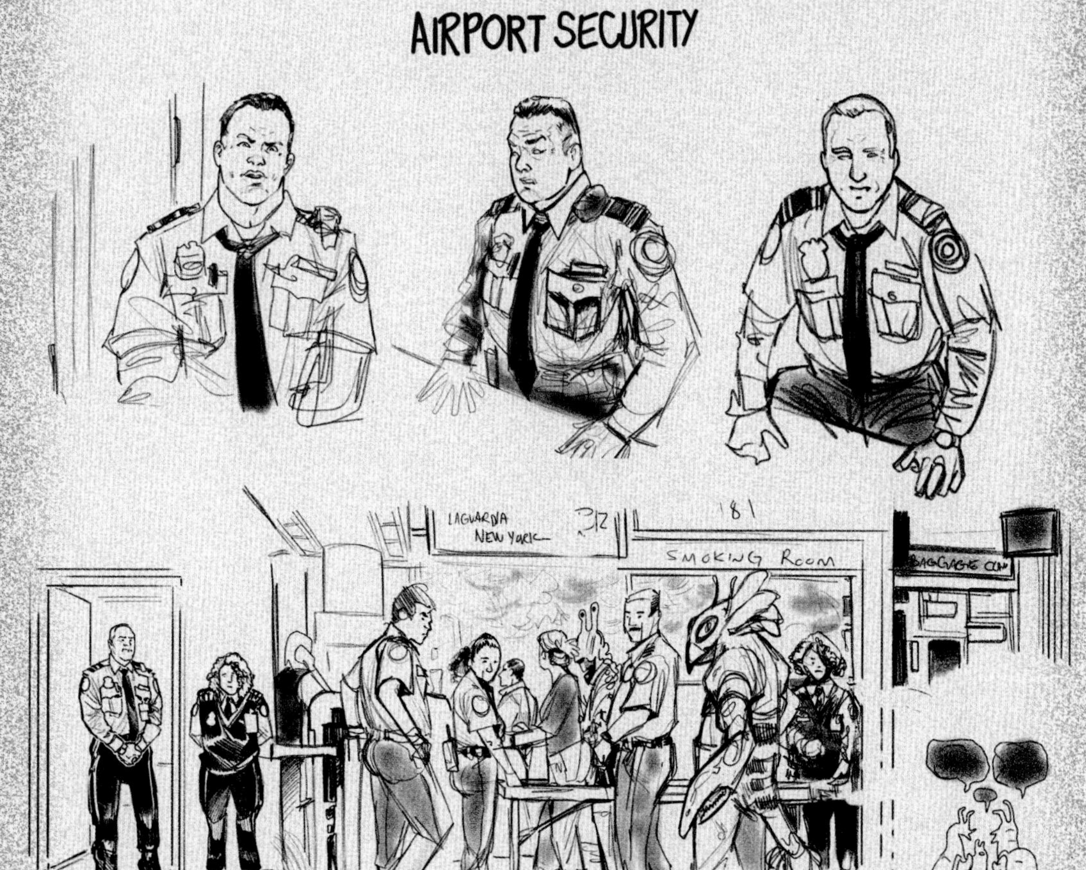
AIRPORT SECURITY
LAGUARDIA NEW YORK
312
181
SMOKING ROOM

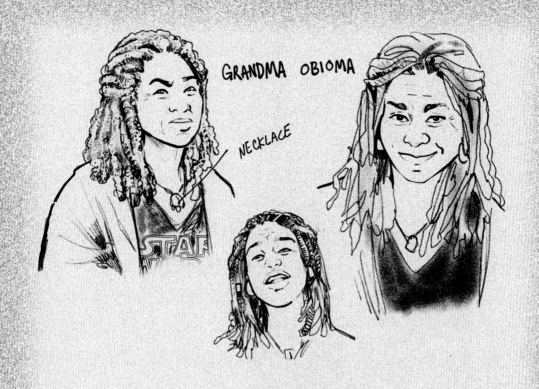

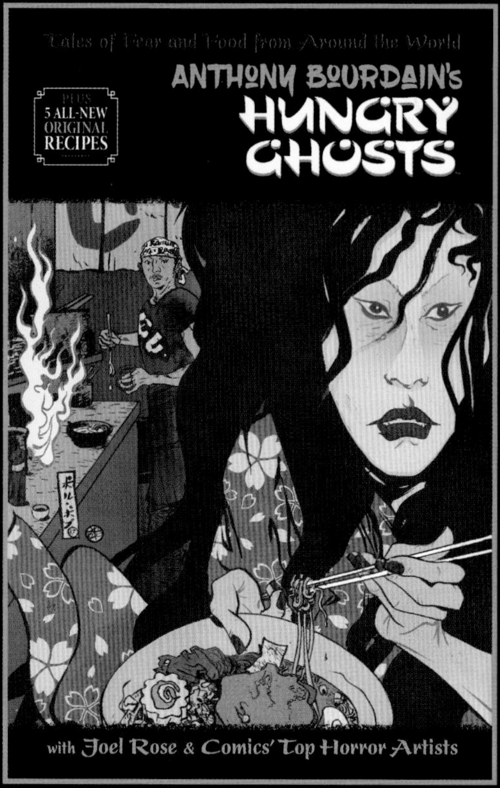
Tales of Fear and Food from Around the World
ANTHONY BOURDAIN's
HUNGRY GHOSTS
PLUS 5 ALL-NEW ORIGINAL RECIPES
with Joel Rose & Comics' Top Horror Artists

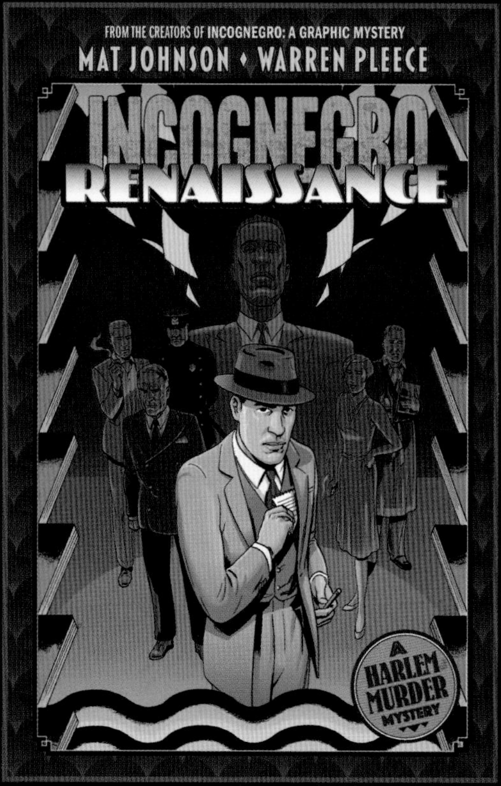
FROM THE CREATORS OF INCOGNEGRO: A GRAPHIC MYSTERY
MAT JOHNSON • WARREN PLEECE
INCOGNEGRO
RENAISSANCE
A HARLEM MURDER MYSTERY

DARING

DISTINCTIVE

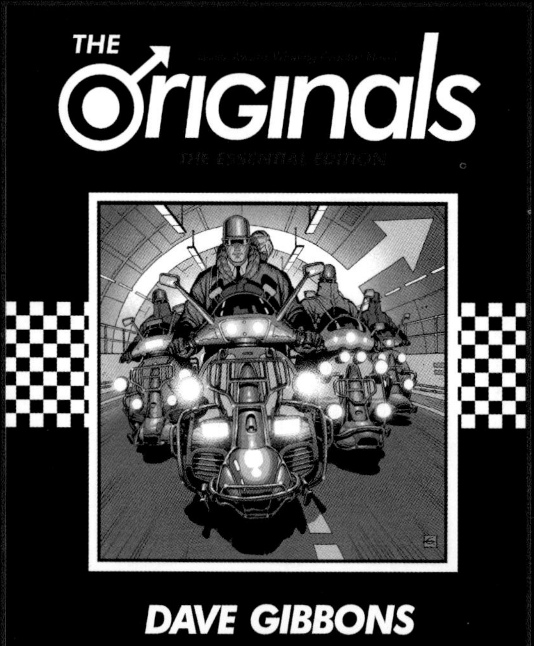
THE Originals
DAVE GIBBONS

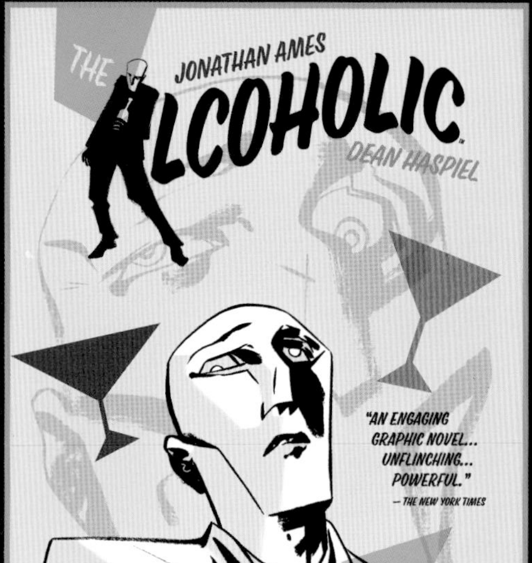
JONATHAN AMES
THE ALCOHOLIC
DEAN HASPIEL
"AN ENGAGING GRAPHIC NOVEL... UNFLINCHING... POWERFUL."
— THE NEW YORK TIMES

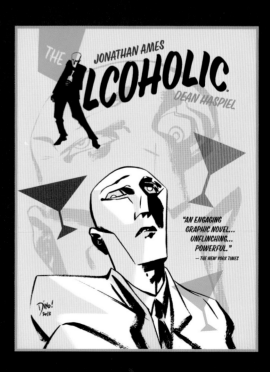

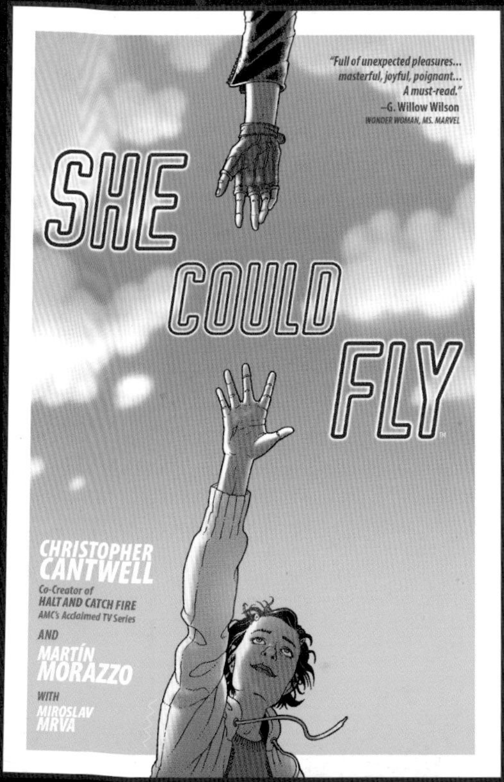
"Full of unexpected pleasures... masterful, joyful, poignant... A must-read."
–G. Willow Wilson
WONDER WOMAN, MS. MARVEL
SHE COULD FLY
CHRISTOPHER CANTWELL
Co-Creator of HALT AND CATCH FIRE
AMC's Acclaimed TV Series
AND
MARTÍN MORAZZO
WITH
MIROSLAV MRVA

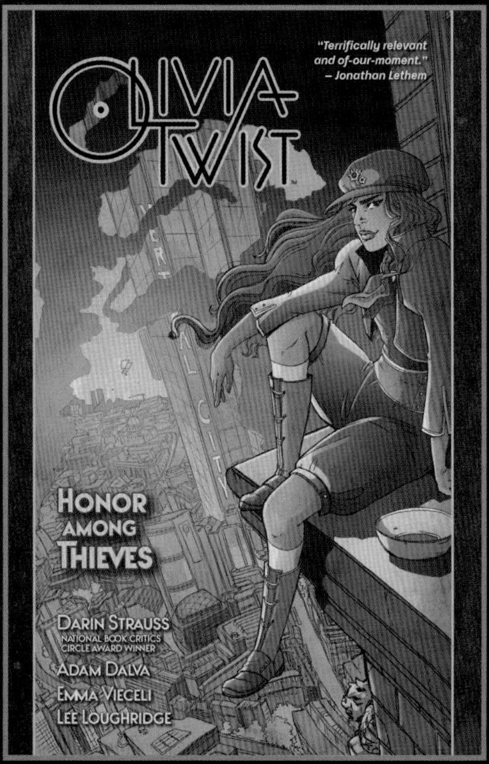
"Terrifically relevant and of-our-moment."
– Jonathan Lethem
OLIVIA TWIST
HONOR AMONG THIEVES
DARIN STRAUSS
NATIONAL BOOK CRITICS CIRCLE AWARD WINNER
ADAM DALVA
EMMA VIECELI
LEE LOUGHRIDGE

GRAPHIC NOVELS

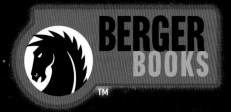

BERGER BOOKS ™

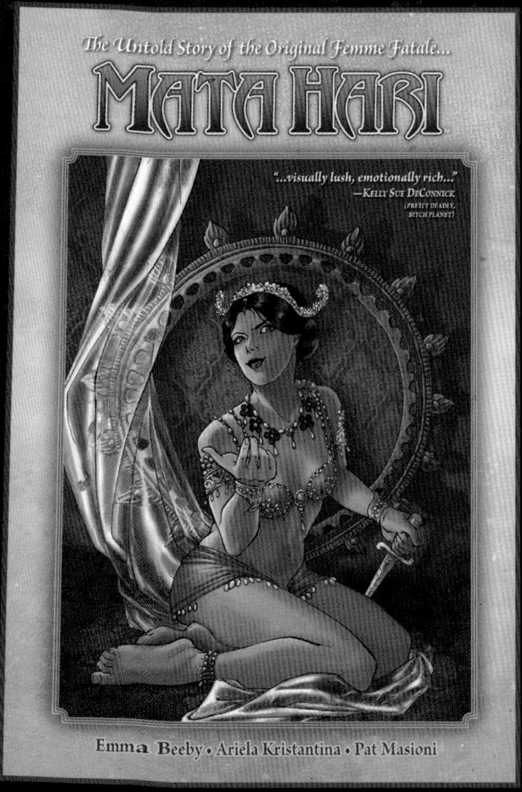
The Untold Story of the Original Femme Fatale...
MATA HARI
"...visually lush, emotionally rich..."
—Kelly Sue DeConnick
(PRETTY DEADLY, BITCH PLANET)
Emma Beeby • Ariela Kristantina • Pat Masioni

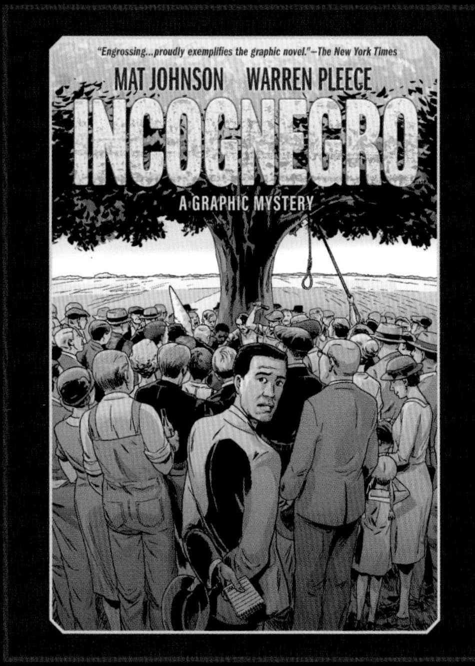
"Engrossing...proudly exemplifies the graphic novel."—The New York Times
MAT JOHNSON WARREN PLEECE
INCOGNEGRO
A GRAPHIC MYSTERY

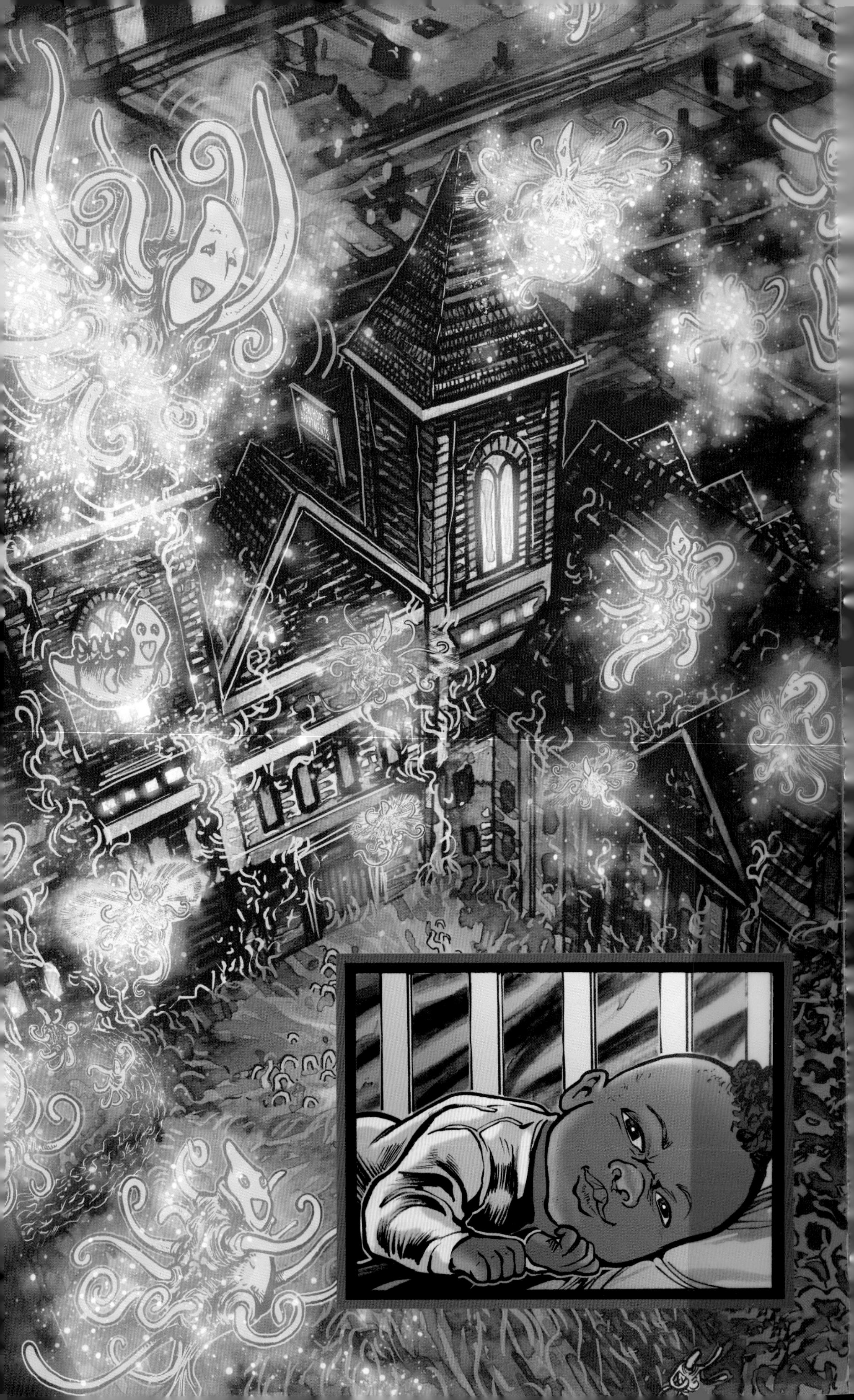